Waynesburg College Library
Waynesburg, Pa. 15370

C816f

320.3
Cornford, James
AUTHOR
The failure of the state
TITLE
123365
BORROWER'S NAME

320.3 C816f
Cornford, James
The failure of the state
123365

THE FAILURE OF THE STATE

THE FAILURE OF THE STATE

ON THE DISTRIBUTION OF POLITICAL AND
ECONOMIC POWER IN EUROPE

EDITED BY JAMES CORNFORD

CROOM HELM LONDON
ROWMAN AND LITTLEFIELD TOTOWA N.J.

© 1975 James Cornford
First published 1975

Croom Helm, 2-10 St. John's Road, London SW11
ISBN: 0-85664-280-0

Rowman and Littlefield, 81 Adams Drive, Totowa, N.J.

Library of Congress Cataloging in Publication Data

Cornford, James
   The failure of the state.

Includes bibliographies.
1. Decentralisation in government – Europe.
2. Europe – Economic policy.
3. Europe – Politics – 1945 – I. Title
JS3000.3.A3C67 1975 320.3 74-22235
ISBN 0-87471-607-1

Printed in Great Britain
by Biddles of Guildford

CONTENTS

Introduction *James Cornford* — 7

1. Regionalism in France *R.E.M. Irving* — 14
2. Italy: Regionalism and Bureaucratic Reform *Martin Clark* — 44
3. Great Britain: The Quest for Efficiency *Michael Clarke* — 82
4. Decentralisation of Power in the Federal Republic of Germany *John Holloway* — 107
5. Models of Reform in Eastern Europe *David Holloway* — 141
6. The EEC Dimension: Intended and Unintended Consequences *Richard McAllister* — 174

All the contributors to this volume are members of the Department of Politics, University of Edinburgh.

INTRODUCTION

Governments today are in a paradoxical situation: they face demands for the protection or enhancement of local autonomy, and for increased opportunities for citizens to contribute to the decisions which affect their lives. At the same time governments are not only held responsible for the general welfare of society, and in particular the level of material prosperity, but they also come under pressure from every conceivable interest to exert the powers of central government on their behalf. In addition to this political counterpoint, there is concern about the ability of central government to cope with its accumulated burdens, and a desire on administrative grounds to discover at what levels different kinds of decisions can most appropriately be taken, while maintaining effective control of strategic planning at the centre.

It is the purpose of this book to examine how these dilemmas have been perceived and debated in Europe, East and West, and what solutions have been proposed or attempted. It has been written as a cooperative enterprise and the choice of countries covered reflects the interests and knowledge of a small group of colleagues. We are conscious of how much we would have gained from an examination of Scandinavia and the Low Countries, and from more detailed enquiry into particular Eastern European systems. It will also be apparent that we have not tackled here two major determinants of the success or failure of European States; first the problem of over-mighty allies; and second, the international economy within which domestic economic management has to be practised. To the military division of Europe I shall briefly return, but on the economic front it is clear that recent developments have increased longstanding difficulties.

The rapid emergence of the Eurocurrency market has hastened the disintegration of the Bretton Woods system and threatens to undermine intergovernmental controls of the monetary system and hence control of the impact of monetary factors on the domestic economy. The rise of the multi-national corporation, and particularly the immense increase in direct US investment in Western Europe, equally poses problems for European governments. These are undoubtedly threats to the viability of nation states, but we have been concerned primarily with internal institutional problems and have considered these external factors only by implication: that is by looking at the likely success of the attempt to overcome the weakness of the individual states (Chapter VI); and, secondly, by looking at the institutional problems which remain even in command economies (Chapter V). Nor have we looked at more fundamental conflict over the nature of regimes, open in Ireland, Belgium and Greece, emergent in Portugal and Spain, and hovering in the wings in the rest of Europe. We have concentrated on the problems which remain when the boundaries of the political community are settled and the most ardent reformer would not appeal to force. 'The failure of the State', in our limited definition, involves two related problems. The first is the failure of governments to satisfy the expectations which their assumption of wider responsibilities has raised. The second is the sacrifice of political values entailed by the steps found necessary to fulfil these new obligations. The responsibility for material welfare has resulted in a steady pressure for the concentration of power: just as economies of scale have been the engine of growth, so the role of central governments has expanded from the guarantor of the legal framework of economic activity, to the provider of basic services, director of investment, supplier of capital and controller of the distribution of welfare. This concentration of responsibilities has taken place within different constitutional settings, some more readily adaptable than others, but all exhibiting in some degree the same complaints: centralisation is inefficient in its own terms; and it involves a loss of responsiveness and accountability to the people on whose behalf it has been undertaken. The first four chapters deal with the reaction to these problems in the major Western European states. Though these reactions have much in common, they tend to emphasise different approaches to the dilemma of centralisation, approaches which may be crudely summarised thus:

		Basis	
		Territorial	*Functional*
Motive	*Managerial*	Deconcentration	Hiving off
	Participatory	Devolution	Interest group representation/ workers' control

Much of the rhetoric of reform in France, Italy and Britain has concentrated on devolution, on increasing the autonomous powers of elected regional and local government. Most of what has been done has been prompted by managerial considerations, more openly in France where Jacobin tradition supports the continued primacy of central government, but equally clearly in Britain and Italy where the reform of local government has been undertaken with the aim of improving its efficiency as an agent of central government. The effect of reform has been to increase the size of local government units in the name of efficiency, reduce their powers and lock them more effectively into the mechanisms of central administration. This is not simply because the Jacobins are unconcerned about participation, but because they rightly perceive that territorial devolution (and the inherited systems of local government) bear little relation to the developing realities of the social and economic structure. The Jacobins are not in fact indifferent to participation, but they see it as an aspect of efficiency. It is a mistake to see the demands for efficiency coming from above and for participation from below. Rather the reverse is the case. The central administrators, conscious of the impossibility of their task, look for consultation, information, understanding, assent and compliance with their plans, in order to have any chance of satisfying the demand for efficiency from below. It is striking how much regional discontent, though it may be focused on symbols of local identity, is concerned with the failure of policies, such as regional economic policy, over which the central government is bound to retain control. But to the Jacobin, participation is concerned more with responsiveness than accountability. It rests on a consumer model of citizenship, in which feedback is necessary to the government as the provider of services, but which does not assume citizen initiative. This of course is in contrast to the participatory model of the devolutionists which is one of self-government, in which essential ends are not agreed but are a matter for debate and determination through institutions controlled by and answerable to citizens, and not merely responsive to their views. The weakness of the devolutionist case has been to tie the demand for active participation to territorial decentralisation. In the first place, this will not give effective control over key areas of economic and social policy; and second, the institutions of regional and local government are easily converted into the agents of central government, instruments therefore of *deconcentration,* rather than of *devolution.* It does make a difference whether a local administrator is a direct employee of central government or of a locally elected government, but the difference may be scarcely perceptible to those whom he serves. Territorial decentralisation involves a balance between administrative convenience and political control: even the purest case of *deconcentration* will probably enhance local influence. But territorial decentralisation, whatever the balance, is mainly an answer to the problems of government as the provider of services, rather than as director and controller of production. In the field of services the demand for uniformity, fiscal control, and doctrines of accountability submerge central departments in an avalanche of detail: greater autonomy for local governments or increased administrative discretion for local agents of central departments are alternative and even complementary means of avoiding suffocation. On the production side, similar models have been followed in the effort of the states to guarantee economic growth and to control its direction. To match the growing concentration of economic power, governments have resorted to familiar strategies: total control, shared control and combined control. In Eastern Europe the Jacobin model has been adopted and central government control exerted over all economic activity. This 'solution' has resulted in the familiar complaints of inflexibility, unresponsiveness and inefficiency; of rule by a repressive and unaccountable bureaucracy punctuated by explosions of discontent. In Western Europe, shared control has resulted both in the use of traditional fiscal and monetary powers of government for new purposes and in the acceptance of direct public responsibility for large sectors of industry. This too has posed a problem: to avoid apoplexy, the congestion of the traditional channels of control, governments have resorted to functional decentralisation: 'hiving off' responsibility for particular industries or services to public corporations, which have unfortunately managed to combine the worst of all worlds: lack of effective political control and insulation from the demands of clients and customers. There is no more evidence of political imagination here than in the Jacobin solution. Indeed there has rather been a loss of nerve on the part of public administrators and a temptation to look to the success of the private corporation and 'to imitate the action of the tiger'. No doubt there is much to be learned from the techniques of corporate management, especially in the central organisations of government, but the fact remains that industries or services have generally been taken into the public sector because private ownership has failed and because the standards and concerns of private bureaucracy are unacceptable.

The third approach, combined control, has taken the form of an attempt to recreate in Western Europe the liberal order on a supranational scale: to avoid in effect the problems of direct political control over the private sector, and of the limited capacity of the nation state, by creating a larger order in which the benefits of the market can be combined with economies of scale and political institutions to match. The difficulties of this enterprise are notorious, and success in its present form might prompt as much gloom as failure. Failure would certainly not restore autonomy and independence to national governments, as some seem to hope, but success would reinforce the indifference to accountability already entrenched at national level. The EEC is a monument to bureaucratic stealth, at the mercy of national governments because it has no constituency, no base in common assent or understanding.

In confronting these dilemmas national critics and reformers feel, like Sir George Sitwell, that there is always more laughter in the next room. In France they want devolution, the sharing of powers between central, regional and local government; in Britain and Italy, the reinvigoration of local government by the creation of effective regional bodies. But in West Germany where such bodies already exist, the pressures are reversed and the reformers seek salvation in greater central control and in experiment with new forms of representation through economic rather than political institutions. And in Eastern Europe where political control of the economy is established, reformers want to restore some influence to the consumer, to give greater autonomy to the enterprise, and to create more opportunities for participation by workers in its management.

The debates have been carried on in different terms: in France, Britain and Italy the accent has been on political reform; in West Germany and Eastern Europe on economic. But there can be no doubt that what is being debated is the same thing; it is a question of different taboos. Those who ask for political devolution in the west are rejecting the analogy between citizen and consumer. But if the citizen is to be politically effective, his participation cannot be limited to the political sphere. It must extend also into economic institutions. And if workers' participation is to mean anything, it will involve drastic changes in the size of enterprises and the relations of authority within them. There is little point in reproducing in the economy representative practices already discredited in the political system. In Eastern Europe any change in the pattern of economic control must equally have major political repercussions.

The case for decentralisation, for the granting of greater autonomy either to territorial or functional units, must rest on two propositions: first that the logic of centralisation is at fault; and, second, that public institutions are not *ipso facto* any more accountable than private ones. The logic of centralisation is economic: it is predicated on growth, on the need to adapt political institutions to guarantee the conditions for increasing wealth. The commitment to growth is made at the expense of discussing the distribution of wealth and at the expense of alternative values, both political and economic. The strength of the centralist case is that there is a vast unsatisfied demand for the blessings of the corporate economy. But even if that continues to be the case, the political diseconomies of scale will become more apparent as growth becomes more difficult to sustain. Three aspects of centralist dogma must then be questioned: the irrelevance of place, the need for uniformity, and the indifference towards means. The first proposition of the centralist case is that the most important relationships in our society are functional and not territorial and that what matters is to coordinate centrally the activities of functional organisations. But the irrelevance of place to many of the organisations which govern our lives does not mean that place is irrelevant either to ourselves or to the decisions which these organisations take. Central administration by function transfers decisions from the places where they take effect and ignores the costs and irrationalities of failure to coordinate locally. Central coordination itself is difficult to achieve and may have little effect locally: it enables central organisations to rub along together, which is important but not at all the same thing as local coordination. The striking feature of centralisation is in fact the energy and skill absorbed just to keep the machine ticking over.

Again uniformity, whether of benefits or obligations, is supported in the name of equity, as a principle of common citizenship, and as a condition of mobility and 'economic rationality'. But it is seldom achieved in practice, though much effort is expended in the attempt. And where it is achieved the effect is often rebarbative. Nostalgia for the market economy is not only ideological, but reflects general discontent with the style of public services which do not provide even the illusion of choice, and are often administered in contemptuous, arbitrary and punitive ways. Private bureaucracy at least takes the trouble to manipulate its clients. Finally the centralist dogma depends on the assumption not only of a consensus about ends but of indifference to means. But it is quite rational for people to be satisfied by how much they get without being at all satisfied with the means by which they get it. The feebleness of representative institutions in the contemporary state may be compensated by the activities of interest groups, but it is one thing to have decisions taken after public debate and another to have public debate about decisions which have been arrived at already after negotiation between governments and interest groups. Privacy is as important to this system as it is to the clandestine politics of the Eastern European bureaucracy. In either case the effective representatives of the people become either suitors or adversaries to governments which are themselves accountable only in the most indirect and indiscriminate ways.

The case for decentralisation may indeed be that beyond a certain size no institution, public or private, can be made answerable, and that whatever costs or absurdities small units may involve, they cannot be worse than the alienation caused by remote control.

However that may be there are two things devolutionists must face: that political and economic devolution must go hand in hand; and that there will be costs, very large costs, in scaling down. Even if these are accepted, we all know that devolution will be a matter of compromise and experiment. The real tragedy for Europeans, who of all people are committed to reconciling their traditions of individual liberty and self-determination with the demands of collectivism, to the achievement of 'Socialism with a human face', is that they have so little room for experiment. As a consequency of their past divisions, the only effective cooperation among them is the enforced discipline of military alliances. These alliances not only divide Europeans against each other, but freeze their political institutions in the image of the antiquated and irrelevant systems of the USA and the USSR. Anybody who thinks that an exaggerated sentiment should watch closely forthcoming events in Yugoslavia and Portugal.

1. REGIONALISM IN FRANCE

R.E.M. Irving

'Avec la centralisation vous avez l'apoplexie au centre et la paralysie aux extrémités' (Lamennais).

'This measure (the 1972 Regional Reform) ... does not transfer any of the attributes of the State to the Regions ... It does no more than continue the policy of administrative deconcentration.' (J. M. Jeanneney, *Le Figaro*, 26 April 1972).

'Functional regional representation ... cannot act as an effective democratic counterweight to centralising administrative pressure because it lacks the necessary legitimacy in a liberal democratic culture.' (J.E.S. Hayward, *Political Studies*, March 1969, p.73).

Taken together the above quotations focus admirably on the nature of France's governmental structure (extreme centralisation), her predominant political culture (liberal democracy), and her tentative steps to reconcile the two (administrative deconcentration and functional representation at the regional level). But the fundamental dilemma, as Jack Hayward points out, has not been resolved. Can administrative deconcentration, even if complemented with ideal institutions for consulting regional interest groups, ever be a substitute for political devolution? In this chapter I shall attempt to answer this question, which lies at the heart of the French regional debate, by discussing the nature of the French governmental-administrative system, the recent attempts to modernise and reform this system, and the arguments for and against political and administrative devolution to the regions.*

The Nature of French Centralisation

France claims to be a 'liberal democratic state', and in so far as this rather vague epithet has any meaning, she is. Even if her radio and television are largely state-controlled, she has a free press. Her judiciary is independent. Her interest groups are free to organise themselves within the framework of the law. Her citizens are constantly being called upon to vote in free elections, whether presidential,

*I am indebted to Professor Jack Hayward of the University of Hull who was kind enough to read and criticise the first draft of this chapter.

parliamentary, departmental or municipal — not to mention the six national referenda of the last fifteen years. And yet in spite of all this 'evidence' of liberal democracy at work, French citizens have remarkably little influence in national or local politics. This state of affairs is, of course, by no means exceptional in liberal democracies. Nevertheless, the French situation is arguably worse than that applying in most other Western democracies. The President has far-reaching power in both domestic and foreign policy (the *domaine réservé*). The powers of Parliament were emasculated under the Constitution (and even more by the practice) of the Fifth Republic. Moreover, there is no tradition of strong local government in France. In so far as local government institutions exist at the communal and departmental level (and embryonically at the regional level), they are very much subject to central government control. This brings us to the heart of the problem. France is by any standards a very centralised State. She is, claims Pierre Fougeyrollas without undue exaggeration, 'a perfect example of bureaucratic despotism'.[1] The enormous influence of France's senior civil servants in the Third and Fourth Republics was not surprising. Like Ripolin paint, the bureaucracy could easily outlast a few governments. But paradoxically the situation has worsened in the Fifth Republic in spite of a degree of political stability which might have been expected to allow the politicians to reassert themselves. First of all, General de Gaulle was not particularly interested in domestic affairs, that is until 1968, when characteristically (but too late for once) he focused on the main issue — *participation,* or rather the lack of it. Secondly, political stability also produced administrative stability — senior civil servants became set in their ways at a particular ministry or in a ministerial *cabinet*. Thirdly, as a number of senior civil servants themselves admit, the *Ecole Nationale d'Administration* (ENA) system, established in 1945 to democratise the civil service, has had exactly the opposite effect; by the 1960s ENA graduates — an élite within an over-hierarchical bureaucratic structure — controlled most of the key positions in the senior civil service (notably in the Ministry of Finance), whence they exuded a *mélange* of technocratic brilliance and political virginity.

The technical competence of France's senior civil servants is unquestioned — indeed it is one of the reasons why the Hudson Institute in early 1973 reported so optimistically about the prospects for the French economy in 1985 — but the paralysing effect of a system in which a few hundred senior civil servants are responsible for both major and minor decisions has been brilliantly analysed by the sociologist Michel Crozier.[2] He notes the absence of channels of communication between senior and junior civil servants:

'Everything is so organised in this service, as in many other French organisations, that people who know the difficulties at first hand have not the least power of decision, and those who have the power of decision have no way of being objectively informed.'[3]

The civil service is seen by Crozier as a microcosm of the French State. Lack of communication results in delays; the hierarchical structure encourages conservatism; the *administré's* complete lack of control over the *administrateur* breeds both servility and scorn. Crozier criticizes the civil service in words which could appropriately be applied to the whole French governmental structure:

'It is only to the extent to which authority can be democratised, social distances minimised, humiliations eliminated, that one can re-establish the necessary means of information, hence of communication.'[4]

This is exactly what the whole regional debate of the past twenty years has been about: how France can be governed both democratically and efficiently in the 'post-industrial' world, i.e. in a world of rapid economic and social change, in which traditional ways of life, like peasant farming, or traditional industries, like coal mining, are in steady decline, resulting in structural imbalances in some parts of the country, whilst in other parts social and environmental problems are being caused by exceptionally fast industrialisation and economic growth.

In the days when the chief tasks of the State were diplomacy, the army, the police and the budget, a large degree of centralisation was probably an advantage rather than a disadvantage. But since the War the huge extension of the economic and social role of the State has resulted in a mushrooming of the Parisian bureaucracy and a slowing down of the decision-making process.[5] Many decisions which ought to be taken locally (e.g. about such matters as the building of primary schools) have to be referred to Paris. And the situation has been worsened by the 85 per cent dependence of mayors and departmental councils on central government finance, as well as by the conservatism of provincial notables, for both mayors and departmental councillors have frequently shown their reluctance to change the present system, in which they retain a certain status locally and can at the same time pass the buck on to Paris for unpopular or delayed decisions. Indeed, in recent years *'la complicité des notables'*[6] has been at least as important in delaying fundamental reforms of the French State as has the desire of Parisian 'technocrats' to hold on to their powers. Meanwhile, decision making — often of the most trivial kind — goes on quite outwith the control of the *collectivités territoriales*,[7] much less that of individual citizens. Mayors and departmental councillors claim that they are 'intervening', Prefects that they are 'pushing the *dossiers* in Paris', Members of Parliament that they are 'trying to see the Minister' ... but the village in the Auvergne continues to wait for its new primary school. The present situation has been described by a political club (whose membership includes senior civil servants of Gaullist sympathies) as ' a game of Box and Cox between blind tyrants and begging slaves ... in which neither the State nor the local authorities can any longer fulfil their allotted functions'.[8] The club goes on to argue that the system is not only inefficient, it is also undemocratic and potentially dangerous: frustrated citizens are liable at any time to take the law into their own hands, as happened in May 1968. Or, as Joseph Martray, the moderate and respected founder of the National Movement for Decentralisation and Regional Reform, has put it, the danger today is not the separatism feared by Jacobins like Michel Debré and Alexandre Sanguinetti, but a popular loss of confidence in the whole governmental and administrative system.[9]

The growth of executive and bureaucratic power has, of course, been a transnational phenomenon in the post-Keynesian world, but the French problem of overcentralisation has been aggravated by a number of historical legacies, which make its solution both more urgent and more difficult. For the past six hundred years monarchs, emperors and republicans have been 'Jacobins' almost to a man. In contrast to Italy and Germany, the French State preceded the French Nation: monarchs from Louis XI to Louis XIV forged Celts, Flemings, Germans, Provençals, Basques, Occitans and Franks into one nation, the present Hexagon. Republicans then emphasised 'la République une et indivisible', and strove to destroy particularism with their emphasis on *laïcité* and linguistic uniformity. Napoleon I gave France a military-administrative system based on the prefectoral corps and began to centralise higher education in Paris. Napoleon III — like most Roman emperors — had megalomaniac tendencies in so far as his capital was concerned: to him bigness was greatness. (Incidentally, de Gaulle's first Delegate-General for the Paris Region, Paul Delouvrier, seems to have been under the same illusion, but his 1965 plan for creating a greater Paris of sixteen million by the year 2000 has now been largely abandoned.) Even France's one constitutional monarch, Louis Philippe, succeeded in aggravating the problem of overcentralisation by allowing the *Polytechnicien,* Baptiste Legrand, to create a railway system, a map of which still looks like a bicycle wheel axed on Paris. (Owing to a lack of transversal lines it is, for example, still quicker to travel from Bordeaux to Lyons via Paris.) The First World War led to vast industrial expansion around Paris (the creation of the 'Red Belt');

it also made the fortunes of André Citroën and Louis Renault, and so by a strange historical accident Paris became the French Detroit. In the eighty years up to 1936 the Paris Region (i.e. Seine and Seine-et-Oise) gained 4½ million people, i.e. 87 per cent of the national gain of 5 million (from 36 million to 41 million), whilst the population in 95 per cent of French departments declined. These developments, in no way controlled or discouraged by the government, resulted in a Paris in which administration, commerce, industry and population were concentrated to the detriment of the rest of the country, creating what Jean-François Gravier called in a famous book (published in 1947) *Paris et le Désert Français*. Or, as Robert Lafont put it, the provinces had become the colonies of Paris.[10]

In the immediate post-war period governments had to concentrate first of all on reconstruction, but from 1950, and more especially under the Fifth Republic, efforts have been made to divert industry from the Paris area, and to decentralise a limited amount of administrative decision making. The 1968 census indicated that the policy of diverting industry was beginning to work,[11] and some progress has also been made in the field of regional policy *(aménagement du territoire)*. But in the area of administrative decentralisation — not to mention political devolution — successive governments have acted with great caution. Twenty-two economic planning regions were set up in 1955,[12] and their institutional structure was strengthened in 1964 with the establishment of consultative councils (CODER)[13] and the appointment of regional prefects, and again in 1972 with the creation of deliberative regional councils with (very limited) financial resources. But all these steps have been in the realm of *administrative* deconcentration and decentralisation and not in that of *political* devolution, which in one form or another is what is demanded by committed regionalists (like Pisani and Servan-Schreiber), moderate regionalists (like Martray and Gravier), and those senior officials who believe that regional policy without devolution of decision making can never be really effective (like Monod and Castelbajac). The regionalists claim that France cannot hope to solve the problems of the post-industrial age with a State apparatus which dates from Louis XIV and Napoleon, an apparatus which moreover brings democracy into disrepute by its failure to carry out its tasks effectively and quickly. But the regionalists are well aware that they are faced by conservative, Jacobin politicians in all parties, by senior civil servants who have no wish to share or lose their present powers, and by local government notables who prefer status and a quiet life to real administrative responsibility.

France's Experience of Regionalism

Before discussing the pros and cons of regionalism, i.e. of the devolution of decision-making powers to the regions, something must be said about recent developments in this area. Two preliminary points need to be made. Firstly, in spite of the setting up of twenty-two economic regions in 1955 and subsequent steps to consolidate their existence and structure, the department (*département*) remains *the* basic administrative unit in France. The country has been divided into departments (of which there are now ninety-five) and communes (just under 38,000) since 1790. They alone are constitutionally recognised as administrative units *(collectivités territoriales)*,[14] and of the two the department, under its prefect, is the more important unit. Regions, on the other hand, are recognised only as *établissements publics* (Law of July 1972), i.e. their legal status is no higher than that of state schools. In a country like France where legal niceties (not least in the fields of constitutional and administrative law) are very important, such a distinction is significant. It indicates that no government has, as yet, taken regionalism seriously. The second preliminary point is that regionalism is not the prerogative of any one party or group. It has been advocated by conservatives from Alexis de Tocqueville to Olivier Guichard, who have seen it as a check upon the totalitarian tendencies of centralised government; by Christian Democrats from Albert de Mun to Jean Lecanuet, who have seen it as an aspect of functional decentralisation; and by socialists from P.J. Proudhon to Michel Rocard, who have been anxious both to reconcile authority and liberty and to make democratic participation meaningful. Equally it has been (and is) opposed by conservatives like Michel Debré, who are afraid that the corollary of devolved power is a weak state, and by socialists like Guy Mollet, who believe that an egalitarian society cannot be achieved if 'reactionary', 'clerical' provinces have the right to shape their own future.

What has been achieved so far? In a nutshell, quite a lot in regional policy *(aménagement du territoire,* dispersion of industry, economic planning); a certain amount of administrative deconcentration (external services of Paris ministries, regional prefects); almost nothing in the field of political devolution, and not much in that of genuine administrative decentralisation, although the 1970 Law increased the autonomy of regional prefects, and the 1972 Law holds out the possibility of greater powers for the new regional councils. The steps towards regionalisation have all been noticeably pragmatic, a remarkable fact, as Philippe Brongniart has emphasised, 'for a nation which loves theories'.[15] There is, for example, no reference to the region in the Constitutions of 1946 and 1958, although the regional reform of 1969, rejected at the April referendum of that year, would

have given the regions constitutional status as *collectivités territoriales*.
As regards regional policy, the first official step was taken in 1950
with the setting up of the *Fonds National d'Aménagement du Territoire*
(FNAT) by Eugène Claudius-Petit, the Minister of Reconstruction and
Urban Development from 1948-53. It is important to realise that this
first step resulted from regional pressure, notably from the Breton
Comité d'Etude et de Liaison des Intérêts Bretons (CELIB), the
famous precursor of the various regional expansion committees formed
in the early 1950s.[16] Claudius-Petit argued that regional planning was
necessary in order 'to reverse the tendency for all the country's
forces vives to converge on the major industrial centres, notably Paris,
and to create new life in those regions, whose resources are under-utilised
and which are tending to become deserts in spite of their rich potential'.[17]
The Fund set up in 1950 (FNAT) was to help such regions to develop
industrial infrastructure. Only a small amount of money was allocated
to the fund (approximately £1 million per annum from 1950-4, or
1 per cent of the amount being spent in Britain on the redistribution of
industry under the 1947 Act). Nevertheless, FNAT helped to finance
fifty-seven decentralised industrial operations, creating over 26,000
new jobs. For example, industrial estates were established at such towns
as Chalon-sur-Saône, Chalons-sur-Marne and Reims, whilst companies
such as Citroën (at Rennes) and Gillette (at Annecy) set up new
factories with help from FNAT. The success of these tentative steps in
regional policy was confirmed by Mendès-France's decrees of
September 1954 (establishing a fund to subsidise companies which
decentralised their operations) and January 1955 (forbidding new
industrial projects of more than 500 square metres in the Paris region
without special governmental authorisation). And later in 1955, when
Edgar Faure was Prime Minister and Pierre Pflimlin Minister of Finance,
a series of decrees was promulgated, introducing tax reliefs of up to
20 per cent for companies expanding outside the Paris area, and
investment grants, also of 20 per cent, for companies setting up new
factories in thirty odd 'critical zones'; at the same time a fund was
established to help medium-sized provincial companies to expand
(the *Sociétés de Développement Régional*, SDR). It has been estimated
that as a result of these measures over 500 factories were built and
113,000 new jobs created in the provinces between 1955-9. Meanwhile,
Paris's share of new industrial development fell to 23 per cent of the
total, compared with 32 per cent in the previous five years. Altogether
about 350,000 jobs of Paris origin were 'devolved' in the period
1950-64, almost half of them, it is true, to less than 200 kilometres from
Paris. Nevertheless, an important start had been made in the new policy
of *aménagement du territoire*.[18]

Of even more significance from a long-term point of view was the

June 1955 decree establishing twenty-two *circonscriptions d'action régionale*. These were the forerunners of today's economic regions,[19] around whose powers and dimensions the regional debate of recent years has centred. The *circonscriptions* set up in 1955 were planning regions. Their *comités d'expansion économique* were *ad hoc* advisory bodies, whilst the roles of the *préfet coordinateur* and the *conférence interdépartementale* were imprecisely defined in the decrees of 1959. However, in 1964 a major regional reform occurred. The regions were given a permanent and uniform structure, without as yet being granted full constitutional recognition. The semi-official *comités d'expansion* were replaced by *commissions de développement économique régionale* (CODER), and the *préfet coordinateur* and *conférence interdépartementale* by regional prefects *(préfets régionaux)*, each assisted by a permanent team of experts *(mission régionale)* and by a committee consisting of departmental prefects (the *conférence administrative régionale)*. Henceforth, the two key regional institutions were the regional prefect and the CODER. In accordance with French administrative tradition the former had (and has) a dual role. He is responsible both for drawing up planning proposals for his region (on a fairly strict procedural basis — he must consult the departmental prefects, departmental councils and CODER before submitting his plans to Paris), and for seeing that the government's final plan is implemented in the region for which he is responsible. The CODER were purely advisory bodies consisting of representatives of the *collectivités territoriales,* i.e. mayors and departmental councillors (one quarter of the total), government nominees (one quarter), and representatives of the region's chambers of commerce, trade unions, agricultural organisations and other socioprofessional groups (one half). The CODER were much criticised as non-elected rather shadowy bodies, whose opinions were frequently ignored by Paris. And it is important to emphasise that the reform of 1964 did not create a new *collectivité territoriale* or impinge on existing administrative structures; nor was a regional budget or civil service established. At the same time the *reality* of the region was recognised in 1964, and the steps which were taken at that time gave considerable impetus to the whole regional debate. Should the regions now be given greater powers? And if so, should regional assemblies be directly elected, with perhaps an executive emerging from them? But before going on to consider these questions, a word must be said about the *central* government reforms of 1963-4 (in so far as they affected regional administration) and about the abortive regional project of 1969 and the regional law of 1972.

The decrees of February 1963 emphasised the central government's interest in regional *policy,* which does not necessarily mean to say that the government was interested in regional *devolution*. If anything, the government's immediate intention was to strengthen Paris's control over the provinces; and the 1964 decrees enhancing the powers of the departmental prefects confirmed that this was so. However, in practice, the government, by giving greater emphasis to regional policy, *nolens volens* encouraged the regionalists to press their case for administrative decentralisation and political devolution.

The essential aspects of the 1963 reform were that the prime minister took over direct responsibility for regional affairs; interministerial committees were set up to coordinate regional planning and policy; and further funds were made available to encourage research into regional problems as well as to finance regional projects.

The first two reforms were part of the same package, and both were in turn closely linked with the whole process of national planning, which has come under increasing governmental supervision in the Fifth Republic. The *Délégation à l'Améngement du Territoire et à l'Action Régionale* (DATAR) was modelled on the *Commissariat du Plan* (Planning Commission). Like the Planning Commission, the DATAR is composed of a small group of senior civil servants and research specialists (there are about fifty *chargés de mission* in the Planning Commission and about thirty at DATAR). Both bodies are also directly responsible to the prime minister, and therefore in practice to the President. The French Plan has never had the force of law despite General de Gaulle's description of it as 'an ardent obligation'. Nevertheless, both the Planning Commission and DATAR are extremely influential bodies owing to their high-powered membership, direct access to the prime minister and President, and ability to cut across departmental boundaries. The Planning Commission works out the national Plan by means of 'vertical' agricultural, industrial and transport committees, whose work is coordinated by 'horizontal' economic, financial, social, regional and urban committees. The most recent Plan (the Sixth, 1971-5), was drawn up in consulation with about 4,500 representatives from industry, agriculture, the trade unions and the universities, (the last two groups being heavily outnumbered by the first two). The Plan was debated in the Economic and Social Council, the National Assembly and the Senate, but despite this outward display of consultation all the main options had already been decided by the Planning Commission and approved by the government. The planning system has been much criticised in recent years on the grounds that it is both undemocratic and irrelevant: undemocratic because all the key decisions are made by a tiny group of civil servants and industrialists (even the CFDT, the Socialist/Catholic trade union confederation, which was enthusiastic about planning ten years ago, has become completely disenchanted with the whole process); and irrevelant because 'national' planning is becoming obsolete in the context of the European Economic Community (decisions about agriculture, for example, are meaningless unless they mesh in with the Common Agricultural Policy). Whatever the demerits of the French planning system, however, there can be no doubt that the Plan is psychologically important in a country which has relied on Parisian economic initiative from Colbert to the present day. At the same time it is quite clear that planning is a political exercise closely supervised by the government.[20] In other words there is no *a priori* connection between regional planning and regional decentralisation and devolution. On the contrary, all the signs are that the Fifth Republic wants to plan more (at all levels), but to keep the planners under strict central government control. Whether this makes sense in terms of efficiency or democracy is of course debatable.[21]

The DATAR, which is run by a senior government minister, works out the details of the regional plans after considering proposals put to it by the *Commission Nationale d'Aménagement du Territoire* (CNAT). The latter body consists of twenty-seven representatives of the ministries concerned and of fifty representatives from the new regional councils (formerly CODER). After the regional plans have been drawn up, the DATAR can establish *ad hoc* inter-ministerial committees to see that the plans are being implemented. This is an important development, because delays in Paris frequently occur owing to lack of contact between the various ministries, a situation which results from inter-ministerial rivalry. Finally, the DATAR has financial resources of its own, the *Fonds d'intervention pour l'Aménagement du Territoire* (FIAT). Although this fund is quite small (it cannot exceed 1 per cent of the total State budget for regional projects), it acts as a catalyst, keeping the process of regional development on the move. Its funds are used only to finance 'urgent projects', defined as those particularly in need of help during the next twelve months. Closely associated with DATAR (though, unlike FIAT, not directly responsible to it) is the *Fonds de Développement Economique et Sociale* (FDES), which allocates grants and helps small companies to raise capital. (It should be remembered that the French private capital market, like the Italian, is much less sophisticated than that of the City of London.)

The above steps in the field of regional development were complemented by the important decree of October 1967 establishing four 'special zones' under *Commissaires à la Rénovation Rurale*. The zones are Bretagne-Manche, Limousin-Lot, Auvergne (plus the departments of Aveyron, Lozère and part of Ardèche) and lastly the mountainous regions (essentially the Massif Central). The special zones are all areas which are particularly in need of government aid owing to their higher-than-average agricultural population, lower-than-average standard of living, and lack of industry. The *Commissaire* responsible for each zone works in liaison with the prefect (or prefects), but he is directly responsible to the central government. He is assisted by a committee of experts and senior civil servants. At the national level there is a *Comité Central de Rénovation Rurale,* consisting of representatives from the various ministries concerned with regional development; it is both an advisory committee and a ginger group which tries to ensure that priority is given to development projects in the special zones. There is some evidence that the special zones' scheme is beginning to work; it has certainly helped to develop tourism in the zones, and there are signs too that the haemorrhage of rural depopulation has been slowed down.[22] Overall, the reforms of the 1960s institutionalising the regions and rationalising the government's control of them have been quite successful from the point of view of regional development and administrative deconcentration. Although only about £50 million per annum was spent on regional policy in the years 1965-70, over 300,000 new jobs were created in the 1960s. The 1968 census showed that between 1962-8 the West had gained 143,000 jobs and the East and South 179,000, whilst Paris had lost 23,000. (Gravier, however, has shown that in spite of encouraging signs, Paris's growth has not been effectively checked yet.)[23] And in the years 1965-70 the Nord-Pas-de-Calais region gained 40,000 new jobs, mainly in the motor industry. Against these successes, however, must be set the fact that a number of rural departments are dying on their feet; one such is Lozère in the southern Massif Central which lost 43 per cent of its population between 1958-68, and where by the late 1960s there was insufficient able-bodied labour left to carry out the necessary structural changes even if adequate funds had been available.[24]

In terms of political and administrative devolution, however, progress has been much more limited, principally because successive governments have been unwilling to face up to the risks (as they see them) inherent in such developments. The Events of May 1968 gave the Gaullist *régime* a severe jolt, and resulted in educational reforms (granting some degree of autonomy to the universities) and industrial reforms (strengthening the *comités d'entreprise),* but the government was able to back-pedal on regional reform as a result of the ambiguous referendum of April 1969.[25] General de Gaulle had, in fact, talked about regional reform *before* the Events of 1968, notably at Lyons in March of that year, when he declared that 'the all-embracing type of centralisation, which was once necessary to realise and maintain the nation's unity, is now outdated'.[26] But there is no reason to think that de Gaulle was ever seriously interested in regionalism (or domestic policy of any sort for that matter) until he was faced with the 'incomprehensible' Events of May 1968. The Events made it clear that 'a hyper-centralised bureaucracy had grown too sluggish and unwieldy to exercise the multifarious and detailed powers of tutelage to which it had traditionally laid claim'.[27] As it turned out, the government, after consulting over 3,000 provincial personalities and local government bodies, brought forth a mouse of a regional reform, a project appropriately described by Jack Hayward as a 'pseudo-democratic camouflage' for regional devolution.[28]

The projected regional reform of 1969 (rejected by 52 per cent of the voters on 27 April) would, for all its failings, have inserted the region into France's constitutional structure for the first time. The regions would have become *collectivités territoriales* (constitutionally recognised local government units like departments and communes); they would have had limited *ressources propres* (independent financial means), supplemented by State funds and equalisation grants; and they — or to be more precise the regional prefects — would have had quite considerable powers in such matters as town planning, industrial development, and primary and secondary education (for a full list of the powers devolved to the region, see Article VI of the 1969 regional project).[29] Even such a strong critic of the 1969 reform project as Edgard Pisani (who labelled it 'un compromis des Jacondins')[30] conceded that it would have marked a real assault on the centralised State, and in particular on the prerogatives of the Ministry of Finance. But for all the advantages that it might have conferred on the regions, it cannot be denied that the 1969 project was in direct line with all post-war regional developments. It was essentially another attempt to deconcentrate administrative power, i.e. the main beneficiary would have been the regional prefect, the central government's representative. The regional councils, which would have replaced the CODER, would have had no legislative role. Like their predecessors they would have been only advisory bodies. Moreover, although they would have contained representatives of the communes and departments, as well as representatives of socioeconomic groups, they would not have been directly elected; indeed the 'regional' content of their membership would even have been diluted by the inclusion of local deputies as *ex officio* members (this provision was included in the project owing to pressure from the Central Committee of the Gaullist party in November 1968). The reform would have been, as its chief *animateur,* Jean-Marcel Jeanneney, frankly admitted, above all a 'transfer of technocrats',[31] i.e. deconcentration not devolution.

As it turned out, the proposed regional reform was rejected by the electorate (52 per cent voting against), partly because it was linked to the reform of the Senate, partly because it was opposed by many local notables (in spite of the fact that a majority of them favoured some sort of regional reform, as shown by the large-scale attempt to consult them which took place during the autumn of 1968), but above all because the French electorate voted on a pro- or anti- de Gaulle basis and not for or against regional or Senate reform.[32] The failure of the 1969 regional project, of course, did nothing to solve France's problem of overcentralisation. It is therefore not surprising that regional reform has remained a matter for debate.

Under pressure from regional groups such as the *Conseil National des Economies Régionales et de la Productivité*, and with the memory of May 1968 still very much in mind, President Pompidou announced at Lyons in October 1970 that the government was working on a 'pragmatic, supple and liberal' regional reform:

> 'The region should not be seen as a new administrative stratum, but rather as the organ through which the departments can come together to plan major regional projects ... It should make it possible for the State to deconcentrate responsibility without creating a new layer of government. Likewise it should make it possible for departments to delegate upwards some of their powers in matters which extend beyond the departmental sphere'.[33]

Pompidou's Lyons speech (followed by a similar one at Brest in October 1971) foreshadowed the regional reform announced by Roger Frey in November 1971, which became the law of 5 July 1972. The Frey Law can only be described as pragmatic and timid. Its saving grace is that the region *can* evolve *if* the national government or *collectivités territoriales* (departments and communes) decide to transfer powers to it. Executive power remains firmly in the government's hands in the person of the regional prefect. No attempt has been made to rationalise the regions by cutting down the present twenty-two (as advocated by many regionalists). The regions have not been recognised as *collectivités territoriales*, but merely as *établissements publics*, defined by the *Conseil d'Etat* as 'organisations sous l'autorité de l'administration'.[34] The CODER have been abolished and replaced by two assemblies, one deliberative and indirectly elected (the Regional Council, consisting of local parliamentarians and representatives of departmental and communal councils),* the other consultative and indirectly elected (the Economic, Social and Cultural Committee, consisting of representatives of the socioeconomic groups). The financial autonomy of the regions has been so strictly limited as to be derisory.

*The first Regional Councils were elected in December 1973.

The regions' income is to consist of driving-licence revenue, plus a local tax of up to 1.20 francs per inhabitant. It has been calculated that the revenue from these two taxes (and the 1.20 francs is optional and maximal) would bring in only 37 million francs in the present region of Picardie, compared with a total annual budget of over 800 million francs for the three departments which constitute Picardie (Aisne, Oise and Somme). Not unreasonably *Le Nouvel Observateur* commented that Pompidou's maxim must be 'No regions which can threaten the central government'.[35] Almost no one except the orthodox Gaullists (and even they were not united) was satisfied with the new law. Departmental notables, as well as traditional Jacobins like Sanguinetti and Mollet, thought it went too far.[36] Not surprisingly Edgard Pisani did not think it went nearly far enough; in his view the new law was 'detestable' — no real power had been devolved to the regions and nothing had been done to reduce their number.[37] Jacques Pelletier of the *Centre Démocrate* called it 'a caricature of regionalisation'.[38] The Communists criticised it because it did nothing to reduce the powers of the regional prefect (who presides over the Regional Council).[39] François Mitterrand, First Secretary of the Socialist party, maintained that the law perpetrated the present system of 'one Napoleon for each department'; in his view elected regional councils, from which executives could emerge, were essential if regional devolution was to have any democratic meaning.[40] Only the moderate Joseph Martray of the *Mouvement National pour la Déconcentration et la Réforme Régionale* was prepared to regard it as 'une base de départ', though he argued that the reform would be meaningless if the government failed to delegate real powers in the future to the regions (this is possible under Article VI of the law). In the meantime Martray was prepared to give the government a chance to show its good faith.[41]

In view of the strength of France's centralised administrative tradition and the attitude of Gaullist governments hitherto, Martray's hopes may well be disappointed, for there is no doubt that up till now all that has been achieved is administrative deconcentration, and the law of July 1972 does nothing to transfer any real prerogatives of the State to the regions. Jean-Marcel Jeanneney, who was responsible for the 1969 regional project and who resigned from the Gaullist party in November 1971 in protest against its failure to tackle the regional problem (amongst other things), said of the 1972 law: 'The power of the State remains intact. The Paris ministries and senior civil servants have retained exclusive control over the central government funds on which local government depends.'[42]

The Regional Debate

In this section I shall attempt firstly to outline the arguments for and against devolving powers to the regions, and secondly to assess the merits of the various regional reform proposals put forward in recent years.

The arguments about regionalism centre on three main themes: efficiency, democracy, and balanced economic growth. The advocates of regionalism contend that regional assemblies (from which would emerge regional executives) would provide quicker, more efficient and more flexible government; quicker and more efficient because the long, slow process of transmitting dossiers to and from Paris would be eliminated; more flexible, because regional governments would be able to adapt central government legislation to fit in with local needs. Their opponents, however, maintain that the creation of a new layer of government would only result in an increased number of civil servants and a plethora of arguments about who was competent to do what; the result would be new legal wrangles and more administrative delays. The partisans of regionalism also believe that the creation of new *collectivités* of sufficient size to wield significant powers (unlike the commune and department), but of such a dimension as to avoid impersonality and remoteness (unlike the State and the European Economic Community), would help to renew political interest and give a boost to democracy by making political participation more meaningful. The new regions would also help to protect cultural minorities faced with the harmonising policies of that remote juggernaut, Community Europe. Ultimately such units could fit into a united, federal Europe, whilst retaining their own cultural and linguistic individuality. Those who oppose such arguments maintain that semi-autonomous regions would discredit democracy owing to the inevitable conflicts which would arise between elected regional governments and elected national governments whenever the political complexion of the two differed. Such conflicts might moreover threaten national unity, and even result in major civil conflicts which could destroy the present (admittedly imperfect) liberal democratic State. Finally, they argue that regionalism has not nothing to do with the building of a federal Europe; if such a Europe ever comes about, it will be the result of political decisions taken by the nation-states, and will not result from the (hypothetical) federal desires of the regions. The last argument about regionalism centres on economic growth. The protagonists of regionalism maintain that regional policy *(aménagement du territoire)* cannot be isolated from political devolution. Balanced economic development, they insist, cannot result from financial hand-outs, however generous these may be, but only from a combination of central government incentives *and* the creation of a broad regional infrastructure (including regional merchant banks, scientific research establishments and cultural centres). Such a regional infrastructure, it is said, will never be created unless important decisions can be taken at the regional level, and this means elected regional governments. Those who disagree with these views argue that economic planning and investment can only be tackled nationally, and some would go further and say that European economic planning alone makes sense today. They also point to the difficulties experienced by the USA, and to a lesser extent by West Germany, in trying to operate equalisation funds. They contend that it is easier for a central government in a unitary state to give preferential treatment to regions requiring it than it is for a federal government to do this, because such treatment inevitably provokes protests about 'favouritism' from the other states (or regions).

It is necessary to go into these broad arguments in more detail. In spite of the administrative reforms of the Fifth Republic there is plenty of evidence of inefficient and arbitrary administration in France. A trivial example of the pettiness of the system is given by J.-F. Gravier, who refers to the case of a widow named Mme Zulmé-Elvire-Estelle Denoyelle, who left a legacy of a few hundred francs to the social welfare office at Bergues (near Dunkirk); the case had to be referred to Paris, where it was decided after a delay of several months that the legacy could be accepted.[43] A more serious matter was the fact that 40 per cent of new primary schools were opening at least a year late in the early 1960s.[44] And René Mayer has pointed out that, whereas in the mid 1950s the Ministry of Building tried to reply to letters about rural road building within one week, by 1970 the average reply took eight months. Moreover, this was not so much the fault of the civil servants at the Ministry as the inevitable result of the twelve-fold increase in the number of decisions which had to be taken.[45] In January 1971 Jean Lecanuet, the Mayor of Rouen and leader of the *Centre Démocrate,* pointed out that the Paris Administration had taken twenty-six years to give Rouen permission to rebuild a residential block in the Place de la Cathédrale. Twenty-eight plans had been rejected (often without any adequate reasons) before the twenty-ninth was finally accepted. Such administrative procedures, Lecanuet emphasised, both destroyed local initiative and discredited the governmental-administrative system.[46] The Rouen case is no doubt an extreme one, but there is adequate evidence that France's serious housing problem has been aggravated by constant administrative delays. The promising scheme introduced in 1959 by Pierre Sudreau, the Housing Minister, to obtain more land for development and to beat speculation by the setting up of *Zones à Urbaniser par Priorité* (ZUPs) and *Zones d'Aménagement Différé* (ZADs), foundered (largely) on the rocks of administrative delay.[47]

There have been some improvements in recent years. As a result of the 1964 and 1970 reforms enhancing the powers of the prefects, the decision about the widow of Bergues' legacy could now be taken locally. But the basic problem remains. The senior civil servants in Paris are no doubt extremely competent and hard-working, but they are over-burdened with administrative matters which could well be devolved elsewhere. But the question is where. The present local government structure based on departments and communes is hopelessly outdated. Departments are supposed to be major local government units, but their elected *conseils généraux* do not run them (virtually all they do is to ratify the annual budget); it is the prefect and his officers who administer the department. The communes are supposed to 'administer themselves by means of their elected council', but for at least 36,000 out of 38,000 (all those with less than 5,000 inhabitants) this is a myth; they are in fact largely run by the sub-perfect and the engineer from *Ponts et Chaussées,* who are of course both central government agents.[48] The protagonists of regional reform argue that there is no point in pouring good money after bad in the sense of refurbishing a local government structure designed for rural France of the nineteenth century. The answer is to create a new local government structure suitable for an urban France which is already confronted with the problems of the twenty-first century. Men like Edgard Pisani, Jean-Jacques Servan-Schreiber and Claude Glayman support such initiatives as the 1971 law to encourage communal amalgamations and the attempt to deconcentrate central government departments (such as the removal of the department responsible for army pensions to La Rochelle), but they also argue that such 'reforms' are only scratching the surface.[49] France, they contend, can only be run efficiently (not to mention democratically) if a great many more political and administrative powers are devolved to the regions.

But it is the democratic argument which is at the centre of the regional debate. Arguably France could be run more efficiently if more powers were deconcentrated to regional administrators, but this would have nothing to do with 'democracy' or 'participation'. Edgard Pisani (with not untypical hyperbole) compares French citizens to de Tocqueville's slaves who prefer to accept equality in servitude rather than struggle for equality in freedom. He maintains that the main argument for regional reform is that Frenchmen would be released from their present 'slavery' and rediscover freedom through political participation.[50] Robert Lafont also sees regionalism as a 'liberalising' force; elected regional assemblies would bring to an end the unholy alliance of reactionary local notables and conservative civil servants.[51] Michel Rocard argues along similar lines except that he brings in the issue of class. He maintains that the bourgeoisie of the civil service and the bourgeoisie of local élites, who are two of the pillars of the capitalist system, must have their powers severely curtailed if socialism and democracy are to come into existence. Rocard, like Gravier, is also much concerned with the 'quality of life', which, he maintains, will be improved for everyone once a participatory democracy has been achieved. In Rocard's view the region is the ideal unit for the birth of this new participatory (and socialist) democracy, because it would be big enough to wield power and therefore attract the interest of the voters, but small enough for them to be able to identify with it.[52] Men of very different political views to those of Rocard, namely the (largely) Gaullist senior civil servants of the Club Nouvelle Frontière, have also argued that 'seven centuries of bureaucracy' have produced a *blocage* in French society. Although their vision of society is very different from Rocard's, they come to a similar conclusion, viz., that local life can only be 'revitalised' by meaningful participation at the regional level.[53] No doubt some of these ideas and hopes about democratic participation would be disappointed if semi-autonomous regions were created in France. No doubt, too, quite a number of Rocard's 'reactionary notables' would find their way into the new assemblies. But in spite of these doubts, the argument about democracy and participation, especially when linked with arguments about preserving the cultural heritage of the regions and improving the overall quality of life, is the most powerful one in the regionalists' armoury. Even if the 'democratic' and 'participatory' effects of regionalism are very difficult to forecast or quantify, it is difficult for liberal democratic politicians to reject out of hand the argument that an increasingly educated 'sovereign people' should have more say in running its own affairs.

The economic arguments for devolving power to the regions have been outlined most convincingly by Jérôme Monod and Philippe de Castelbajac, both senior officials at DATAR (the important central government regional planning group), and by Michel Rocard, leader of the PSU and a former *inspecteur des finances.* Monod and Castelbajac lay particular emphasis on the need for regional planning within the overall context of national planning. They contend that 'the whole concept of regional planning rests on the assumption that a geographical dimension exists for social and economic problems',[54] and the corollary of this is that those who live in the regions should be able to influence the planning decisions which are made for them; the only way that this can be done effectively is through elected regional assemblies. Theoretically regions could simply be administrative sectors, and local opinion could be consulted through bodies representing interest groups (such as the old CODER and the new Economic, Social and Cultural Committees), but Monod and Castelbajac argue that in such a scenario (similar to the present one in France) regional opinion cannot be properly consulted, nor can it have much effect on the central government, because it is not channelled through a fully representative body. Hence effective regional planning requires a regional body which can take decisions. Bernard Kayser and Claude Glayman have both shown that even a relatively successful region such as Rhône-Alpes is constrained by its inability to take planning and investment decisions at the local level.[55] And Michel Rocard has pointed out that, as the Common Market develops, it will become increasingly important for regions such as Alsace and Brittany, whose natural trading partners are respectively Baden-Württemberg and England, to take economic decisions on their own account. Indeed Edgard Pisani and Jean-Jacques Servan-Schreiber attribute the relative economic backwardness of Alsace and Lorraine (compared with Baden-Württemberg and Rhineland-Palatinate) to the economic subservience of these regions to Paris: investors, including French businessmen, are attracted to the other side of the Rhine, because they can get quick, autonomous decisions from the governments of the German Länder. Michel Rocard makes much of the argument that Parisian economic dominance will inevitably continue unless real power is devolved to regional governments, because no company will consider moving its headquarters out of Paris so long as all economic decisions continue to be taken there. And Monod and Castelbajac contend that the designated *métropoles d'équilibre* (Lille-Roubaix-Tourcoing, Nancy-Metz, Strasbourg, Lyon-Saint Etienne-Grenoble, Aix-Marseille, Toulouse, Bordeaux and Nantes-Saint Nazaire) will never develop into effective 'poles of attraction' unless they are granted a measure of economic autonomy, which in practice means elected regional assemblies with decision-making powers.[56] The only alternative would be to convert regional prefects into virtual economic dictators, which would presumably be unacceptable in a so-called democratic state.

It is now time to turn to the various schemes put forward by the advocates of regionalism. Roughly speaking the regionalists can be divided into two groups, gradualists and maximalists. Both are agreed that in the interests of efficiency and democracy some degree of devolution is essential. The gradualists are more inclined to take account of the difficulties arising from France's centralised tradition. They realise that the old local government units (departments and communes) retain a certain affection, even if they are unsuitable for the second half of the twentieth century. They suspect that an attempt to push through a far-reaching administrative reform might back-fire by provoking into existence an alliance of traditionalists and conservatives of all parties and political complections. But their ultimate aim is nevertheless regional government. The maximalists, on the other hand, argue that the problem is so serious that it must be tackled in a 'revolutionary' manner. Tinkering with the cancer of overcentralisation will do nothing to cure it, and might even worsen the situation by curing some of the symptoms without tackling the source of the disease. They rule out half measures such as partially elected assemblies with limited powers and small financial resources. They want to reduce the number of regions rather than trying to give some degree of autonomy to the present twenty-two, which are very unequal in size and resources.[57] And they want to deal with the problem of the communes and departments at the same time as that of the regions.

A good example of the gradualist approach is the scheme put forward by the Gaullist-oriented Club Nouvelle Frontière.[58] Although in favour of devolving powers to the regions, the Club came out against directly elected regional assemblies, even if ultimately they might be desirable. Instead the assemblies should consist of indirectly elected territorial representatives (elected by communal and departmental councillors) and interest-group representatives. The latter could either be nominated or elected, the decision being left to the interest group. Alternatively there could be elected representatives for 'macrogroups' such as wage-earners, farmers, civil servants, students, etc. The regional assembly would have its own financial resources (perhaps based on the British rates system) and would be responsible for such matters as tourism, higher education and hospitals. The reform would apply to the present twenty-two regions, because it would be a mistake to create a dozen or so 'purely technical and administrative'[59] regions even if such units would make more sense from an economic point of view. The Club recognised that the communal and departmental structure was far from ideal but was against tampering with it except for its proposal that an additional layer of government should be created (inter-communal councils representing at least 25,000 voters). There would thus be four levels of local government — the commune, the inter-communal group, the department and the region — but the two new units would be the key ones, whilst the two traditional ones might eventually wither away.

Another advocate of a gradual approach to regionalism is Joseph Martray, president of the National Movement for Decentralisation and Regional Reform. Ultimately he would favour directly elected regional assemblies, but as a first step he proposes indirect election by communal and departmental councillors. The regional prefect would preside over the executive committee emerging from this assembly, but the assembly would nevertheless have an important decision-making role in the field of regional planning. It would also have its own financial resources and be responsible for regional planning, tourism, communications, higher education and hospitals, but in so far as possible it would not impinge on the areas of competence of the departments and communes. Unlike the Club Nouvelle Frontière, Martray proposes that there should be fifteen regions instead of the present twenty-two. One of the reasons why both the Club Nouvelle Frontière and Martray are against direct election of the assemblies is that they suspect that this would 'politicise' them, and they regard this as undesirable. Martray refers to the highly successful CELIB as an example of an inter-party regional body which functioned very well. But both he and the Club Nouvelle Frontière are on weak ground when they talk about taking 'politics' out of regional government. Inevitably (and quite legitimately) there would be political conflicts within regional assemblies because of the nature of their tasks. To try to avoid such conflicts by indirect elections would do nothing to eliminate them. Moreover, indirectly elected assemblies would inevitably lack the power and legitimacy of directly elected assemblies, and Martray at least wants to see these assemblies wielding definite and considerable powers.

J.F. Gravier's proposals are similar to those of Martray except that they are spelt out in more detail.[60] Gravier also opts for fifteen regions and an indirectly elected assembly (consisting of departmental councillors). The assembly would have no more than thirty members (otherwise, in Gravier's view, it would spend too much time debating and too little getting on with the job). It would be presided over by a *préfet-intendant* (in effect a regional prefect who would be more independent of the central government, as were the *Intendants* of the eighteenth century), and when the assembly was not in session a permanent executive committee would see that the *prêtet-intendant* carried out the policies decided by the assembly. There would also be a socioprofessional advisory council (like the Economic, Social and Cultural Committees created by the 1972 Regional Law). Gravier's regions would have their own financial resources (partly local taxes, partly government subsidies), and their responsibilities would be similar to those outlined by the Club Nouvelle Frontière. Gravier would also introduce inter-communal groups. He suggests that there should be about 3,000 of them (to be called *cantons* in the countryside and *villes* elsewhere), and that like the regions they should have their own financial resources. Gravier's carefully worked out scheme would be unlikely to arouse the hostility of the local notables, whilst at the same time it would result in considerable devolution of power. The chief criticism which can be levelled against it is that an indirectly elected assembly would lack political legitimacy and at the same time be unacceptable to the Communists, Socialists and *Réformateurs,* i.e. all the opposition groups in the present National Assembly.

The maximalist schemes put forward by Edgard Pisani, Claude Glayman, the Club Jean Moulin, Jean-Jacques Servan-Schreiber, Michel Rocard and Pierre Fougeyrollas could not be criticised on the above grounds, but they would be more likely to encounter opposition from other sources, notably from all those with a vested interest in the status quo (including the three parties of the present Gaullist *majorité,* traditionalists of all sorts, and many senior civil servants). The maximalist schemes all have certain points in common, such as their advocacy of relatively large regions (ten to twelve altogether), directly elected regional assemblies which would elect their own executives, considerable powers in the hands of these executives, and the linking of other local government reforms to regional reform. The maximalist schemes of course differ in detail. Rocard and Servan-Schreiber, for example, would abolish regional prefects whereas Pisani would not. Fougeyrollas would like to convert France into a federal State, whereas the others talk of a decentralised unitary State. In practice, of course, there would not be much difference between the two. Certainly if the maximalists got their way, it would be a nice academic point to decide whether the Federal Republic of Germany was more or less 'federal' than unitary France.

Rather than discussing all the maximalist schemes, those of Pisani, Rocard and Fougeyrollas will be examined in some detail. The Pisani and Rocard schemes are similar, whilst Fougeyrollas's scheme is the most far-reaching of all. Pisani and Rocard both propose a dual reform: at the same time as ten to twelve regions are established, new style communes (about 4,000-5,000 instead of the present 38,000) would be set up. The regional assemblies and communal councils would both be directly elected, and would elect their own executives and mayors. Pisani would also like an advisory economic and social council, whose members would be directly elected by the various interest groups. Rocard makes no reference to such a body. Pisani's regional prefect would in effect be the head of the regional civil service. He would have an important role of 'command, definition and synthesis'[61] in implementing the policies of the regional government. Rocard would simply abolish the prefectoral office, but would no doubt have to create something similar with a different name but comparable role to that outlined by Pisani. Without discussing the powers of the regional governments in any detail, both men say that every power which is not clearly a national prerogative should be devolved to the regions, just as in turn every power which can be sensibly devolved to the new communes should be. Both regions and communes would have their own financial resources, although the central government would also run a regional equalisation fund.

The Pisani and Rocard schemes would result in a complete *bouleversement* of France's administrative-governmental structure, but Pisani and Rocard are convinced that a far-reaching reform of this type is necessary to deal with the problem of overcentralisation; half-measures would simply produce more *étatisation* (central government interference). But the trouble with their schemes is that they would arouse a great deal of opposition. Pisani's suggestion that departments ('designed for the age of horse-drawn carriages')[62] should gradually be phased out would certainly arouse fierce opposition from France's 3,300 *conseillers généraux*. Nor is it likely that the 30,000 mayors who would lose their jobs would accept the reform without a bitter fight. Others, with less interest in the status quo, would regard the new regions as artificial creations; after all it has taken almost twenty years to confer some reality on the present ones. Moreover, the Gaullists will never agree to directly elected regional assemblies so long as they are relatively weakly implanted in local government. Altogether it is most unlikely than any maximalist scheme will get off the ground in the present political and social climate in France.

The same can be said with even more confidence of Pierre Fougeyrollas's proposals for a federal France.[63] Fougeyrollas contends that France should become both properly presidential and federal, like the USA. Assured of stability through the separation of powers, the President of the Federal Republic of France would choose his own ministers, who would be responsible to him. He would be responsible for foreign policy, defence, monetary policy and the coordination of regional planning. The Federal Assembly (which would replace the National Assembly) would be elected as at present; it would be responsible for federal legislation. The Senate would represent the states like the American Senate or German *Bundesrat*. France would be divided into eleven regions or states, and the regional governments emerging from directly elected regional assemblies would wield all powers not specifically reserved for the President or devolved to large, reorganised communes. To complete the picture, a new federal capital *(Franceville)* would be built in the centre of France, and Paris would become a mere regional capital. The chances of such a scheme being accepted are minimal. Not only would it arouse the opposition of all those who would be against the Pisani and Rocard proposals, it would also be rejected by committed regionalists such as Gravier, who points out that France, unlike Germany, Switzerland or the United States, has no strong particularist traditions, and without such traditions a French federation would be artificial and therefore most unlikely to succeed.[64]

Some Conclusions

In spite of the regionalist movement of the last twenty years, France remains a very centralised country. It is difficult to quantify the success of regional policy in any country, but it is clear that the establishment of twenty-two economic regions in 1955, their consolidation under regional prefects and CODER, responsible to a high-powered central government *délégation* (DATAR) in 1964, and the creation of four special regional zones in 1967, helped to re-establish confidence and economic growth in provincial France. Regional imbalances certainly remain, and some regions are noticeably poorer than others (parts of Brittany and of the Massif Central to name but two), but the 1968 census indicated rapid economic growth in regions other than the Paris basin, notably in Rhône-Alpes and in the Bouches-du-Rhône, as well as in and around major provincial cities such as Toulouse in the South and Rennes in the West. Paris (or at least the Paris region) continues to be economically dominant, but J.-F. Gravier's 1972 version of *Paris et le Désert Français* is much more optimistic (at least in economic terms) than the original edition of 1947.

In the area of administration the picture is less bright. There has been some administrative decentralisation. As a result of the 1964 reform creating regional prefects, and the 1964 and 1970 reforms increasing the powers of the departmental prefects, a number of decisions which previously had to be referred to Paris can now be taken on the spot by the appropriate prefect. But the basic local government units (the 95 departments and 38,000 communes) are poorly adapted to the administrative needs of the second half of the twentieth century. To make matters worse, they are almost entirely dependent on national subsidies for carrying out their tasks. So far virtually nothing has been done to reform local government. The 1971 law providing a 50 per cent increase in subsidies to communes which amalgamate on the advice of the prefect has only scratched the surface of the problem. In 1972 only 268 communes agreed to amalgamate.

The Frey Regional Law of July 1972 was described by President Pompidou as 'pragmatic, supple and liberal'. This law, creating indirectly elected regional councils with very limited powers (and minute financial resources), aided by advisory economic and social committees, may be said to be pragmatic in the sense that it should work, as it entails such a limited change that it is unlikely to upset the status quo in any way, but it is not particularly supple unless article VI (allowing for a further devolution of powers to the regional councils) is generously interpreted, and it is certainly not liberal if that word is meant to be synonymous with progressive. The reform could hardly be more timid. The regions will be neither powerful nor democratically governed. But in fairness to Pompidou and the Gaullists, it must be conceded that devolving powers to the regions is a very sensitive political issue. It is not simply that the government is acting in a pusillanimous manner when faced by traditionalists in the provinces and powerful civil servants in Paris. Nor is it simply that France's whole historical tradition is against a reform of this sort. Experienced political commentators such as Roger Priouret and Georges Vedel have pointed out that serious conflicts could arise both between semi-autonomous regions and Paris, and between the regions themselves.[65] The experience of Italy is not very encouraging in this matter, whilst Germany's inability to carry through much needed educational reforms owing to *Länder* control of education confirms the sceptics in their opposition to regionalism.

There is no simple solution to France's governmental-administrative problems. The State is failing its citizens because it is overcentralised and therefore frequently inefficient. At the same time the traditional local government structure, largely a nineteenth-century creation, is in desperate need of modernisation. The regional reforms of the last twenty years have helped to adjust the governmental-administrative structure to the economic conditions of the second half of the twentieth century, but so far they have amounted to a political *coitus interruptus*. The regions which have been created are too small as planning units, too uneven in size, too weak financially, and too undemocratic institutionally. The devolution of greater powers and more functions to the regions would not of itself be a panacea, but it would almost certainly improve the governmental-administrative structure by making it more efficient, more flexible and more democratic. However, the greatest obstacle to such a reform is the traditionalism of most Frenchmen. Michel Rocard has rightly emphasized that 'the centralising current in this country can only be reversed by a major effort of political will'.[66] But up till now this political will has been lacking. A SOFRES opinion poll of December 1970 found that only 15 per cent of respondents wanted a far-reaching regional reform (63 per cent favoured gradual changes, whilst 22 per cent wanted no change). At the 1973 General Election regionalism was not an issue except for the centrist *Réformateurs* who won only 12.5 per cent of the votes and 32 seats. There is therefore no political weight behind the regional movement. It remains the prerogative of a number of Bretons and Alsatians who have a strong sense of regional identity; of cultural enthusiasts like Lafont and Fougeyrollas; of academics like Gravier and Vedel; of Parisian 'technocrats' like Pisani and Rocard; and of senior officials like Monod and Castelbajac. But regionalism has failed to arouse any popular enthusiasm except perhaps for a brief period between the Events of May 1968 and the regional referendum of April 1969. It is therefore not surprising that only a limited number of administrative functions have been deconcentrated under the Fifth Republic, whilst no attempt has been made to devolve real power to the regions and to subject it to democratic control. The dilemma remains: in the interests of democracy and efficiency the balance of power within the governmental-administrative structure needs to be altered to reduce the all-pervading influence of Paris, but the majority of politicians and civil servants have no desire to tackle such a politically sensitive problem, and their inaction is widely approved by conservative local notables and apathetic electors.

Appendix: Present 22 Regions

	Area Km²	Pop. 1968 (000's)	Estimated Pop. 2000 (000's)
Région Parisienne	12,008	9,251	9,300
Champagne-Ardennes	25,600	1,279	2,500
Picardie	19,411	1,579	2,600
Haute-Normandie	12,258	1,497	2,150
Centre	39,061	1,990	4,100
Basse-Normandie	17,583	1,260	2,100
Bourgogne	31,592	1,503	2,900
Nord	12,379	3,815	4,700
Lorraine	23,540	2,274	3,200
Alsace	8,310	1,412	2,000
Franche-Comté	16,189	993	1,800
Pays de la Loire	32,126	2,582	3,900
Bretagne	27,184	2,468	3,700
Poitou-Charentes	25,790	1,481	2,800
Aquitaine	41,407	2,460	4,400
Midi-Pyrénées	45,382	2,185	4,100
Limousin	16,932	736	1,400
Rhône-Alpes	43,694	4,423	6,300
Auvergne	25,988	1,312	2,200
Languedoc-Roussillon	27,448	1,707	2,950
Provence-Côte d'Azur	31,436	3,299	5,300
Corse	8,681	220	500
	534,998	49,778	75,000

Notes

1. Pierre Fougeyrollas, *Pour Une France Fédérale* (Denoël, 1968), p.9.
2. Michel Crozier, *Le Phénomène bureaucratique* (Seuil, 1963); *La Société Bloquée* (Seuil, 1970); *Esprit*, Dec. 1957, pp.779-98.
3. M. Crozier, 'La France, terre de commandement', *Esprit*, Dec. 1957.
4. M. Crozier, 'La France, terre de commandement', *Esprit*, Dec. 1957.
5. For details, see pp.17-18 & 29.
6. A phrase used by the Club Nouvelle Frontière, *Autonomie pour les Régions?* (Paris, 1968), p.3; for conservatism of mayors see, for example, *Le Monde*, 26, 27 and 28 May 1973.
7. I.e. departments and communes, the only local government units recognised by the Constitution (Article 72).
8. Club Nouvelle Frontière, *Autonomie pour les Régions?* (Paris, 1968), p.65.
9. Joseph Martray, *La Région pour un Etat Moderne* (France-Empire, 1970), p.17. For Debré's Jacobinism, see *Au Service de la Nation* (Paris, 1963), pp.235-8; for Sanguinetti's, see *Le Figaro*, 6 Jan. 1971.
10. R. Lafont, *Décoloniser en France* (Gallimard, 1971).
11. See also J. Monod and P. de Castelbajac, *L'Aménagement du Territoire* (PUF 1971), and J. -F. Gravier, *Paris et le Désert Français en 1972* (Flammarion 1972).
12. Reduced to twenty-one in 1960, increased to twenty-two in 1969 (when Pompidou, honouring an electoral promise, granted Corsica regional status).
13. *Commissions de Développement Economique et Régionale.*
14. Article 72 of the 1958 Constitution. There are also *arrondissements* (about 450), now important only as electoral units, and *cantons* (groups of communes, about 3,000), but neither is recognised as a *collectivité territoriale*.
15. P. Brongniart, *La Région en France* (Colin, 1971), p.13.
16. On CELIB see R. Pleven, *Avenir de la Bretagne* (Calmann-Levy, 1961); M. Phlipponneau, *La Gauche et les Régions* (Calmann-Levy, 1967); and J.E.S. Hayward, 'The Battle of Brittany', *Political Studies*, March 1969.
17. E. Claudius-Petit, *Pour un Plan d'Aménagement du Territoire* (Paris, 1950).
18. For figures in this paragraph, see J. -F. Gravier, *Paris et le Désert Français en 1972* (Flammarion, 1972), pp.94-7.
19. Officially recognised as such in 1960.
20. For increased 'politicisation' of planning under the Fifth Republic see J.E.S. Hayward, *The One and Indivisible French Republic* (Weidenfeld & Nicolson, 1973), pp.168-9. For detailed accounts of the planning process, see Hayward, *op.cit.*, Chapter 6; A. Shonfield, *Modern Capitalism: the Changing Balance of Public and Private Power* (Oxford University Press, 1965); J. and A.M. Hackett, *Economic Planning in France* (Allen & Unwin, 1963); and S.S. Cohen, *Modern Capitalist Planning: the French Model* (Weidenfeld & Nicholson, 1969). On DATAR see B. Pouyet, *La Délégation à L'Aménagement du Territoire et à l'Action Régionale* (Cujas, 1968).
21. See pp.28-39.
22. See J. Monod and P. de Castelbajac, *L'Aménagement du Territoire* (PUF, 1971), pp.86-94.
23. J. -F. Gravier, *Paris et le Désert Français en 1972* (Flammarion, 1972), p.204.
24. See D.I. Scargil, *Economic Geography of France* (Macmillan, 1968), p.25.
25. See p.26.
26. *Le Monde*, 26 March 1969.
27. J.E.S. Hayward, 'Presidential suicide by plebiscite; de Gaulle's exit, April 1969', *Parliamentary Affairs*, Autumn 1969, p.296.

28. Ibid., p.296.
29. E.g. in P. Brongniart, *La Région en France* (Colin, 1971), pp.75-9.
30. E. Pisani, *La Région . . . Pour Quoi Faire?* (Calmann-Levy, 1969), p.155.
31. Quoted, J.E.S. Hayward, 'Presidential suicide by plebiscite: de Gaulle's exit, April 1969', *Parliamentary Affairs*, Autumn 1969, p.297.
32. Ibid., p.317.
33. *Le Monde*, 2 November 1970.
34. *Le Monde*, 26 April 1972.
35. 20 September 1971.
36. *Le Figaro*, 6 January 1972; *Le Monde*, 26 April 1972.
37. *Le Monde*, 23 November 1971.
38. *Démocratie Moderne*, 17 February 1972.
39. *Le Monde*, 12 February 1972.
40. *Le Monde*, 23 November 1971.
41. *Le Monde*, 26 April 1972.
42. *Le Figaro*, 26 April 1972.
43. J.-F. Gravier, *Paris et le Désert Français en 1972* (Flammarion, 1972), p.20.
44. P.M. Williams and M. Harrison, *Politics and Society in de Gaulle's Republic* (Longman, 1971), p.249.
45. J.-J. Servan-Schreiber, *Le Pouvoir Régional* (Grasset, 1971), p.25.
46. *Démocratie Moderne*, 7 January 1971.
47. For details about the housing problem and the failure of the ZUPs and ZADs scheme, see R.E.M. Irving, *Christian Democracy in France* (Allen and Unwin, 1973), pp.129-37.
48. See B. and J.-L. Kayser, *95 Régions* (Seuil, 1971); Club Jean Moulin, *Les Citizens au Pouvoir, 12 Régions et 2000 Communes* (Seuil, 1968), and J.P. Worms, 'Le préfet et ses notables', *Sociologie du Travail*, No. 3, 1966.
49. E. Pisani, *Une Région . . . Pour Quoi Faire?* (Calmann-Levy, 1969); J.J. Servan-Schreiber, *Le Pouvoir Régional* (Grasset, 1971); Claude Glayman, *Liberté Pour Les Régions: Bretagne et Rhône-Alpes* (Fayard, 1971).
50. E. Pisani, *Une Région . . . Pour Quoi Faire?* (Calmann-Levy, 1969), p.59.
51. *Esprit*, December 1968, pp.643-7.
52. M. Rocard, *Décoloniser La Province* (Grenoble, 1966), esp. pp.8, 15 and ff.
53. Club Nouvelle Frontierè, *Autonomie Pour Les Régions?* (Paris, 1968), pp.11-28.
54. J. Monod and P. de Castelbajac, *L'Aménagement du Territoire* (PUF, 1971), p.44.
55. B. and J. Kayser, *95 Régions . . .* (Seuil, 1971) p.39, and ff. G. Glayman, *Liberté pour les Régions: Bretagne et Rhône-Alpes* (Fayard, 1971).
56. J. Monod and P. de Castelbajac, *L'Aménagement du Territoire* (PUF, 1971), p.116.
57. See Table, p.39.
58. Club Nouvelle Frontière, *Autonomie Pour Les Régions?* (Paris, 1968).
59. Ibid., p.33.
60. J.-F. Gravier, *La Question Régionale* (Flammarion, 1970), pp.161-82.
61. E. Pisani, *La Région . . . Pour Quoi Faire?* (Calmann-Levy, 1969), p.122.
62. Ibid., p.122.
63. Pierre Fougeyrollas, *Pour Une France Fédérale* (Denoel, Paris, 1968).
64. J.-F. Gravier, *La Question Régionale* (Flammarion, 1970), pp.164-5.

65. Priouret in *L'Express*, 11 January 1971; Vedel in *L'Express*, 28 February 1971.
66. M. Rocard, *Décoloniser la Province* (Grenoble, 1966), p.25.

Select Bibliography

K. Allen and M. MacLennan	*Regional Problems and Policies in Italy and France* (Allen and Unwin, 1970).
P. Brongniart	*La Région en France.* (Colin, 1971).
Club Jean Moulin	*Les Citoyens au Pouvoir: 12 Régions et 2,000 Communes.* (Seuil, 1968).
Club Nouvelle Frontière	*Autonomie pour les Régions?* (Paris, 1968).
M. Crozier	*Le Phénomène Bureaucratique.* (Seuil, 1963).
	La Société Bloquée. (Seuil, 1970).
Esprit. (December 1968)	Special No. on Regionalism.
T. Flory	*Le Mouvement Régionaliste Français* (PUF, 1971).
P. Fougeyrollas	*Pour Une France Fédérale.* (Calmann-Lévy, 1961)
C. Glayman	*Liberté pour les Régions: Bretagne et Rhône-Alpes.* (Fayard, 1971).
J.F. Gravier	*La Question Régionale.* (Flammarion, 1970).
	Paris et le Désert Français en 1972. (Flammarion, 1972).
P. Grémion and J.-P. Worms	*Les Institutions Régionales et la Société Locale.* (Copédith, 1968).
	Sociologie du Travail. (July-September 1966), special No. on 'L'administration face aux problèmes du changement'.
O. Guichard	*Aménager la France.* (Laffont, 1965).
J.E.S. Hayward	*The One and Indivisible French Republic.* (Weidenfeld & Nicolson, 1973), Chapter II.
	'The Battle of Brittany', *Political Studies*, March 1969.
Institut d'Etudes Politiques de l'Universite de Grenoble	*Aménagement du Territoire et Développement Régional.* (6 vols., 1968-73). (University of Grenoble and DATAR).
B. and J.L. Kaiser	*95 Régions.* (Seuil, 1971).
R. Lafont	*La Révolution Régionaliste.* (Gallimard, 1967).
J. Martray	*La Région pour un Etat Moderne.* (France-Empire, 1970).
R. Mayer	*Féodalités ou Démocratie.* (Arthaud, 1968).
J. Monod et P. de Castelbajac	*L'Aménagement du Territoire.* (PUF, 1971).
M. Philipponneau	*La Gauche et les Régions.* (Calmann-Lévy, 1967).
	Debout Bretagne. (Presses Universitaires de Bretagne, 1971).
E. Pisani	*La Région: Pour Quoi Faire?* (Calmann-Lévy, 1969).
R. Pleven	*Avenir de la Bretagne.* (Calmann-Lévy, 1961).
B. Pouyet	*La Délégation à l'Aménagement du Territoire et à l'Action Régionale.* (Cujas, 1968).

P.J. Proudhon *Du Principe Fédératif, in Oeuvres Complètes.* (Rivière, 1959).

M. Rocard *Décoloniser la France.* ('Rapport général sur la vie régionale en France' presented at Rencontre Socialiste de Grenoble, 1966).

J.-J. Servan-Schreiber *Le Pouvoir Régional.* (Grasset, 1971).

2. ITALY: REGIONALISM AND BUREAUCRATIC REFORM

Martin Clark

Introduction

Italy is an excellent illustration of the main themes of this book. She is seen by many of her own citizens as the European country where the 'failure of the State' has been most acute. Public confidence in politicians appears exceptionally low; rumours of impending *coups d'état* are frequent; and the civil service is widely regarded as inefficient or corrupt. Moreover, her regional disparities are greater than those of any other country in Western Europe; the 'southern problem' in particular affects all aspects of the Italian economy and of the Italian political system. In an attempt to remedy this situation, the Italians have recently embarked upon an ambitious reform of the State machinery and administration, including the setting up of regional governments throughout the country. This essay will examine the new measures, and will assess how far they are likely to provide solutions for the country's problems. However, for reasons of space it will not include discussion of the weakness of the judiciary, the police forces or the legal system, where the failure of the State has been equally apparent.

The administrative tradition of united Italy has always been highly centralist. In 1861 the Prefectoral system of Piedmont (based on that of France) was extended to the new Kingdom of Italy; and for nearly a century the Prefect, a centrally appointed official, remained the most important political figure in each province, responsible (among much else) for securing a government majority at the next General Election. The provinces themselves (numbering ninety-two at present) were, like the French *départements,* simply convenient areas for structuring the State's field administration; they had negligible powers of their own. They were (and are) 'artificial constructions, without traditions or distinctive economic or social conditions that can justify their existence as a separate level of local self-government'.[1] There was also no question of 'autonomous' local government at town or village level. The basic unit of local government was the 'commune' (8,056 at present), which varied in size from tiny Alpine villages to big cities like Rome or Milan. A uniform legislation applied to all of them, and they were all supposed to carry out the same — very limited — functions. The mayors were government appointees until 1896 — and even afterwards the most important local official, the commune secretary, remained a central civil servant. Moreover, the Prefect was expected to exercise close supervision over the mayors and commune councils in his province, and he could normally prevent any effective independence.

The reasons for this centralisation were simple. The new governing class was perfectly aware that local feelings were strong, and that Piedmontese domination was much resented in other regions. But they were also aware that their own power base was extremely restricted, and that the local elites in the country — Bourbonists, Clericals, Republicans and Extreme Left — could only be kept in check by the smack of firm (centralised) government. In short, they adopted the classic 'Jacobin' solution, and justified it by the need to 'make Italians'.

Although their opponents continued to campaign against excessive centralisation, after the 1860s the arguments were normally about the virtues of local democracy at commune level, or the iniquities of the Prefect system in the provinces, rather than about the need for regional governments or for a more 'federal' State. Sicily, indeed, was perhaps the only region which had to be taken seriously as a historical and geographical unit. Most of the other regions (the so-called 'historic regions') were invented in 1864 by the Statistical Office to group its data, and consisted of clusters of provinces.[2] They remained a statistical fiction until after the Second World War, with no political or economic reality. There were, and are, extreme disparities among them in population and resources: compare, for example, Lombardy's largely industrial population of eight and a half million with Molise's 300,000, half of whom are peasants (see Table 1, p.74). There were also marked intraregional conflicts, notably the traditional rivalries between neighbouring cities (Messina-Palermo, etc.). Above all, the 'regions', like the provinces, lacked a natural political base, and except in Sicily (and to a much lesser extent in Sardinia) there was little demand for any measures of regional devolution.

The discovery and increasing importance of the 'southern problem' in late nineteenth and early twentieth century political debate was only marginally a contribution to 'regionalism'. The south is, of course, a supraregional area (it consists of eight regions, plus parts of two more, out of the total twenty), and any attempt to deal with its problems obviously requires supraregional economic development planning (or possibly a political revolution throughout Italy). Paradoxically, the very intensity of the southern regions' problems — for which, it was argued, the local land-owning elites were largely to blame — provided an additional justification for Jacobinism; and this has remained true to this day.

This centralist tradition was powerfully reinforced during the Fascist period. Mussolini restored government appointment of mayors, and campaigned vigorously against the Sicilian elite. He also pursued a rhetorical (and tragic) policy of 'Italianisation' in the newly acquired German-speaking and Slav provinces of Northern Italy.[3] Indeed, it was the resentment aroused by Mussolini's policies that led, after the collapse of Fascism in 1943, to serious threats of secession or revolt in these outlying regions. These threats were so serious that they could only be countered by granting some measure of regional autonomy, in a desperate attempt to pacify the local elites. By 1947, therefore, there already existed four so-called 'regions of special statute', with varying legislative and administrative powers, in Valle d'Aosta, Trentino-Alto Adige, Sicily and Sardinia (see pp.47-49).

Even in the rest of Italy, there was a strong reaction after the war against the old centralised machinery of the strong State, which was associated with Fascist oppression, and which had in any case collapsed in 1943. Some of the victorious Resistance parties (especially the Christian Democrats and the Party of Action) had long been committed to measures of political devolution. All these factors ensured that the new Republic set up after 1945 would not be completely centralised. The 'historic' regions, including those of special statute, were written into the new Constitution which came into force in January 1948 (Article 131). It is worth mentioning – in the light of later developments – that there was little debate about their boundaries, and virtually no consideration of economic criteria or of the concept of 'city-region'.

The Constitution also laid down the main guidelines for the organisation of regional administration (Articles 114-33). Each region was to have a single, directly elected Council, a regional government *(Giunta)* responsible to the Council, and a President of the Giunta to act as head and representative of the regional government. The regions were given considerable legislative powers, within the framework of national legislation, on certain named matters, the most important of which were agriculture and public works.[4] They were also to have administrative powers on these same matters, although they were supposed to work through the existing commune and province administrations, rather than set up their own additional bureaucratic stratum. A Government Commissioner was to be set up in each region, to supervise and coordinate the administration, and to act as government watchdog over proposed regional legislation.[5]

Despite the constitutional commitment to regionalism, however, the new Republic did not introduce in practice a marked break with Italy's centralist traditions. Only in the outlying 'special regions' were regional governments actually set up, that is, only where they had to be. Elsewhere the constitutional provisions were simply ignored. The Prefect system was restored in full, and indeed from January 1946 the Prefects themselves were the old career officials, who

had served Mussolini as they now served De Gasperi, and who
personified the continuity of the State. By 1948 the Roman bureaucracy
had recovered from the shocks of the previous five years, and for the
next two decades continued to govern the country on much the same
lines as before. The greater complexity of the tasks facing civil
servants, and the increased demands upon the modern State
administration, made this traditional centralised system seem
completely inadequate by the late 1960s.

The Special Regions

As has been seen, four 'regions of special statute' existed officially by
early 1948, in Sicily, Sardinia, Valle d'Aosta and Trentino-Alto Adige.[6]
They were all in outlying parts of the country, where there were strong
ethnic or linguistic differences from mainland Italy, and where there
had been revolts or threats of secession to foreign powers at the end of
the war. By 1963 a fifth special region, Friuli-Venezia Giulia, was set up,
with its capital in Trieste; this was another region with important
linguistic minorities and where a foreign power (Yugoslavia) had a
substantial interest. These special regions were clearly much more
meaningful entities — with much more obvious political bases — than
the others, and it is not surprising that the local elites were originally
conceded greater — sometimes, as in the case of Sicily, considerably
greater — powers than were envisaged for the 'ordinary' regions. The
special regions are an example of an attempted 'political devolution',
forced on the Italian State by the circumstances at the end of the war.
Such political devolution seems to me extremely unlikely to occur
anywhere without great pressure from disaffected ethnic or linguistic
groups.[7]

In fact, however, there is not all that much that is 'special' about
the special regions. They are organised in much the same way as the
other regions, with elected Council, regional Giunta and President,
and in practice have much the same sort of legislative powers — the
so-called 'exclusive' legislative powers of the special regions are
exclusive only in name.[8] Even Sicily, whose Statute was issued in
May 1946, before the Constitution itself, has seen its 'exclusive'
legislative powers whittled away since 1956 by successive decisions
of the Constitutional Court. The main distinguishing feature of the
special regions' powers is that they, unlike the 'ordinary' regions, may
legislate on matters other than those listed in Article 117 of the
Constitution, so that in principle they can have considerable say over
local industry, commerce, education and social affairs, as well as the
usual agriculture and public works. However, it seems that the bulk
of the special regions' legislative activity over the years has been

concerned with agriculture, especially the granting of various concessions and subsidies to individual farmers; the special regions have been inhibited from legislating on contentious areas like, say, education in Trentino-Alto Adige, for fear of being ruled unconstitutional.[9]

Similarly, the special regions' administrative powers have been greatly restricted in practice. Not only have special sections of the Court of Accounts exercised close supervision over regional administration,[10] but there has been very little delegation of administrative functions.[11] The State has maintained its field services in the regions, with the result that regional administration has been of marginal importance.[12] Above all, the special regions have enjoyed little financial independence. Their expenses have been largely met by all or part of certain state taxes, unilaterally decided by the Treasury; the Tupini Commission estimated that in 1958 82 per cent of the special regions' receipts came from the central authorities.[13] The system of 'special contributions' made by the Treasury gives the State great control over the execution of particular projects, even when these clearly lie within the region's area of competence.[14] This picture is even true of Sicily, which nominally enjoys much greater financial independence.[15]

It is interesting to examine how regionalism has operated in some of these special regions, and to see how the original aims of the regionalists have been frustrated. For example, the Valle d'Aosta (where much the largest local source of finance is the Casino) is instructive in showing that regionalism does not necessarily guarantee the position of the local elite or the local (French-speaking) culture. Assimilation has been very rapid since 1945. The largest local parties are the Christian Democrats, who are strong in the rural areas, and the Communists. The Communist vote is largely immigrant (Italians from other regions), and the Communist Party normally controls the town of Aosta, where most of the immigrants settle. It is a splendid paradox that the main effect of granting regional autonomy has been to increase the number of jobs and services available in Aosta town, compared with the rural areas, thus providing a stimulus to immigration and hence to assimilation.[16] In retrospect, the secessionist crisis of 1944-8 looks like a last desperate attempt by a cultural minority (and an old elite within it) to safeguard its position. This attempt has proved unsuccessful, so much so that French is no longer the normal language of the Valdostani. It seems that small regions wishing to preserve their sense of community should concentrate more on controlling immigration than on securing political devolution.

Sicily illustrates another important phenomenon. The regional government's powers to allocate public works contracts, and to create posts in the regional administration, has modified the whole power structure of the island. A recent study of the composition of the regional Council shows that there has been a steady decline of landowners and men of independent means (local notables) since the war, to the benefit of full-time professional politicians (party officials), public employees, and teachers.[17] These men are of course members of national parties, and the local separatist parties have never done well since 1947. The new groups now exercise a virtual monopoly of worthwhile local patronage. This interpretation of the changing power scene in the south is confirmed by studies at village level in many other areas, including Sardinia.[18]

The most obvious example of the failure of a special region to satisfy local demands for political devolution has been Trentino-Alto Adige, which consists of the two provinces of Trento (Italian) and Bolzano (two-thirds German-speaking in the 1971 Census). After a great deal of agitation in Bolzano province in the 1960s, the recent Italo-Austrian packet agreement has led to a new Regional Statute,[19] in which the two *provinces* have been given most of the powers of regions elsewhere, and the province of Bolzano some extra ones as well (e.g. to discriminate in job allocation in favour of its own residents). Powers are now being transferred from the region to the provinces, although there are still important unsolved problems (e.g. the Italian State TV monopoly, and whether legislative powers on hydroelectric schemes can be given to the province of Bolzano). Perhaps more interesting, and less well-known, has been the conflict over immigration and industrialisation (which are obviously linked). Whereas the Bolzano politicians in the dominant local party, the SVP,[20] have resisted industrialisation strongly, Trento province has encouraged industrial development. Thus the intraregional conflict has not been merely over linguistic or ethnic questions, but over the nature of the region's future economy. A recent study of the regional councillors elected in Bolzano province shows that most of them are still landowners and men of independent means. There are very few professional politicians (the SVP being purely a local party), and, unlike Sicily, there appears to be no growth of a professional political class. However, patronage — in the form of jobs in Cooperatives, Peasants' Banks, charities, etc. — seems to be as important as in the South.[21] The new measures of further political devolution have probably come just in time to enable the local notables in the SVP to maintain their power, although of course they (as in Valle d'Aosta) may find their position eroded eventually, despite regional autonomy.

The Advent of the Ordinary Regions

Altogether, the special regions were not a happy precedent; and this is no doubt one of the reasons why the Constitutional commitment to hold elections to the other, 'ordinary' regions' Councils within a year was not observed. But there was another, more pressing, reason. After 1947 the regional question became a party political issue at national level. The Communist and Socialist ministers were expelled from the government in May 1947, and by January 1948, when the Constitution came into force, the cold war was a reality. Anti-Communism was the main theme (and a highly successful one) of the Christian Democrat campaign in the first post-war parliamentary election, in April 1948. In these circumstances it was unthinkable for the Christian Democrat leaders to allow regional devolution to go ahead, and thus set up their arch-rivals, the very enemies of Western civilisation itself, in positions of power and influence in central Italy. The electoral strength of the Italian Communist Party (and of the Socialists, who maintained their alliance with the Communists until the mid-1950s) in Emilia, Tuscany and Umbria, was a powerful argument against introducing regional government anywhere.

Moreover, by 1948 the Christian Democrats were established in Rome, with all the powers of the centralised State at their command. The party could, and did, use the Prefect system to control local governments (especially Communist and Socialist local governments); and regionalism would probably mean the abolition of Prefects, or at least the curtailment of their powers. Above all, by 1948 the political situation had changed greatly from the heady days of the armed Resistance and the apparently revolutionary situation of three years earlier. The 'wind from the north' had died down to the gentlest of breezes, and there was very little pressure on the Christian Democrat governments to introduce any further sweeping constitutional change. Indeed, the pressures were in the opposite direction, for not only were the civil servants themselves naturally opposed to any disruption, but the Liberal Party was often an indispensable coalition ally of the Christian Democrats in the years after 1948, and it remained implacably hostile to any alteration in the old centralised structure inherited from the golden Liberal age of pre-Fascist Italy.

However, the ordinary regions were not entirely forgotten after 1948. In February 1953 the famous Scelba Law was passed, laying down in minute detail their future internal organisation, but at the same time introducing some very severe limitations on regional autonomy.[22] However, this law omitted the vital financial and electoral clauses, so that the regions could still not be set up.

In the 1950s more sophisticated voices were heard. Many Christian Democrats were uneasy at the party's abandonment of what had been a central plank in its platform (and indeed of the whole Christian Democrat and Popular Party tradition). To placate them, it was argued that it was vital to build up the party (and State) organisations in the regions (especially the southern regions, where the Christian Democrats were not strong) before any measures of regional autonomy could safely be granted. Failure to do so would mean that regional government would fall either into the hands of the traditional reactionary landowning and commercial groups, or into the even more grasping hands of a new class of locally based professional politicians. In the mid-1950s, in fact, Fanfani as party secretary made a determined effort to reorganise the Christian Democrats in the south, so as to exclude the old notables from control of the party at local level, but he was dismissed from his post before his work was complete. The activities of the Land Reform Boards, and indeed of the Fund for the South *(Cassa per il Mezzogiorno)* itself in its early years, may also be seen as part of an attempt to create a centralised patronage network outside the old notables' control, in order to undermine their political power. The power of the local notables, and the relationship between them and local party organisations, was (and still is) a serious problem in the south. Its importance has been revealed again very recently, by the riots at Reggio Calabria in 1970-71 when a rival city was chosen as seat of regional government, with consequent loss of patronage for the ruling elite in Reggio. Regional governments were, therefore, unlikely to be set up in the ordinary regions until the governing parties in Rome had some confidence (however misplaced) in their local party organisations and in their command of worthwhile patronage, especially in the south; in other words, until they could ensure that regional governments would remain under central control.

By the mid-1960s this condition had largely been fulfilled, because of the economic — and hence political — importance of the various public agencies and public works schemes. The great population movements of these years also played their part. To quote one acute observer, 'the decreasing importance of internal sources of income (in the south) and the existence of possibilities of migration help to free the poorer classes from the crippling system of social relationships within the community, and help to free them from the hegemony of the traditionally dominant classes'.[23] Once the economic dominance of the local notables was over, it was thought safe to introduce regional governments into the mainland south. Indeed, national politicians could look forward to strengthening their own positions in the intense faction fights of their respective parties by the judicious use of regional patronage. Socialist politicians were particularly active in this field, most notably the Party secretary, Giacomo Mancini, in Calabria.

The advent of 'Centre-Left' governments in 1963, and the increased importance of the Socialist Party in the Italian political scene in the 1960s, was in fact one of the main reasons for the introduction of 'ordinary' regional governments in 1970. The Socialists insisted on this as a precondition for their joining the government coalition in 1963; and they were well placed to benefit from the new party-based organisation of patronage in the South.[24] Moreover, the new 'Centre-Left' governments excluded the Liberals, who were thus unable any longer to oppose regionalism effectively; and they relied more heavily on the Left-wing factions of the Christian Democrats, who were more regionalist in tradition and ideology than the party's Right. Most important of all, with the gradual lessening of cold war tensions the Communist Party became regarded as much less of a threat — even, by the late 1960s, as a pillar of Republican legality. It was clear to most observers that, sooner or later, the Communists would have to be given an even more important role in the parliamentary system than they had already; and it might be an advantage for them to acquire useful experience of government, at regional level, in central Italy. This might even be an advantage one day to the Christian Democrats, if ever they felt it necessary to attempt a 'Grand Coalition' between themselves and the Communist Party. In the meantime, a further safeguard was provided by the establishment (since 1956) of a Constitutional Court, which could be relied on to adjudicate conservatively in cases of conflict between the central State and the regions.[25] In other words, in the changed political situation of the 1960s, many of the previous political obstacles to regionalism had disappeared.

There were also new reasons for many prominent politicians to favour some kind of reform. Rapid industrialisation and large scale migration had brought about a desperate need for new infrastructures at local level, especially in the northern cities, and the existing government machinery was apparently incapable of tackling these problems with the required urgency. Italy's first experiments with planning in the mid-1960s also showed the importance of greater coordination with local planning bodies. The rising generation of 'technocratic' Christian Democrat leaders (Gaspari, Malfatti *et al.*) argued, as did the central planners and some constitutional lawyers, that the planning problems could not be solved without effective deconcentration of the State administration. There were, therefore, persistent demands for 'efficiency', for regional administration as an essential aid to planning, and as part of an ambitious reform of public administration; and these demands came from the top of the government machinery. This reasoning implied a regional reform of a very different kind, introduced for very different motives, to that envisaged by the Constituent Assembly back in 1946-7. The technocrats' emphasis was on territorial deconcentration, for reasons of 'efficiency', rather than on political devolution or increased citizen participation.

Indeed, it is striking how little *popular* demand for regional government still existed by the late 1960s. The wave of social unrest and labour agitation of 1968-9 produced many calls for reforms — of housing, pensions, health services, education, etc. — but in virtually all cases it was the *central* government that was urged to respond and produce the goods. Inasmuch as popular demands for more 'participation' were important at all, they were so in universities and in industry (the factory delegates' movement, trade union rights in the workshops) rather than in the formal political system.[26] The introduction of the 'ordinary' regional governments was a response to the wishes of politicians and technocrats, rather than a response to popular demands.

Thus in 1968-70 the Centre-Left governments moved cautiously towards their only major reform. In February 1968 the electoral system — a form of proportional representation — to be used for the regional elections was laid down.[27] In 1969 various government projects on the regions' financial, planning and legislative powers were discussed.[28] Finally, in May 1970 the vital law on regional finance was passed,[29] enabling the ordinary regions to be set up at last, after twenty-two years' delay.

The first elections for the legislative Councils of the 'ordinary' regions were held on 7 June 1970.[30] They were fought on national, not regional, issues. To some extent local issues were deliberately excluded from the campaign. In particular, announcements about where the regional capitals were to be situated were made only after the elections, in order to avoid the campaigns being too confused by squabbles among local politicians over the patronage that the seat of regional government would be able to dispense. This precaution was wise, as the subsequent rioting at Reggio Calabria showed. Despite the rioting in Calabria (and also in the Abruzzi) the nature of the campaign, and indeed of the candidates, indicates that 'on the whole it looks as if most regional governments will be run by new 'technocratic' party-based elites, with a lot more patronage of their own'.[31] In Emilia-Romagna, for example, the majority of those elected to the regional council, for whatever party, had held party jobs previously; over half the Communist candidates, in this Communist Party stronghold, were paid party officials.[32]

The elections themselves produced few surprises, except that the stability of each party's vote since the 1968 General Election was itself a surprise. Despite the social agitations of the intervening two years (student riots, and the 'Hot Autumn' of workers' agitations in 1969), there was very little net transfer of votes. The only significant change was the loss of votes suffered by the Left-wing Socialist party, PSIUP; but even this can be more easily explained in 'national' terms (i.e. the return of former Socialist voters to the Italian Socialist Party in 1970, after temporarily registering a protest vote for PSIUP in 1968), and was indeed reflected later at national level in the 1972 General Election. This is not, of course, to say that the parties fared uniformly throughout the country. On the contrary, the usual big regional differences in party strength appeared once more. The Communists and (usually) their Socialist allies took control of regional government in the 'Red Belt' of central Italy (Emilia-Romagna, Tuscany, Umbria); and the traditional Christian Democratic hegemony was clearly revealed once more in the Veneto, where the Christian Democrats were able to form a single party regional government. Most of the regional elections produced a majority for the 'Centre-Left' parties (Christian Democrats, Socialists, Republicans, and Social Democrats); and so most regional governments shared the political complexion of the national government, which remained 'Centre-Left' until early in 1972.

The first elections in the 'ordinary' regions gave little sign, therefore, of any popular feeling in favour of regionalism, or even of any independent-minded regional elites. Even so, central party control is by no means complete, especially in the south; and it seems likely that the issues of patronage and party organisation will continue to be a theme of the regionalist debate in Italy for many years to come. It is also worth noting, in assessing the possibility of regionalist sentiment becoming stronger in the future, that in the 1972 General Election there was no sign of the regions or the regional councils providing the recruits for the national Parliament.[33] Regional councillors are in any case ineligible for Parliament, and must resign if they become parliamentary *candidates*. Thus it seems unlikely that success at regional level will provide the basis for many later parliamentary careers; and this factor in itself may well make central party control of the regional councillors more difficult, and make future regional elections more liable to be fought on regional issues.

The Powers of the Ordinary Regions

Legislative Powers
The precise limits of the ordinary regions' legislative powers are still far from clear. As we have seen on p.46, the Constitution declares that the regions can legislate on certain matters, notably agriculture and public works; but regional legislation is subject to approval by the Government Commissioner in each region. If this approval is not given, and if the law is passed again by the regional Council, it can be referred by the

government either to the Constitutional Court, for a final decision on its constitutional legitimacy, or to the national Parliament, for a decision on its political acceptability (the vexed, and much discussed, 'question of merit').

As far as constitutional legitimacy is concerned, there seem to be four main provisions: regional laws, obviously, must not apply outside the geographical limits of the region; they must not conflict with Italy's international and Treaty obligations (including those arising from membership of the EEC); they must not conflict with the Constitution itself (for example, any attempt to set up regional tariffs would conflict with Article 120 of the Constitution); and — at least for the ordinary regions — they must not conflict with the 'fundamental principles established by the laws of the State' (Article 117 of the Constitution). The 1953 Scelba law had interpreted this last provision in a draconian fashion; the regions were denied the right to legislate at all unless the 'fundamental principles' had first been clearly established. However, in 1970 the regionalists won an important victory, when the 1953 clauses were superseded by Article 17 of the law on regional finance. This declared that 'the promulgation of legislative norms by the (ordinary) regions in matters laid down in Article 117 of the Constitution occurs within the limits of the fundamental principles, such as result from laws which expressly decree them for each separate subject matter, or *such as are inferred from the existing laws*'.[34] It seems that the 'ordinary' regions are not to be much worse off than the 'special' regions in this respect, for the latter have a very similar provision written into their regional Statutes: their laws must not conflict with 'the fundamental rules of the economic and social reforms of the State' (the Sicilian Statute omits this provision).

As for the 'question of merit', regional legislation can be invalidated by the national Parliament if it is deemed to be contrary to the national interest, or to the interest of other regions. Thus the laws of the national parliament (or at least the 'fundamental principles' of them) are to be valid in the regions; whereas regional legislation may be over-ridden by Parliament on the grounds of 'national interest'.

In practice, the extent of the regions' legislative powers will depend on the Constitutional Court's decisions, and it is perhaps significant that one of the important political issues of 1970-72 was the composition of the Constitutional Court. A great deal will also depend on whether the government of the day chooses to refer unwelcome regional legislation to the Court, and here the experience of 1971-2 was particularly discouraging for committed 'regionalists'. In 1972 the Centre-Right government of Sig. Andreotti referred many regional laws (normally passed by Centre-Left regional governments) to the Court, even on such innocuous issues as nursery schools and assistance to emigrants returning home to vote at General Elections. It remains to be seen whether the return of 'Centre-Left' governments at national level in 1973 will alter this policy.

Financial Powers

The May 1970 Law also established the rules for the future finances of the ordinary regions.[35] There is clearly no question of them enjoying any financial independence. The regions were given very few revenue sources of their own, mainly income from their own property and tax revenue from former State concessions transferred to the regions; it was estimated that these would provide only about one-seventh of their total income and would not exceed 120 milliard lire (£85 million) per annum.[36] The bulk of the regions' revenue would come from two sources: the State would grant to them half the proceeds of the road tax paid by vehicles registered in their region; and, even more important, there would be a 'Common Fund', consisting of fixed proportions of the proceeds of certain State indirect taxes, collected and administered nationally (e.g. 25 per cent of the tobacco tax would go to the Common Fund). The Common Fund's moneys would be distributed among the regions according to a complicated formula, carefully laid down in the Act.[37] It is clear that the Common Fund will account for at least three-quarters of the ordinary regions' revenue: in 1973 it amounted to 564.6 milliard lire (about £380 million) (see Table 3).[38] It should also be emphasised that the bulk even of these provisions are simply to enable the regions to carry out their 'normal' administrative tasks. If extraordinary circumstances arise — and these are very liberally interpreted — the State will always have to provide the cash, as it does, for example, for economic development in the south.

There is no doubt, therefore, that the central State has not loosened its grip on the purse-strings. The unfortunate financial experiences of certain special regions, and the fear that regional administrators might prove less competent and indeed less honest than national ones, have played their part in this outcome. However, the financial law of 1970 is not quite so one-sided as has been alleged by many regionalists. The quotas, both for the regions' share of the indirect taxes and for the distribution of the Common Fund among the regions, cannot be altered by the government at will. Similarly, the regions are allowed, within certain limits, to float loans for capital expenditure, and to take shares in regional firms operating in certain sectors of the economy. Even so, one can foresee some real problems arising in the future, either from inflation or from any major indirect tax reform, which might leave the regions without sufficient income to meet their necessary expenditure. In any case, neither the regions' own financial resources, nor even the State's regular financial contributions, are sufficient to enable the regions to pursue an independent policy on important issues.

Administrative Powers

Since 1 April 1972, the ordinary regions have enjoyed administrative (as well as legislative) responsibility in the spheres listed in Article 117 of the Constitution (see note 4, p.77). This responsibility is subject to 'control of legitimacy' by a State body, and the State also retains general powers of co-ordination and direction.[39] In addition, the regions are to exercise other 'delegated' administrative powers, even in spheres not listed in Article 117, at the State's discretion; in doing so, of course, the regional administration will act essentially as an organ of the central administration and will remain responsible to it. This power of 'delegation' has been rarely used towards the special regions, except Sicily, but it seems intended to form an important part of the restructuring of public administration being attempted in the early 1970s. Thus regional administration will be of two kinds, using different procedures and subject to different methods of central control. The situation will be further complicated by the Constitutional provision (Article 118) that 'the Region normally exercises its administrative functions by delegating them to the provinces, communes or other local bodies'; although perhaps it should be said that this provision has been much honoured in the breach in the special regions. Finally, many of the State's field agencies will remain in operation at the local and regional level, and indeed it is intended that much of the work now being done in Rome will henceforth be carried out in the 'peripheral offices of the State'.[40] Many commentators forsee great problems in coordinating their activities with those of the regional administrations.

The main burden of coordination will fall on the Government Commissioner in each region (see p.46). He is supposed to act as the link between the regional administration and Rome, and also has powers of supervision over the State's peripheral offices in his region. In addition, a 'Commission of Control'[41] was set up in each ordinary region towards the end of 1971. It consists of the Government Commissioner, who acts as President, a Vice-President chosen by the Commissioner, two representatives of the Ministry of the Interior (usually Prefects), one Treasury official, one councillor of the Court of Accounts, and two experts on administrative law or public administration (these last two are chosen from a short list submitted by the regional council).[42] The 'Commission of Control' exercises 'control of legitimacy' over the region's administrative acts, i.e. it can quash them if it thinks they are illegal (there is, of course, provision for the region to appeal to the Council of State). It cannot quash them on other grounds, although it can refer them back to the regional council for final decision. A similar system has been operating in the Valle d'Aosta for years, but in the other special regions 'control of legality' is exercised, not by any 'Commission of Control', but by special sections of the Court of Accounts.[43] Even in the ordinary regions, the Commission does not, of course, control the *State's* field offices — this too is done by local branches of the Court of Accounts. To complete the picture, it should be added that the regions are themselves supposed to set up their own Commissions of Control, to exercise 'control of legitimacy' over the acts of communes and provinces.[44] Italy's traditional system of local government remains in being, as yet unreformed, but subjected to regional 'control'.

This complicated system of overlapping competences and different controlling bodies is bound to have teething troubles. The special regions have complained for years that 'control of legality' of their administrative acts can often veer over into what is in effect political control; and the 'administrative acts' include, of course, most financial matters. Much will depend on the Government Commissioners, whose role as 'super-Prefects' may be regarded as a continuation of the traditional importance of the Prefectoral Corps in Italian public administration.

One important innovation connected with the transfer of administrative responsibilities to the regions deserves particular mention. Since 1889 the Italian Council of State has been operating a system of administrative justice; it even survived the Fascist period more or less intact. In 1971 Regional Administrative Tribunals (TARs) were set up in each region, to act as administrative courts of first instance. They will hear cases brought by aggrieved citizens against the regional administration, or against the State field offices in the region, or against local (province, commune) administrative bodies. Financial matters, including disputes over taxation and pension rights, are excluded (these are the concern of the Court of Accounts' regional offices), and the TARs have no jurisdiction over public economic agencies; moreover, they can act only on legal grounds, such as excess of power, incompetence, or actual violation of the law. Even so, their powers are considerable, and include the right under some circumstances to 'replace the act' — i.e. take over administrative powers themselves.

Enthusiasm for such administrative courts is running high in Britain at the moment, and it may well be true that the TARs will provide a useful — and much needed — check on maladministration in Italy. Nevertheless, it should be recognised that they may also prove a useful instrument for maintaining central control of public administration. As local branches of the Council of State, the TARs are simply another example of territorial deconcentration, in line with the deconcentration to regional level going on in other fields of Italian administration. Their members are appointed centrally, and they are given jurisdiction over competence (i.e. whether particular fields of administration belong to the region or to the State). Moreover, in future at least one quarter of the members of the (central) Council of State will be promoted from the ranks of the TAR members. There have even been authoritative proposals that all Councillors of State should eventually be promoted from the regions, precisely because the regional Tribunals are courts of first instance for the Council of State.[45] In these circumstances, it seems at least possible that the TARs will prove to be one of the instruments through which the prestigious Council of State maintains its authority over the 'deconcentrated' Civil Service and over the regional administrations themselves. Advocates of a system of administrative law in Britain should note carefully its potential centralising implications.

The earliest administrative responsibilities transferred to the ordinary regions have naturally been those listed in Article 117 of the Constitution (see Note 4, p.77), and it is therefore worth examining precisely what has — and indeed who has — been transferred.[46] The State has retained responsibility even for matters listed in Article 117, when they are of a national or inter-regional character; and this seems to be liberally interpreted. For example, although fairs and markets are transferred to the regions, the more important ones can be regarded as 'national', or even 'international', and thus retained.[47] The position of various national 'functional' agencies dealing with matters listed in Article 117 (e.g. ENIT, the main national tourist office, or ENAPI, the national agency for artisans and small industry) is therefore unaffected, since they are national or multiregional. Even more striking is the case of agriculture, where the State has retained all the most important responsibilities — for research and experimentation, for agricultural credit, and for the application of EEC directives and regulations. Moreover, all the transfer decrees emphasise that the State (i.e. the Council of Ministers, or the Inter-Ministerial Planning Committee) retains a general power of 'direction and co-ordination' over the regions' own administrative activities, and that there must be a mutual exchange of relevant information through the Government Commissioner. The decree on Town Planning and Public Works is, not surprisingly, the most explicit: the State exercises its powers of direction and coordination 'in order also to ensure uniformity and coordination to the activity of urban planning at the various territorial levels . . . [the Minister of Public Works defines] the methodological and procedural aspects to be observed in the formation of regional territorial plans, as well as the town-planning and housing standards that are the inderogable minimum and maximum to be observed in the formation of town plans'.[48] Thus the administrative autonomy of the ordinary regions, even in matters listed in Article 117, is not to be as great as many regional politicians had hoped.

By contrast, the 'delegation' of administrative tasks to the regions (see p.57) is frequently envisaged. For example, many of the functions of the Ministry of Health (infectious diseases, transplants, blood transfusion services, accident prevention etc.) are retained by the State, but 'delegated' to the regions. Most of the new regional officials carrying out these tasks will, of course, be former State officials working in field offices, who will have been 'transferred to the regions' in order to carry out the same tasks, in the same offices, subject to the same directives coming from the same Ministry in Rome. It is difficult to see this even as an example of territorial deconcentration! At best, it presumably represents an attempt to avoid the confusion that has arisen in some of the special regions (especially Sicily) from the coexistence of two bureaucracies working in the same field.

The total number of civil servants involved in this first transfer of administrative responsibilities to the regions is considerable. Public Works and Agriculture are the Ministries most affected, with 6,500 and 5,825 respectively. However, it should be remembered that most of them are 'transferred' only from field offices of the State (all but 644 in Public Works, and all but 150 in Agriculture). Even so, most of the spending Ministries in Rome will lose some of their staff, including their top-grade staff; and the process of deconcentration has a long way to go yet.

Bureaucratic Reform

One of the main reasons for the establishment of the 'ordinary' regions in 1970 was the urgent need for a general reform of the Italian civil service. For many years the centralised civil service has been almost universally regarded as archaic, over-powerful, over-manned, slow-moving and excessively legalistic; in addition, it has often been accused of corruption.[49] In fact, the most serious difficulty has been that the civil service has become over-loaded by a great many new functions, as the State has taken over supervision or control of more and more areas of society and of the economy. Consequently, the reform has had two main aims: the transfer of many administrative tasks from Rome to offices in the regions; and the adoption of new managerial techniques within the central Ministries in Rome.

The first of these aspects has already been partially outlined, in the previous section. The 'transfer' of administrative responsibilities from Rome to the new regional governments forms part of this general attempt to reform the central bureaucracy, and so too does the practice of 'delegation' to the regions (see p.57). In addition, there is supposed to be a considerable 'deconcentration' in the strict sense, i.e. the shifting of administrative functions from the Ministries in Rome to field offices (of the State administration) at various lower levels, including the regional level. Indeed, this 'deconcentration' is supposed to include 'all administrative functions except those which affect national or inter-regional interests, or which involve a considerable commitment of expenditure'.[50] The field offices are to be fewer in number, but they are to have greater decision-making powers, and the system of administrative controls is also to be decentralised (e.g. the TARs). It is worth emphasising that eventually most ordinary administration will be dealt with at local or regional level, where the mass of civil servants will be employed. Needless to say, there has been considerable resistance to these plans by the civil servants themselves,[51] and so far little appears to have changed.

However, it is the attempt to 'rationalise' the central administration in Rome along 'functional' lines that has attracted the most attention within Italy. The civil service now faces exactly the same problems as any other European bureaucracy, those of managing the economy and society efficiently. Not surprisingly, therefore, Italy is adopting much the same solutions, based upon a 'managerial model' that is believed to flourish in the USA and in neighbouring European States, and can also be seen operating near at hand, in the State-owned economic agencies (IRI, ENI, etc.). The old picture of the upper civil service as an 'army of ill-paid law graduates', and of public administration as — at best — the impartial application of law to cases, is to be replaced by a more modern image, that of a handful of thrusting technocrats, steeped in the social sciences, skilfully managing the industrial society of the future. The central Ministries in Rome will be reorganised on a 'functional' basis. Many General Directorates *(Direzioni Generali)* of these Ministries will be supressed, 'according to a rigorous criterion of functionality',[52] and the remaining offices will be given competence over distinct branches of administrative activity. Much greater responsibility is being given to the officials in charge of these offices, including the power to authorise expenditure up to a stated sum (300 million lire, or about £200,000, for the top civil servants).[53] Similarly, the career patterns of the civil servants themselves are being altered 'on the basis of functional qualifications'.[54]

Above all, a new class of top grade civil servants, called *dirigenti* (which may be translated as 'managers') is being set up, corresponding to the former Directors of Division and above; their number is to be restricted to 6,975.[55] In order to be promoted to *dirigente,* civil servants must pass successfully through a fourteen-month course of management training *(formazione dirigenziale)* with final examinations; but only those officials who have already given five years satisfactory service as section directors in a Ministry are eligible to be admitted to it. It is clear that this course, taken in the Higher School of Public Administration in Rome, is intended to provide much of the specialist training for the bright young (or youngish) men in each Ministry. As the decree establishing it proclaims, 'the course of management training is on distinctly professional lines, and is concerned essentially with the techniques designed to ensure the most rational organisation of the Administration, and the cheapness and efficiency of its operations'.[56] For half the period pupils will be sent to Ministries other than the ones to which they belong, or to private firms or state-owned agencies, in order to study the management structure and organisation. They will then draw up a report, including a critical analysis of the services and organisations studied, and proposals for adapting any rational solutions that they have come across in these organisations to their own Ministry. These reports will be debated in seminars and given a mark, which will count for a third of the total credit for the course. Thus, at least in theory, future top civil servants in Italy will be successful management consultants. On the other hand, this is no 'ENA solution' in the French manner. Not only are the pupils already established civil servants, but there is no suggestion of creating a mobile elite in the top ranks, and it is noticeable that the pupils on the course will be divided up by Ministry for much of their instruction. In this respect, at least, the reform proposals are remarkably timid and fail to tackle one of the most serious problems of Italian public administration, the jealousy and mutual incomprehension between the various Ministries.

In other ways, also, the reform is not all it might seem. Although the number of top-grade civil servants has been reduced to just under 7,000, the position of those existing civil servants not chosen to be *dirigenti* has been remarkably well safeguarded. There have been no dismissals. Voluntary resignations have been encouraged by extremely generous terms (automatic promotion to the next highest grade, plus seven years extra seniority, for pension and gratuity purposes). Over 10,000 senior civil servants took advantage of this opportunity for even greater leisure, and these included nearly two-thirds of those at the Ministry of Finances (which was about to introduce a major tax reform).[57] Those super-numerary top administrators who are left (approximately 2,000) will continue to draw four-fifths of their normal salary, plus extra allowances; and promotion to nonexistent jobs will still be made from the existing *carriera direttiva* (administrative grade). In other words, the bitter battle that occurred in 1971-2 between Gaspari (Christian Democrat Minister for Reform of Public Administration) and the top civil servants has largely resulted in the victory of the latter.[58] This victory was crowned after the 1972 elections by the replacement of Gaspari by Gava in the new government of Sig. Andreotti (himself very close to the Roman bureaucracy). The top civil servants also secured a very large pay rise in 1972, in order to compensate them for their increased 'functional responsibilities'. This pay rise was defended on the grounds that the best managerial talent in Italy needed to be attracted into the civil service, and also, perhaps more realistically, on the grounds that it was essential to put an end to all the other perks and extra payments with which civil servants had supplemented their salaries; it involved nearly doubling the salaries of top civil servants (Prefects and equivalent).[59]

Thus the innate Italian scepticism about the likelihood of any 'managerial' reform of the civil service actually occurring has some justification. The political power of the bureaucrats in Rome should not be underestimated. Little has been changed so far except the titles of the top posts: the new *dirigenti* are the old senior *direttori*, writ large. Moreover, various important issues have hardly been tackled at all. For example, if responsibility for spending large sums is given to the *dirigenti*, what happens to the central accounting procedures and to the role of the Court of Accounts? It is significant that the decree establishing these changes (and the new pay scales) was held up for months in the second half of 1972 by this Court, which is now very concerned to maintain its position as custodian of the financial probity of the State's administration. Similarly, the Prime Minister's Office remains intact, and it looks as if the need for its coordinating role will increase, rather than diminish, in the future. Above all, there is the problem of the specialist agencies based on Rome, often with peripheral offices. Not only do the functions of these 'para-State' agencies overlap with those of the Ministries, but they are extremely important politically as centres of patronage. In present political circumstances, it is unlikely that any reform of these agencies will be seriously attempted.

To summarise, the reform of the bureaucracy has a long way to go yet, despite the implementation of regional governments; and one of the outstanding problems is the relationship between the regions, the allegedly new 'functional' civil service, and the old functional agencies — especially, perhaps, the economic agencies.

Economic Planning and the Regions

The past few years have seen a considerable increase in the demand for efficient economic and social planning, and a corresponding increase in the powers and influence of the central planners in Rome. Although the Minister of the Budget and Economic Programming is formally responsible for national economic planning, for steering plans through Parliament and ensuring that the plans' objectives are being realised, most of the planning work is done by the office of the Secretary General of Economic Programming, under the Ministry of the Budget, whose position is comparable to that of the French *Commissaire du Plan*. In the summer of 1972 the Ministry of the Budget was reorganised to give increased power to the Secretary General, Giorgio Ruffolo, who became head of ISPE (Study Institute for Economic Programming), as well as becoming responsible for international relations and EEC matters affecting planning. ISPE is the main research and statistical body involved in economic planning, and its annual budget was doubled in 1972.[60]

Above all, the Secretary General was put in charge of 'relations with the regions for the aims of economic planning'.[61] Henceforth, the main channel for the regions to make their voices heard in the national planning process will be through the office of the Secretary General, to which they will have direct access. The main channel of communication will no doubt be the inter-regional consultative committee, set up in 1967 to examine regional problems and help in the national planning process.[62] After the ordinary regions were established in 1970, the composition of this committee was altered, so that it now consists, not of government appointees as previously, but of the Presidents of each regional government (or their representatives). It seems likely that membership of this committee will provide the most effective way — perhaps the only effective way — for a region to take an important part in economic planning.

The views of the leading planners on the regions' role in the planning process are, therefore, of particular interest.[63] They see the problems almost entirely in 'managerial' terms — i.e. regional devolution is necessary in order to achieve certain functional ends. The regions will be able to give valuable help in the formulation of plans and particular programmes (more detailed information, etc.). They will also be able to set up regional functional agencies (e.g. agricultural development agencies) which should prove more efficient at their tasks than the traditional regulation-bound centralised bureaucracy (this is of course simply the old general argument in favour of administrative deconcentration — see pp.60-61). Some such bodies have already been set up by the regions, e.g. zonal (inter-commune) sanitary committees on preventative medicine.[64] Thirdly, the regions will be of use in 'coordinating' various projects – 'the region is the political coordinating base, upon which attempts to solve the key problem of territorial administration – that of the city – must be founded'.[65] To this end, 'autonomous functional enterprises' *(aziende funzionali autonome)*, normally responsible to the regions, must be set up to implement large scale intervention in metropolitan areas. Emphasis is laid, however, upon the need for over-riding central control of these new functional agencies, and it is stressed that 'the necessary collaboration with autonomous administrations (i.e. regions, provinces and communes) would concern mainly the phase of implementation of works and management of equipment and services'.[66] Finally, the creation of functional metropolitan agencies would provide the impetus for a reform of local government structure, especially designed to merge and increase the size of communes (again on grounds of functional efficiency). Of these various aims, only the first two have been achieved as yet, but it seems probable that, with their newly enhanced position in the governmental machinery, the central planners will continue to press for political action on the others.

It should be clear by now that the regions are far more likely to help the central planners in Rome, than they are to do any effective regional planning themselves. It is true that regional economic development committees have existed off and on since 1959 on an advisory basis, and that since 1970 the regions have been able to appoint their members.[67] But the regions have extremely limited planning powers. In the central and northern regions, for example, the government made 21,760 million lire (over £15 million) available in 1971 for public works in their 'depressed zones', but the Interministerial Planning Committee (CIPE) lays down the criteria for the selection of projects, and the work is normally entrusted to provincial or commune administrations. The new Higher Council of Finances, set up to advise the Treasury on tax questions, including those affecting relations with the regions, contains no regional representatives.[68] The law of March 1971 giving 110 milliard lire (£75 million) for government 'intervention for restructuring and reconverting industrial enterprises' creates a new national financial society, GEPI, acting under the directives of the Interministerial Planning Committee. The regions are conspicuous by their absence in this Act. Indeed, an attempt in Parliament to involve them in the planning processes was firmly rejected, on 'functional' grounds (Hon. Compagna: 'I am contrary to the amendment, because the less the region interferes [sic] in industrial policy the better I think it is').[69]

The main concession to the regions in this field has been the creation of a Regional Development Fund, which amounted in 1973 to 140 milliard lire (£100 million). However, even this concession is

more limited than might appear. Not only is the amount of the Fund
determined quinquennially by the National Plan, and annually by the
Budget, but it is allocated to the regions 'on the basis of criteria which
will be laid down annually by the Interministerial Committee for
Economic Planning (CIPE)'.[70] In 1973 this committee, while recognising
'the regions' autonomy in evaluating the sectors for investment,
provided they are included within the matters of regional competence',
indicated the priorities as being agriculture, transport, artisans, tourism
and health.[71] In practice, it seems that the regions will merely be
able to give fairly minor technical and financial assistance, mainly to
agricultural improvement schemes.[72] The fund — at least 60 per cent
of which is to be spent in the south — does not cover the important
matters, such as industrial development or large infrastructural public
works, which in the south have been left firmly in the hands of the
Fund for the South *(Cassa per il Mezzogiorno)* and its associated agencies.

Regional economic planning in Italy has, of course, been closely
associated with — often coterminous with — attempts to solve the
'southern problem'. Since 1950, a series of institutions have been
set up to draw up and implement development programmes; they have
nearly all been centrally controlled and financed. The most important
of them, the Fund for the South *(Cassa per il Mezzogiorno)* is run
by a Council of Administration consisting of government-appointed
experts, and is subordinate to the Minister for the South; it contains no
representative elements, and has been described as 'an interesting
example of purely functional administrative decentralisation'.[73]
As has been argued above (p.45), the existence of very large, very
backward areas, with many problems in common, has diminished the
chances of regional economic planning in the south, and has also made
it more difficult for the northern and central regions to persuade
anyone to take their economic problems seriously.

The increased emphasis on industrialisation as a remedy for the
'southern problem' has also played its part in this process. When the
Fund for the South turned its attention to industrial development
after 1957, it found it needed specialised technical agencies at local
level. Consortia were therefore formed, consisting largely of local
government representatives and members of local Chambers of
Commerce, to draw up plans and buy land needed for the projected
'industrial development areas' and 'industrial nuclei'. Industrialisation
implied, therefore, the selection (by the government) of a few zones of
potential development, which were then organised by Consortia working
in increasingly close cooperation with the Fund.[74] The regional
framework laid down in the Constitution was largely irrelevant to
this scheme, and indeed throughout the 1960s some of the poorest
regions (e.g. Calabria, Basilicata) remained without any industrial

development areas.[75] There was one exception to this rule, in
Sardinia, where the normal hierarchy of Minister – Fund for the South –
Consortia and local government was replaced even in the 1960s by a
genuine regional plan, drawn up and implemented by the regional
government.[76] However, Sardinia was a unique case. The island can
be seen as a distinct economic region, the regional government has
'special' powers, and above all the work on the Sardinian plan began
in 1962, before the national planners had begun to operate effectively.
It seems very unlikely that other regions, in the south or elsewhere, will
be able in the future to secure the same degree of control over regional
economic planning.

An indication that they will not is provided by the new Law on the
Fund for the South, passed towards the end of 1971.[77] The Fund
was reconfirmed in its function as the leading development agency
for the south, and given increased funds.[78] The new law also ratified
several recent tendencies in Italian thinking on regional development.
Much less emphasis was placed on industrial 'nuclei' or 'areas of
development', which have given disappointing results (see below, p.69)
Attention was focused instead on the need to create networks of small
industries and small firms, through improved capital grants,
tax concessions, etc., and on the need to develop the backward (hilly)
areas of depopulation. The regions may well have an important role
here. But the bulk of the Fund's activities will be concerned with the
so-called 'special projects', of an intersectorial and often of an inter-
regional kind. These projects will be decided on by the Interministerial
Planning Committee itself, will be centrally planned and administered,
and will be implemented by the Fund and its affiliated bodies. The
first batch of 'special projects' was announced in August 1972, and
give a clearer idea of how the system is to work. They include such
items as the depollution of the Bay of Naples, the creation of an
industrial port at Cagliari, and the provision of major infrastructural
works in the new industrial areas of S.E. Sicily.[79] It is true that the
regions can suggest proposals for 'special projects' to the
Interministerial Planning Committee (CIPE), and that the Act also sets
up a consultative committee, consisting of the Presidents of the
regional governments in the south, to give its views on proposals coming
before CIPE; but these are concessions in what remains a very centralised
development programme. There are still to be no regional representatives
on the Fund's Administrative Council. Even apart from the 'special
projects', CIPE lays down the directives and priorities of industrial
policy in the south, including the siting of new factories. A firm
centralised control is kept over such matters as credit facilities, tax
concessions, etc. Thus although the regions now have their own economic
planning committees, which are beginning to produce regional, sector

and zonal plans, and although they are given some powers and more influence by the new law, it is clear that the bulk of the money voted for the economic development of the south is going to remain firmly under the control of the central planners in Rome.

Indeed, the real importance of the new Act lies in its centralising aims. One of its main purposes has been to bring the Fund for the South itself under more centralised control, and to tie southern development more closely to the aims of the national planners. The increased powers given to CIPE is one indication of this, as is the whole concept of 'special projects'. The other public economic agencies are similarly disciplined by the new law. Henceforth they must submit each year their development plans for their southern activities over the following five years (including the number of new jobs to be provided). All firms, both public and private, will have to submit their large-scale investment plans (in the south or elsewhere) to the Minister of the Budget, and these plans can henceforth be vetoed by CIPE where it considers that the areas chosen are already congested or that suitable labour is unavailable.[80] In short, the new Law on the south not only demonstrates the irrelevance of historical-geographic regions to large-scale economic planning, and imposes greater centralisation on the relationship between government and regions; it also attempts to tackle the perennial problem of the relationship between the central government and its functional economic agencies.

The Drive for Central Control

Indeed, the role of these public sector economic agencies and holding companies (IRI, ENI, etc.) is central to any discussion of regional policy in Italy. For many years the best approximation to a regional policy has been the investments of these agencies. The public sector in Italy is extremely large, and by 1971 over 350 firms of various sizes were State-owned or State-controlled, usually via holding companies ultimately responsible to the Ministry of State Participations.[81] The firms operate in practically all sectors of industry and in many services, and are dominant in heavy engineering, shipping, ship-building, energy, etc.[82] Their share of Italy's industrial investment has risen steadily since the early 1960s, and in 1971 came to over forty per cent of the total.[83] Since 1957 the holding companies and the firms they control have been compelled by law to place forty per cent of their total investment, and sixty per cent of their investment in new industrial plant, in the south; and the 1971 Act raised these figures to sixty per cent and eighty per cent respectively.[84] In fact, in 1971 they made new industrial investments of 691.5 milliard lire (£495 million) in the south; the vast majority of this total (649 milliard lire) was by firms controlled by IRI, the Institute for Industrial Reconstruction.[85]

This policy of directing the State firms' investments to the south has, however, proved much less successful than anticipated. The emphasis has been on the so-called 'cathedrals in the desert', i.e. major capital-intensive projects, above all in petrochemicals and steel (e.g. Taranto), which have so far produced very little in the way of extra employment. The largest State holding company, IRI, has been especially noted for this policy. 'Steel investments for the period 1958-69 accounted for about eighty per cent of IRI's Southern manufacturing investment, and indeed a very high proportion (about forty-eight per cent) of its total southern investment'.[86] The number of industrial jobs in IRI firms in the south rose from 1960 to 1968 only from 25,120 to 36,148.[87] Although this policy may, of course, eventually start working (the new Alfa-Sud plant near Naples is supposed to employ 15,000 workers when in full production), so far little has been achieved by forcing the large State-backed companies to invest heavily in large capital-intensive projects in backward regions. Such a policy necessarily does little for the smaller private firms in the south, which have been particularly badly hit by the recession of 1969-72, and by the abolition after 1969 of regional differentials in national wage agreements. To quote a recent report by the European Investment Bank:

> 'the jobs engendered (i.e. in 1966-70) as a result of the new industrial ventures were barely sufficient to maintain industrial employment at its 1965 level. As for the cutback in jobs, due to the termination of low productivity ventures which could offer no competition faced with the new conditions brought about by the general regional development, this partly cancelled out the effects of the new ventures. Unemployment could be kept at a level below five per cent solely because of emigration to the other regions (622,000) or abroad (386,000), and the creation of jobs (260,000) in tertiary activities'.[88]

The political, as well as economic, crisis of the south since 1969 is indicative of the failure of this sort of centralised 'top-heavy' investment planning.

The failure of 'investment planning' by State-controlled firms to remedy economic backwardness in the regions is not the only reason why this policy has lost a good deal of political support in recent years. The Right-wing parties — especially the Liberals — have regarded it as an abandonment of the State firms' duty to pursue economic rather than political ends. Northern industrial interests — especially in the recent recession — have resented paying taxes in order to have privileged competition stimulated elsewhere. The Communist Party has regarded the policy as catering for the needs of the northern industrial monopolies (cheap steel for Fiat, etc.) and as failing to meet the pressing need for jobs in the south.

Above all, critics have pointed out the enormous cost of the State firms' operations. Each major holding agency has an Endowment Fund, to meet the social costs involved in uneconomic activities. IRI's Endowment Fund is currently 220 milliard lire p.a. (£150 million), but its annual losses are greater, and its financial requirements considerably greater; ENI is estimated to need 400 milliard lire (£250 million) in 1973; and 663 milliard lire (£450 million) went to the various other public agencies' Endowment Funds in 1972.[89] In early 1973, one relatively small agency alone (EGAM, the Mines and Metal Management Agency) was demanding 330 milliard lire (£230 million) for its 1973 Endowment Fund, as well as permission to borrow more.[90] Parliament's willingness in recent years to vote very large sums to the agencies, without even a serious parliamentary discussion, has aroused much unfavourable comment, including the familiar accusation that the para-state agencies are the main source of *sottogoverno* and corruption in Italian public life. The Endowment Funds have not only become a vital financial resource for public enterprise; they have also contributed to Italy's alarming budget deficit, which reached an estimated 8,800 milliard lire (£6,000 million) in 1973.[91]

It is not surprising that at the end of 1972 there were serious attempts by Parliament — for the first time — to establish the truth about these agencies' finances, to lay down new budgeting procedures common to all of them, and to establish criteria for judging new investment proposals.[92] It was suspected that the Endowment Funds were being used, nor merely to cover social costs, but to conceal 'normal' operating losses. In any case, the use of Endowment Funds as investment capital is not only a drain on the Treasury, but clearly undermines the famous 'IRI Formula' (according to which the private investor is supposed to provide much of the capital requirements of State-controlled firms). The whole debate was intensified by the row in 1972-3 over control of the giant petrochemical firm, Montedison, and the revelation that in the previous four years IRI and ENI had invested 200 milliard lire (£140 million) of State money in this firm. In short, by late 1972 the 'IRI Formula' was in crisis. Public agencies were increasingly regarded — even by Socialists and Left-wing Christian Democrats — as ineffective at regional planning, enormously expensive, and too independent of any parliamentary control.

This is, indeed, the central problem of economic management in Italy. The economic agencies have traditionally enjoyed a great deal

of independence, partly owing to the weaknesses of governments and
of the normal bureaucracy; even the decision on where the new Alfa-Sud
factory was to be sited was apparently taken within IRI itself,
'leaving CIPE very little alternative but to endorse it'.[93] Both Parliament
and the central planners are anxious to establish greater control over
the agencies' activities, and the conflict over the Endowment Funds, as
well as the provisions of the 1971 Law on the South, should be seen
as an attempt to implement an important part of the general
restructuring of public administration in Italy. The 'delegated
management' aspect is an important element in current Italian politics,
but the problem with the State economic agencies has not been
whether to set them up, or how many sectors they should control,
or even — until recently — how to improve their performance. It has
been how to stop them being centres of patronage and/or independent-
minded baronies, and how to convert them into reliable instruments
of central policy.

Conclusion

It is obviously too early to assess the strengths and weaknesses of the
nascent structure of public administration in Italy. However, this
essay has shown that the 'failure of the State' in Italy is being tackled
in a highly centralising manner. The legislative, administrative and
financial limits to the regions' autonomy are great. The regional
governments are faced by a tenacious civil service, and a hostile
Constitutional Court. They are also handicapped by the absence of
any reform of the outdated system of local government (communes
and provinces), on whose administration they are supposed to rely, and
by the absence of any real political base at regional level. It has been
argued that devolution on a geographical basis is largely irrelevant
to the problems of regional planning. It is little wonder that the
introduction of regional governments has generally been regarded
within Italy as yet another example of *'gattopardismo'*[94] — a change
introduced so that everything may remain the same.

Above all, regional autonomy is unlikely in Italy because of the
insistent demands for far-reaching economic and social reforms, of
housing, health, pensions and education. The 'failure of the State' in
Italy has meant, to most people, the failure of central governments
(especially the 'Centre-Left' governments of 1963-72) to provide these
reforms, which are perceived as much more important than political
devolution or citizen participation in local democracy. Only the
central government can tackle these issues — and, indeed, the central
government's machinery will have to be made a great deal stronger and
more efficient yet if it is to be able to tackle them successfully. It is the

strength of this popular demand for reforms that has indirectly increased the influence of the central planners and provided the stimulus to the reform of the bureaucracy.[95]

The first major reform to be tackled since the introduction of the regional governments provides an instructive example of the tenacity of the centralised system. One of the most serious administrative and social problems in recent years has been the failure to provide enough cheap public housing, especially in areas of immigration: public investment for housing amounted to only 29.4 per cent of the planned targets in the period 1966-70.[96] The new reform has abolished the untidy medley of previous housing institutions, and set up a new unified system. 'General directives' are to be laid down by the Interministerial Committee for Economic Planning (CIPE); and CIPE will also take the final decision on the allocation of housing funds to each region. A new national body has been set up, under the Ministry of Public Works, called the Committee for Residential Building (CER). This body, which consists of civil servants, is to submit proposals to CIPE and supervise the financing of the various housing schemes. The Ministry of Public Works will remain responsible for the technical side, including the power to lay down maximum allowable costs on which loans can be granted. The regions' main role seems to be to inform the CER of their priority needs, to press their claims in the inter-regional consultative committee which advises the CIPE, and to set up regional Consortia to supervise the house-building agencies, which in turn are organised at provincial level. The regional Consortia are clearly intended to be 'participatory' bodies, and contain representatives from all the main political parties on the regional Council, from trade unions, tenants' associations, etc. However, control over most of the important aspects of housing will be exercised by central functional agencies, including over such matters as the criteria for allocation of houses and for the fixing of rents.[97] It is noticeable, incidentally, that Left-wing criticism of this legislation has been surprisingly muted, presumably because any measure that looked as if it might produce more houses has seemed acceptable. Communist criticism has focused on the inadequacy of the funds provided, on the possible benefits to big building firms, and on the absence of adequate compulsory purchase powers, rather than on the centralised nature of the reform.[98]

Nevertheless, there is another side to the ledger, and the regions may prove to be not completely irrelevant, even to economic and social reforms. As the example of the regional Consortia in the new Housing Law shows, the regions may be able to involve local associations and pressure groups more closely in the process of government. With all its limitations, 'participation' of this kind (which represents, perhaps, as much as governments are prepared to allow in current conditions) may prove very important in providing a safety-valve for potentially disaffected groups, and thus in helping to secure 'social peace'. This is particularly true for trade unionists. The trade unions have led the campaigns for various social reforms in recent years, and are now much more powerful at local level than before 1969. Moreover, they obviously have a new and vital role to play if governments are to secure the acceptance of any kind of 'income policy'. In short, despite the absence of much *popular* or 'grass-roots' interest in regionalism, the regions may still be important in securing the adhesion of organised interest groups to the political system.[99] In this sense, regional governments may yet provide a point of convergence for demands from below for 'participation', and demands from above for 'efficiency'.

In other ways, too, the regions may prove a useful innovation. They may be able to act more *quickly* and competently than the old centralised State administration. Above all, they provide local politicians with an opportunity to inform, influence and take part in the national economic planning process, thus (presumably) making national planning more effective. Paradoxically, therefore, the real importance of the regions lies in the help they may give to the *centripetal* tendencies of the modern State and of the modern economy.[100] The familiar rhetorical declarations that the regions are 'a dynamic active component of the reform of the State'[101] have more truth in them than listeners often realise. Italian regionalism is part of an ambitious attempt to 'rationalise' the country, to force it to adopt a 'European', northern, rather than a 'Mediterranean', southern, perspective. It is the old Piedmontese centralism, by other means.

Appendix

Table 1 The Italian Regions

Region	Population (Present on Census Day 24 Oct 1971)	% of Total Population (Census 1971)	% of Contribution to Gross Domestic Product (1969)	% of Active Population Engaged in Agriculture (Census 1971)
Piedmont	4,461,527	8.30	10.53	12.1
Valle d'Aosta	111,239	0.21	0.25	13.7
Lombardy	8,504,061	15.82	22.47	5.5
Trentino-Alto Adige	845,111	1.57	1.47	17.4
Venetia (Veneto)	4,122,697	7.67	7.48	14.0
Friuli-Venezia Giulia	1,244,347	2.31	2.34	9.5
Liguria	1,868,630	3.48	4.55	7.6
Emilia-Romagna	3,853,434	7.17	8.43	20.0
Tuscany	3,501,568	6.54	6.98	11.5
Umbria	779,926	1.45	1.32	20.7
Marches	1,350,879	2.51	2.12	25.3
Latium	4,754,484	8.84	9.22	9.9
Abruzzo	1,129,576	2.10	} 1.86	{ 27.7
Molise	302,060	0.56		46.5
Campania	4,997,401	9.29	6.12	24.5
Apulia	3,493,265	6.50	4.55	37.0
Basilicata	565,252	1.05	0.66	39.4
Calabria	1,856,586	3.45	1.89	33.2
Sicily	4,582,541	8.52	5.87	28.9
Sardinia	1,445,787	2.69	1.88	21.6
Italy	53,770,371	100.00	100.00	17.3

Sources: Census Data (provisional), from Bollettino Mensile di Statistica, June 1972, p.221 and pp.223-4. Gross Domestic Product figures from EEC Commission, *Regional Development in the Community* (Brussels 1971), p.294.

Table 2 Composition of Regional Councils

A. Ordinary Regions (Elections of 7 June 1970)

	PCI	PSIUP	PSI	PSU (PSDI)	PRI	DC	PLI	MSI	Total Seats
Piedmont	13	1	5	4	1	20	4	2	50
Lombardy	19	2	9	5	2	36	4	3	80
Venetia	9	1	5	3	1	28	2	1	50
Liguria	13	1	4	3	1	14	3	1	40
Emilia-Romagna	24	2	3	3	2	14	1	1	50
Tuscany	23	1	3	3	1	17	1	1	50
Umbria	13	1	3	1	1	9	0	2	30
Marches	14	1	3	2	1	17	1	1	40
Latium	14	1	4	3	2	18	3	5	50
Abruzzo	10	1	3	2	1	20	1	2	40
Molise	5	0	3	2	1	16	2	1	30
Campania	13	1	7	4	2	25	2	6	60
Apulia	14	1	5	2	1	22	1	4	50
Basilicata	7	1	4	2	0	14	1	1	30
Calabria	10	1	6	2	1	17	1	2	40

Special Regions

	PCI	PSIUP	PSI	PSDI	PRI	DC Pop	DC	SVP	PLI	MSI (DN)	Others	Total Seats
Sardinia (16/6/1974)	21	-	8	4	1	-	33	-	1	6	1	75
Sicily (13/6/1971)	18	1	11	4	3	-	29	-	3	15	6	90
Valle d'Aosta (10/6/1973)	7	-	3	1	0	8	7	-	1	1	7	35
Friuli-Venezia Giulia (17/6/73)	13	-	8	4	1	-	26	-	2	4	3	61
Trentino-Alto Adige (18/11/73)												
Prov. of Trento	3	-	4	2	1	-	21	-	1	1	3	36
Prov. of Bolzano	2	-	2	1	0	-	5	20	0	1	3	34

PCI: Italian Communist Party. PSIUP: Italian Socialist Party of Proletarian Unity (Left Socialists, merged with Communist Party in 1972). PSI: Italian Socialist Party. PSU: Unified Socialist Party now called PSDI, Italian Social Democrat Party). PRI: Italian Republican Party. DC: Christian Democrats. DC Pop.: Popular Christian Democrats (Left DC, in Valle d'Aosta only). SVP: Süd-Tirolische Volkspartei (German-speaking DC, in Bolzano province only). PLI: Italian Liberal Party. MSI: Italian Social Movement (neo-Fascists; from 1972 called DN, National Right).

Source: for Ordinary Regions, J. Nobécourt, *L'Italie à Vif* (Seuil, Paris 1970), p.342.

Table 3   Regional Finance in Italy, 1973

Region	Allocation from Common Fund[1]	Allocation from Regional Development Fund[2]
	(Ordinary Regions only) (millions of lire)	
Piedmont	49,398	6,500
Valle d'Aosta	–	1,000
Lombardy	78,974	8,000
Trentino-Alto Adige	–	3,400 (1700 to prov. Trento; 1700 to prov. Bolzano)
Venetia	44,540	6,800
Friuli-Venezia Giulia	–	4,000
Liguria	19,309	3,800
Emilia-Romagna	47,257	6,500
Tuscany	39,444	6,200
Umbria	11,393	3,800
Marches	17,190	3,800
Latium	44,552	7,000
Abruzzo	19,368	7,000
Molise	6,055	4,200
Campania	75,911	16,000
Apulia	60,047	12,500
Basilicata	12,516	6,000
Calabria	38,693	9,000
Sicily	–	15,500
Sardinia	–	9,000
	564,646	140,000

1. For the criteria for allocation from the Common Fund, see p.56.
   Source: Ministerial Decree 9 November 1972 (in *Gazzetta Ufficiale* 14 February 1973). The relevant legislation is in Law of 16 May 1970, n.281, Article 8.
2. See pp. 65-66.
   Source: Ministerial Decree 7 September 1973 (in *Gazzetta Ufficiale* 9 October 1973). The relevant legislation is in Law of 16 May 1970, n.281, Article 9.

Notes

1. L. Cappelletti, 'Local Government in Italy', in *Public Administration* Autumn 1963, p.253.
2. They were first used in P. Maestri's book, *Statistica del Regno d'Italia nell' anno 1863*, although the actual term 'regions' was not used by the Statistical Office until 1912. See E. Rotelli, *L'Avvento della Regione in Italia*, Milan 1967, p.369.
3. D. Rusinow, *Italy's Austrian Heritage*, Oxford University Press, 1969.

4. They are listed in Article 117 of the Constitution, as follows: the organisation of services and administrative bodies dependent on the Region; the boundaries of communes; local urban and rural police; fairs and markets; public welfare, health and hospital assistance; museums and libraries; town-planning; tourism and the hotel industry; roads, aqueducts and public works of regional interest; navigation and lake ports; mineral and thermal waters; quarries; hunting and fishing in inland waters; agriculture and forestry; artisans; other matters as laid down by Constitutional Laws.
5. For his powers, see p.57.
6. The four regional Statutes were issued as Constitutional Laws on 26 February 1948. The Sicilian Statute simply repeated word for word the text of the 1946 Decree Law.
7. As my contribution to Political Science, I have formulated this as a general Law of Politics, to be known henceforth as the Metternich Principle: regions will always remain mere 'geographical expressions' unless the elites within them can harness popular disaffection to pseudo-nationalist sentiment.
8. They are limited by the regional Statutes of all the special regions except Sicily. See p.55
9. C. Palazzoli, *Les Régions Italiennes*, Librairie General de Droit et de Jurisprudence, Paris 1966, pp.108 and 131.
10. See p.58.
11. See p.57.
12. A. Piras, 'Les Régions Italiennes à statut ordinaire', in *International Review of Administrative Sciences* 1971, p.36.
13. Palazzoli op. cit., p.310; G. Woodcock, 'Regional Government: The Italian Example' in *Public Administration*, Winter 1967, p.407.
14. Palazzoli, op.cit., pp.297-8 on Sardinia and p.317.
15. Palazzoli, op.cit., pp.299-306.
16. A. Passerin D'Entreves and M. Lengereau, 'La Valle d'Aosta, Minoranza di Lingua Francese dello Stato Italiano', in *Quaderni di Sociologia* 1967, pp.65-89.
17. A. Mastropaolo, 'Primi Dati di una Ricerca sull'Assemblea Regionale Siciliana', in *Quaderni di Sociologia* (1969), pp.363-77.
18. R. Catanzaro, 'Il Potere nella Comunità', in *Scienze Sociali* April 1971, pp.91-123.
19. Constitutional Law, 10 November 1971, n.1. A Unified Text of the new Statute was published in the *Gazzetta Ufficiale,* 20 November 1972.
20. Süd-Tirolische Volkspartei, i.e. a German-speaking Christian Democrat party.
21. G. Riccamboni, 'Profilo di una Classe politica regionale: Il Trentino-Alto-Adige' in *Il Politico* June 1972, pp.390-413.
22. Law of 10 February 1953, n.62. The powers of the Government Commissioner were extended, and it was laid down (Art. 9) that the regions could not legislate at all, unless the State had first issued the 'fundamental principles' in its own laws. See p.55.
23. S. Cafiero, *Le Migrazioni Meridionali*, Giuffrè, Rome 1964, p.33.
24. P.A. Allum and G. Amyot, 'Regionalism in Italy: Old Wine in New Bottles?' in *Parliamentary Affairs* Winter 1970-71, p.72. They also point out that the Socialist vote became 'meridionalised' in the 1960s — by 1970 the party was stronger in most southern regions than it was in the north.

25. F. Bassanini, *L'Attuazione delle Regioni,* La Nuova Italia, Florence 1970, ch.20.
26. The agitation for a referendum on the Divorce Law of 1970 is only an apparent exception to this rule. The Divorce Law — a rare example of a social reform actually passed by Parliament — was opposed by the Vatican and most Catholics. The Catholic organisers of the referendum to abrogate the new law had no desire to set up a more 'participatory' political system, merely to return to the status quo.
27. Law of 17 February 1968, n.108.
28. P. Ferrari, *Les Regions Italiennes,* PUF, Paris 1972, pp.45-8, and Bassanini, op.cit, pp.131-62.
29. Law of 16 May 1970, n.281. For its provisions, see p.55 and p.56.
30. For the campaign, and analysis of the election results, see Allum and Amyot, op.cit., and J. Besson and G. Bibes, 'Les Elections du 7 Juin 1970 en Italie', in *Revue Française de Science Politique,* 1971, pp.743-71.
31. Martin Clark and R.E.M. Irving, 'The Italian Political Crisis and the General Election of May 1972', in *Parliamentary Affairs* Summer 1972, p.202.
32. P. Collina, 'Candidati e Eletti nella regione Emilia-Romagna', in *Il Politico*, June 1972, pp.368-89.
33. *Il Mondo,* n.25, (1972).
34. Law of 16 May 1970, n.281, Article 17 *(Gazzetta Ufficiale,* 22 May 1970).
35. For finances of special regions, see p.48.
36. See Ferrari, op.cit., p.42.
37. Article 8, para. 5 of the Law of 16 May 1970, n.281; and also the Table of Coefficients at the end of the Act. 60 per cent of the Fund is to be distributed to the ordinary regions in proportion to their population; 10 per cent in proportion to their area; and 30 per cent according to a points system based on rate of emigration, level of unemployment, and per capita burden of income tax.
38. The 'Common Fund' is quite separate from the famous 'Regional Development Fund' (see p.65), which is allocated annually by the government within the framework of the National Plan, and amounted in 1973 to 140 milliard lire (£100 million).
39. Article 17 of Law of 16 May 1970, n.281: 'the function of direction and co-ordination of the regions' activities which appertain to requirements of a unitary character, including those concerned with the objectives of the national economic programme and commitments deriving from international obligations, remains reserved to the State'. Ferrari, op.cit., p.26, is wrong on this point.
40. See Law of 28 October 1970, n.775, especially Article 3.
41. The Italian word *controllo* has been translated throughout this essay as control. It is, however, less strong than the English word, and 'checking' or 'supervision' might be a more appropriate term in some circumstances.
42. The first nominations were made by the Presidential Decrees of 30 June 1971.
43. Palazzoli, op.cit., p.448, pp.487-93.
44. These Commissions may also exercise a limited 'control of expediency', i.e. they may send back administrative decisions of communes and provinces for reconsideration.
45. Speech by Lucifredi, *relatore* of the Bill on Regional Administrative Tribunals, in Chamber of Deputies, Commission I, 7 October 1970.

46. Decrees of the President of the Republic, 14 and 15 January 1972, nos. 1-11, published in *Gazzetta Ufficiale*, 15 January to 19 February 1972.
47. Decree Pres. Rep. 15 January 1972, n.7, in *Gazzetta Ufficiale*, 27 January 1972.
48. Decree Pres. Rep. 15 January 1972, n.8, Art. 9.
49. Or, more politely, of being imbued with a 'personal morality'. P. Stirling, 'Impartiality and Personal Morality', in J.G. Peristiany (ed.), *Contributions to Mediterranean Sociology*, Mouton, Paris and The Hague 1968, pp.49-64.
50. Law of 28 October 1970, n.775, Article 3.
51. See especially M. Canonica, 'C'è Qualcuno più Statale degli Altri', in *L'Espresso*, 13 February 1972. The most recent government proposals (4 July 1972) are in *Atti Parlamentari*, Senato della Repubblica, VI Legislatura, n.114.
52. Law of 28 October 1970, n.775, Article 1.
53. Decree of President of the Republic, 30 June 1972, n.748, Article 7 (in *Gazzetta Ufficiale*, 11 December 1972).
54. Law of 28 October 1970, n.775, Article 9.
55. The Decree Pres. Rep. 30 June 1972, n.748, has a table at the end, giving the number for each Ministry. There are to be 1210 at the Ministry of the Interior, 1117 at the Ministry of Finances, and 878 at the Treasury.
56. Decree Pres. Rep. 30 June 1972, n.748, Article 23.
57. C. Zappulli, 'La Burocrazia Ghigliottinata', in *Corriere della Sera*, 19 June 1973.
58. See in particular 'La Strage dei Burocrati' in *L'Espresso*, 30 January 1972, for Gaspari's revealing and amusing remarks about this campaign.
59. Decree Pres. Rep. 30 June 1972, n.748, Art. 47, gives the new pay scales *(Gazzetta Ufficiale*, 11 December 1972).
60. To 2 milliard lire (£1.4 million). Law of 23 December 1972, n.822.
61. Decree Pres. Rep. 30 June 1972, n.505, in *Gazzetta Ufficiale*, 7 September 1972.
62. Law of 27 February 1967, n.48.
63. This paragraph is largely based on Giorgio Ruffolo and Luciano Barca's famous 'Progetto 80': Ministero del Bilancio e della Programmazione Economica, *Progetto 80* (Rapporto Preliminare al Programma Economico Nazionale), a cura di Giorgio Ruffolo & Luciano Barca, Sansoni, Florence, 1970.
64. Lombard regional Law, 5 December 1972, n.37.
65. Progetto 80, p.92.
66. Ibid., p.93.
67. For the earliest (1959) bodies see R.C. Fried, 'Administrative Pluralism and Italian Regional Planning', in *Public Administration* Winter 1968, p.384. For the similar bodies operating between 1964 and 1970, see debate in Chamber of Deputies, Commission V, 12 November 1969, esp. pp.64-5.
68. The Council was set up by Decree Pres. Rep. 26 October 1972, n.646.
69. Chamber of Deputies, Commission V, 10 March 1971.
70. Law of 16 May 1970, n.281, Article 9. See Table 3 for the allocation of this Fund in 1973.
71. Ministerial Decree 7 September 1973 (in *Gazzetta Ufficiale*, 9 October 1973).
72. P. Vicinelli, 'I Compiti della Cassa nel Quadro della Nuova Legislazione per il Mezzogiorno', in *Realtà del Mezzogiorno*, November 1972, pp.898-909.

73. M.M. Watson, *Regional Development Policy and Administration in Italy*, Longman, London, 1970, p.11.
74. Ibid., p.49.
75. Although they did have 'industrial nuclei' (restricted to one commune).
76. For the Sardinian 'Plan of Rebirth', see Watson op. cit., pp.80-103, and Palazzoli op. cit., pp.413-26.
77. Law of 6 October 1971, n.853 *(Gazzetta Ufficiale,* 26 October 1971).
78. 3125 milliard lire (£2,100 million) was allocated for the period 1971-5 alone, and the Fund was authorised to assume commitments for the following years as well.
79. For a full list, see Vicinelli op.cit., p.901.
80. Law of 6 October 1971, n.853, Art. 14.
81. OECD Report, *Italy* (1972), p.73.
82. The activity of these agencies, especially IRI, has been amply discussed in recent literature in English, and I will not therefore go into details. See, in particular, S. Holland (ed.), *The State as Entrepreneur,* Weidenfeld and Nicolson, London, 1972. This book, which enthusiastically advocates that IRI's example be followed elsewhere, was published just at the time when Italian disillusionment with the 'IRI Formula' became intense. One is reminded of the spate of books on French planning in the mid-1960s, which suffered the same fate.
83. OECD Report, *Italy* (1972), p.76.
84. Law of 6 October 1971, n.853, Art. 7.
85. Figures given by Taviani, Minister for the South, and by Hon. Isgrò, in the Chamber of Deputies 20 July 1972 *(Atti Parlamentari,* Camera dei Deputati, Seduta 20 July 1972, p.822 and p.789).
86. K. Allen in Holland (ed.), op. cit., p.175.
87. Ibid., p.177.
88. European Investment Bank Research Department, September 1972: *The European Investment Bank and the Problems of the Mezzogiorno,* p.10. I am indebted to Professor Vernon Newcombe for drawing this pamphlet (and others) to my attention.
89. R. Di Rienzo, 'Chi ha l'Assegno Vince', in *L'Espresso,* 14 January 1973.
90. C. Zappulli, 'La Produzione di Fumo', in *Corriere della Sera,* 20 February 1973.
91. This is the estimate for 1973 of the Treasury Minister, Ugo La Malfa, on 1 August 1973. The 1974 forecast deficit was 8,060 milliard lire (£5,750 million).
92. Giorgio La Malfa, 'Finanziamento dello Spreco', in *Il Mondo,* 30 November 1972.
93. Carol Johnson, in Holland op. cit., p.206.
94. From the title of Lampedusa's famous novel *Il Gattopardo (The Leopard).*
95. In July 1973 the Minister of the Budget and Economic Programming, Giolitti, spoke of his Ministry's need to meet the 'strong demand for planning coming from the country, – interview with C. Zappulli, in *Corriere della Sera,* 24 July 1973.
96. OECD Report, *Italy,* November 1972, p.33.
97. This legislation is to be found in the Law of 22 October 1971, n.865, and especially in the Decrees Pres. Rep. 30 December 1972, n.1035 & 1036 (in *Gazzetta Ufficiale,* 3 March 1973).
98. See, for example, V. Pierini, 'La Crisi del Fronte Edilizia', in *Rinascita* 24 November 1972.

99. Trade Union leaders in Italy are a somewhat elite group: a recent survey found that 32.33 per cent of national executive members had degrees. F. Battaglia, 'I Dirigenti Sindacali Italiani – alcuni dati', in *Rassegna Italiana di Sociologia* April-June 1971, p.365. The argument in this paragraph is, of course, also true for the Communist Party.
100. Palazzoli op. cit., pp.550-57.
101. Bassetti, President of the Lombard regional government, interviewed by A. Sensini *(Corriere della Sera,* 11 June 1973).

Select Bibliography

A.E. Alcock	*The History of the South Tyrol Question* (Michael Joseph, London 1970).
K. Allen & M. MacLennan	*Regional Problems and Policies in Italy and France* (Allen and Unwin, London 1970).
P. Ammassari (ed.)	*Il Burocrate di fronte alla Burocrazia* (Archivio ISAP, Giuffrè, Milan 1969).
F. Bassanini	*L'Attuazione delle Regioni* (La Nuova Italia, Florence 1970).
P. Calandra	'Il Riordinamento dell' Amministrazione Statale', in *Rivista Trimestrale di Diritto Pubblico* no.2 (1973), pp.744-805.
P. Ferrari	*Les Régions Italiennes* (PUF, Paris 1972).
R. Fried	*The Italian Prefects* (Yale University Press, New Haven 1963).
S. Holland (ed.)	*The State as Entrepreneur* (Weidenfeld and Nicolson, London 1972).
Istituto Gramsci	*La Riforma dello Stato* (Riuniti, Rome 1968).
J. La Palombara	*Italy – the Politics of Planning* (Syracuse University Press, 1966).
Ministero del Bilancio e della Programmazione Economica	*Progetto 80* (Rapporto Preliminare al Programma Economico Nazionale), a cura di Giorgio Ruffolo & Luciano Barca (Sansoni, Florence 1970).
C. Palazzoli	*Les Régions Italiennes* (Librairie Générale de Droit et de Jurisprudence, Paris 1966).
M. Posner & S.J. Woolf	*Italian Public Enterprise* (Duckworth, London 1967).
R. Ruffilli	*La Questione Regionale in Italia, 1862-1942* (Giuffrè, Milan 1969).
G. Ruffolo	*Rapporto sulla Programmazione* (Laterza, Bari 1973).
D. Rusinow	*Italy's Austrian Heritage* (Oxford University Press, 1969).
E. Santarelli	*Dossier sulle Regioni* (De Donato, Bari 1970).
Lloyd Saville	*Regional Economic Development in Italy* (Edinburgh University Press, 1967).
D. Mack Smith	*Victor Emanuel, Cavour and the Risorgimento* (Oxford University Press, 1971), chapter 12.
M.M. Watson	*Regional Development Policy and Administration in Italy* (Longman, London 1970).
E. Weibel	*La Création des Régions Autonomes à Statut Spécial en Italie* (Droz, Geneva 1971).

International Review of Administrative Sciences, Nos. 1-2, 1971, pp.1-120, contains a number of articles on Italian public administration and administrative law, by M.S. Giannini, F. Benvenuti, *et al.*

3. GREAT BRITAIN: THE QUEST FOR EFFICIENCY

Michael Clarke

Although the 'failure of the State' may sound too apocalyptic a theme for a discussion of British politics, the adequacy of her existing government institutions, with their high degree of centralisation, has been questioned on two grounds. First, that they are too remote psychologically and, often, physically from the average citizen; and second, that their centralisation has brought in its wake rigidity and inefficiency. Those who have questioned have sometimes proposed solutions: the alternatives have ranged from the creation of separate nation-states, through electoral reform, to a simple tampering with, say, the size of the cabinet. The reforms which have been undertaken have been along the lines of improving managerial efficiency rather than increasing participation in the system; of being more concerned with functional rather than regional decentralisation. The politicians and administrators of the centre have decided in recent years that, rather than face the possibility of abrogating power, the must put their own house in order.

Not that there is anything new in this. Governments have always had a penchant for some kind of administrative reform: it is important to be seen to be doing something. Derek Rayner, appointed by the Heath government to review defence procurement (1971) used words from Gauis Petronius in the first century to describe recent administrative history in the defence field. They are apt:

'We trained hard — but it seemed that every time we were beginning to form up into teams, we would be reorganised. I was to learn later in life that we tend to meet any new situation by reorganising, and a wonderful method it can be for creating the illusion of progress while producing confusion, inefficiency and demoralisation.'

During the last decade, however, both politicians and administrators have been more in earnest. The investigation of public expenditure control by Lord Plowden (1961) showed central administration in very bad light, lagging way behind contemporary developments. The criticisms are now bearing fruit: whether the programme of administrative reform is a sufficient, or even correct, response to the problem of centralisation in a period of rapid social and technological change is open to question.

While this programme has been under way, successive governments have been challenged to deal with the remoteness of ordinary people from an overwhelming bureaucracy. Cries have gone up for 'participation' and governments have promised, 'more participation'. What this means nobody says; a singularly arid debate continues. To increase involvement in public affairs has never been a characteristic British ploy. Reform of the franchise was unhurried and parties of left and right have been content to ensure the dominance of a political elite. Government by appointed committee or board is well entrenched: it remains the order of the day for a wide variety of bodies supervising public services and nobody seems inclined to change it. For example the public corporations and the NHS, with a budget in excess of £2,000 million, are run in this way.

As the other chapters suggest, some European countries are interested in the possibilities of industrial democracy. Typically, in Britain even the leadership of the trade union movement itself opposed moves in this direction during the period of nationalisation under the 1945-51 Labour government. It remains unexcited by the prospect and it is left to the minority Liberal party to make noises about co-ownership and the like. It is extraordinary that at a time when large sums of public money are being pumped into private industry in the form of investment grants, tax incentives and other kinds of regional aid – quite apart from government contracts to a wide variety of industry – there is little concern with the public accountability of private capital. Participatory democracy does not appear to be highly valued enought to warrant extension.

Though we shall concentrate on what has gone on inside Whitehall, it should be said that territorial reform has been on the agenda of national politics. Britain inherited a system of elected local government from the late nineteenth century. That it was out-moded by the middle of the twentieth century was not questioned; how to deal with reform was another matter. Proposal followed proposal until the 1970 Heath government finally took the matter in hand and the new system was born. The paternity is not in doubt; the motives are easily miscontrued.

Until the reform measures of the 1880s, county government was still in the hands of justices of the peace, sitting in Quarter and Petty Sessions. After the franchise reform of 1884, male electors called upon to judge national issues in Parliamentary elections had no control over their localities. For the towns, municipal corporations had been established to greet the dawn of Victorian England but, in both town and country, a variety of *ad hoc* bodies had been created to cope with increasing sanitation provision and so on. The 1888 legislation extended the municipal system to the counties, creating a series of elected councils. They were to share functions with the municipal councils and a network of urban and rural districts: between them they were to acquire most of the functions of the *ad hoc* bodies. The immediate response to the plan was protest from the large towns at being swallowed up by the new county authorities. These towns had their way and some sixty all-purpose County Boroughs were created. These same towns were not so successful eighty years later when many of them fought the proposal to include them in the new counties. This time the Tory shires had the ear of those who mattered.

It was the 1888 pattern which persisted until the recent reforms. Some boroughs became county boroughs in the meantime and a few minor boundary changes occurred, but nothing more significant. In Scotland, legislation in 1929 amended the 1888 reforms. Even though the system was not the same as south of the border, the basic balance between town and country, the four all-purpose Counties of Cities and the county councils was not changed. This stability is extraordinary when the intervening social and economic changes are taken into account. Not least among these has been the movement of population: concentration of people in south-eastern England and the general drift from town and city centre to suburb. Small wonder that the present generation sees the old boundaries as meaningless. Increased mobility resulting from improved public transport and, more important, the private car, has upset the coalescence of living, working and leisure patterns. Not only have the old boundaries become irrelevant but many of the authorities created three generations ago proved to be too small for the functions they have acquired over the years.

In England, despite the recommendation of the Maud Royal Commission (1969), the old counties have remained the base of the system. With minor regroupings they have shown extraordinary power of survival. All-purpose authorities have been abolished and the counties divided into districts. Functions are split between the county and the district, the county councils emerging as the stronger. Exceptions to this pattern are found in the six conurbations (West Midlands, Merseyside, Greater Manchester, South Yorkshire, West Yorkshire and Tyneside) where there are metropolitan counties and districts: there is a different division of function and the districts are considerably stronger. Some of the old problems have disappeared but the overall solution is less satisfactory than the one proposed by Maud.

The Welsh pattern is similar but the Scottish more radical. For Scotland the government closely followed the recommendations of the Wheatley Royal Commission (1969) which favoured a more sweeping reconstruction of local government with the division of the country into eight regional authorities subdivided into districts.

All-purpose island authorities were suggested for Orkney and Shetland. The legislation introduced into Parliament added a ninth region (for the border counties) and another island authority for the Hebrides. However, as if to demonstrate that, radical as the Scottish proposals might look, there was no serious commitment on the part of the government, the Scottish Secretary accepted a Standing Committee defeat over Fife. Split between the Tayside and Forth regions in the draft legislation, it emerged as a separate region. The rationality of the Wheatley proposals was completely undermined.

Despite the drawbacks, the new system in all three countries has authorities better suited to the provision of the variety of local functions. The story of these responsibilities is a saga itself. It would be hard to define the rationale which dictated the almost casual addition and subtraction of services to and from local government — unless one sticks at convenience. The significance of this we shall return to. Education and the personal social services have been major additions, public utilities (gas and electricity) notable subtractions.

Almost as if by hallowed convention, the service responsibilities of local government have been organised on a departmental basis. There are two broad views of local government operation: one of them considers it a public agency responsibile for a variety of public services which can be planned for with the minimum of coordination. This 'separatist' view appears to fit the inherited departmentalism bolstered by professional loyalties among the officials. The opposite extreme or 'integral' view sees local government as responsible for the well-being of a locality and so sees the services provided as interwoven, requiring coordinated overall planning. This view has been bolstered by a series of government reports (Plowden (1967) on education, Seebohm (1968) on the social services and Sharpe (1970) on transport) emphasising the broader context of particular services, and by the organisational blueprint for the reformed system. But more of that later. The first view may be modified to the extent of accepting the common facilities of a single organisational framework as providing economies of scale. Espousal of the 'integral' model is a recent occurrence: the lateness of its arrival has been to the disadvantage of local government performance.*

Just as there are two views of the nature of local government responsibilities, there are two views of the role of local government in relation to central government. One is the view of partnership. There is no question in Britain of local authorities being sovreign entities independent of national legislative control: but there is a school of thought which believes in an administrative partnership and a sharing of service responsibilities, with local authorities left to get

*See Stewart, 1973.

on with their side of the business without central interference. The second view is of local authorities as agents of central administration, performing service responsibilities on their behalf and subject to their control. The rhetoric of the local government lobby and of many a politician in opposition matches the former model; the day-to-day exercise of power by the ministers and officials of the central departments ensures that the latter holds sway.

Over the last decades, central government has become more and more concerned with what it sees as the demands of economic planning. This has led, among other things, to rigid control of capital expenditure by central departments. No only this, but increased intervention in social and economic life has produced an attitude of mind which demands the establishment of minimum standards for public services by the centre and monitoring to ensure their maintenance. This is supported partly by the increased acceptance of social and welfare responsibilities on the part of the state and partly by the fiscal situation.

Local authorities have an independent source of revenue: the levy of a tax or rate on property. Over the years the amount which authorities have realistically been able to raise has formed a dwindling proportion of their annual budget. The balance has been provided by specially tailored grants from the national Treasury. Although this is now a block grant and is no longer provided on a service basis it amounts to around 60 per cent of local government income. Because the socioeconomic structure (and therefore property base) of authorities varies considerably the actual proportion of government finance may be over 70 per cent or so, or as low as 40 per cent. The original intent of the property tax was to free town and county halls of the purse strings of Whitehall and, presumably, to provide for a more realistic partnership. Whatever the intent, the fact is that it is now hard to speak of fiscal autonomy. He who pays the piper is able to call the tune. The grounds for intervention are compounded.

As the demand for local government reform grew in the late 1950s and the 1960s, the rhetoric was much concerned with increasing autonomy, recreating partnership, revitalising democracy and so on. Certainly the stage had been reached where it made sense to question the democratic panoply of the system. If it was administratively convenient to use local government as an agency for the provision of certain state responsibilities, whose shape was determined in London, then why not create administrative outposts of Whitehall departments responsible to London? Why perpetuate the mythology of local control? Such questions strike at the heart of the supposed democratic tradition and so were not seriously discussed. The bandwagon of reform began to roll, a succession of proposals was produced and legislation finally passed — all in the name of democracy, autonomy, partnership.

The rhetoric has masked what has actually happened. The proposals enacted by Parliament demonstrate central government to be more concerned with improving the administrative efficiency of their agents under the guise of local democracy, than with freeing authorities from constraint and increasing autonomy and local responsibility. The new boundaries are undoubtedly more appropriate to the contemporary dispersal of population and there is not much doubt that the new authorities will take an integrated view of their responsibilities, recognising the need for overall planning in their localities. But, for all that, the residual power of central government is consolidated in the new legislation. The idea of laying down minimum standards and the maintenance of monitoring system are as much part of the new as they were of the old.

Reorganisation does not include fiscal reform. In the summer of 1971 a Green Paper was produced by the government. Masquerading as a basis for discussion this proved to be a masterly justification of the status quo. A succession of alternatives were paraded before the reader, all to be undermined by arguments of administrative difficulty or inappropriateness, save for one. The rating system is defended to the last and will remain the fiscal base of local government. In all likelihood the rates will continue to provide a dwindling share of the budget and Treasury assistance will increase. The current battle against inflation has involved directives to local authorities to keep the rates down: in some cases this means Whitehall making good the potential loss of revenue. Without a change of attitude to the control of money from the central coffers, the scope of intervention inexorably increases.

It is hard to believe that there is any commitment among national politicians or civil servants for an increase in local autonomy. Not only does action belie proclaimed intention, but the generation of autonomy would mean a voluntary abdication of power by those who most enjoy its use. While not necessarily easy to justify, the growth of central direction of local responsibilities has proved useful to successive governments. It is convenient to those at the centre to hold as firm a rein as possible and it has rooted the belief that the only way the system will work is with centralisation. Occasional murmurings about the possibility of experimenting with forms of devolution are quickly answered by assertions that the advantages are unclear — and, presumably, the disadvantages only too clear.

These murmurings have meant that discussion of other strategies for territorial reform has not been entirely absent. The academic lobby and a small number of 'practitioners' have pressed the case for a regional tier of government. Justification for this is generally the existence of regional economic imbalances and the need to have machinery capable of combating it. Migration to the south-east of England, the dominance of the London-Birmingham axis, the decline of capital industry: all these continuing factors in the post-war decades have contributed to widespread concern.

It had been accepted, with the onset of the Second World War, that regional organisation was convenient for coordination in an emergency. In 1939 a series of Civil Defence Regions were set up, each with a centre and commissioner empowered to coordinate civil defence. Other departments followed suit and created a network of regional administrations. There was never sufficient emergency to utilise the system fully but its rudiments were kept for the period of reconstruction. The post of 'commissioner' was scrapped but departments accepted common boundaries (the Standard Treasury Regions). The Tories scrapped the system when they dismantled controls in the wake of the 1951 election. In this they were backed by the deeply engrained Whitehall attitudes which saw regional offices with any real discretion as unsuited to the traditional departmental system and a threat to Treasury control. Some departments maintained embryonic regional offices but they were concerned with no more than routine administration. At the same time the newly established public corporations and the National Health Service were consolidating regional administrations. What is interesting about the exercise is that the boundaries of these regional units differed as much as they coincided — in the case of twenty departmental regional structures only two were coterminous. This is a reflection of the lack of natural physical or cultural divisions — in England at any rate. Were there a set of natural regions maybe the impetus for territorial reform would have been greater all along the line.

By the end of the fifties the 'stop-go' economic policies of the Conservative government were the catalyst for renewed interest in planning. Not least among the concerns was the need to cope with the peculiar problems of the less prosperous regions. The Distribution of Industry Act (1958), Local Employment Act (1960) and Local Employment and Finance Acts (1963) marked the Macmillan government's concern and acceptance of the need for selective financial aid in the form of loans, grants and then tax incentives. Well-voiced pressure from Newcastle led to the 2nd Baron Hailsham donning cloth cap as Minister for the North-East, and a government blueprint for development.

The advent of a Labour government committed to the notion of a national plan (which paradoxically implied still more centralisation) saw the creation, in 1965, of six planning regions in England (two more were added to cater for the south-east) and one each for Scotland and Wales. Each region was given a council which immediately

set to work to produce collections of economic, land use and
transport plans and a great mass of statistical information. The fact
that these Councils were advisory and had no teeth escaped all but the
most perceptive observers: the enthusiasm surrounding their
inception was remarkable. Meanwhile in Whitehall the battle for
control over the economy raged between the Treasury and the new
Department of Economic Affairs, created without much thought (in
the back of a taxi, according to Harold Wilson and George Brown, its
progenitors) and charged with the production of the National Plan.
Whatever their differences, neither wanted to see real deconcentration:
unity amid adversity.

Characteristically the regional planning machinery was badly
thought out. Regional Boards, comprising officials of all Whitehall
departments, were convened under DEA chairmanship. How these
related to the Councils (appointed — one third from local authorities,
one third from industry and the unions, and one third from other
institutions such as Universities) was never clearly stated. Council
members met monthly but were usually already heavily involved
elsewhere and without much commitment to their new role.
They lacked executive authority and were there as formal
representatives of nobdoy. Resignation and threat of resignation
quickly showed the scheme up for what it was worth. Not only
were there problems at Board-Council level: both bodies were
involved with tasks whose central direction was not the
responsibility of one department but many. Treasury, DEA, Board
of Trade, Housing and Local Government, Agriculture, Fisheries
and Food, Transport and Fuel and Power all had direct links.
Quelle betise!

A spin-off from this regional organisation was to be the growth
of 'little Whitehalls'. Each regional centre in England (the position of
Scotland and Wales is rather different) was to house regional offices
of Whitehall departments. On paper this was a good proposal,
provided that there was a real delegation of authority. Maintenance
of a centre-periphery relationship would be no good: the centre would
retain control and the periphery to be forced to respond to its
directives without the possibility of extensive adaptation to
regional need. If it could be replaced by a network system (to continue
the analogy used by Donald Schon (1972)) with horizontal rather
than vertical communication, and with freedom to carry out this
adaptation without subjection to central control, then there would be
a base for far-reaching changes. Not surprisingly, administrative
orthodoxy had its way. More often than not the officials in the
regional centres were junior in position, more concerned with their own
future and a return to London than with the regional cause. In such

circumstances it is not difficult to imagine where their loyalties would lie in a conflict between the region and their Whitehall masters. No change in departmental practice occurred at the centre: few people seriously contemplated discussion with a regional office before making policy decisions. Old habits die hard, particularly when to change them is to risk loss of status or authority.

Most domestic departments continue to operate some kind of regional decentralisation within these constraints. The general pattern is for each centre to be supervised by a controller of assistant secretary level (or sometimes a professional official; e.g. divisional road engineer). In most cases the controller will have delegated to him authority for small amounts of expenditure. Experience has shown that it is not easy for a controller to exercise much policy influence: for one thing his headquarters will have produced plans of such detail as a result of their internal processes of consultation that it would be difficult to re-think. More important, most regional offices are overburdened with routine administrative work so that controllers simply do not have the time to concern themselves with such matters.

Regional departmental organisation exists alongside the network of *ad hoc* agencies: the administrative boundaries of the health service and the public corporations may not always coincide but often do mark real units of authority. However, even where enabling legislation has made such units mandatory, there is a constant pressure toward national uniformity. Sponsoring ministries continually intervene to ensure consistency of standards wherever they can, be it in hospital building or the development of the telephone service.

Administrative deconcentration does have a reputable pedigree in Scotland; and recently some of the experience gained here has been transferred to Wales. One of the problems of developing a regional framework is to know how to draw the boundaries. There is no simple way and much empty argument surrounds proposal and counterproposal. Economic concern led British governments to tackle the problem, but there are no sure economic criteria. The search for homogeneity and for areas suffering from a common problem requiring a common policy to tackle it, dominated the Conservative government's thinking in the early 1960s. The problem with this is that a fragmented pattern emerges with large areas of the country left out. An alternative is to search for economic units: areas dependent on a city or industrial complex. This was, in part, the foundation of the 1965 Planning Regions, but again there are problems: the sphere of influence of two cities may overlap (Manchester-Liverpool, Leeds-Bradford-Sheffield, etc.) and make it impossible to draw valid boundaries. The problems of both approaches are solved if regions can be found which arise from historical or administrative factors. Some kind of natural attachment or consciousness is evident in Scotland and Wales for instance. Scotland moreover can be seen as a physically distinct region with its own economic infrastructure. Wales is united by a brand of regional consciousness, even if it is not a real economic unit and its physical characteristics make internal communication difficult.

Where there is a regional identity the business of planning and development is probably easier because an enthusiasm can be generated and tapped. Where there is not, regional division creates administrative artefacts which have little meaning either for the people living in them or for the people running them. Their position at the Whitehall conference table is so much the weaker. What kind of common reference do the people of Worcester or Swanage have with those of Plymouth or Penzance (the S.W. Planning Region): of Bournemouth or Brighton with Luton (S.E. Region), of Lincoln with Huddersfield or Halifax (Yorkshire and Humberside)?

Scotland is different; it emerged as an administrative unit in 1895. The Gladstone government responded to separatist pressures with legislation creating a Secretary for Scotland in whom was vested the function of Scottish administration previously exercised by the Home Secretary, Privy Council, Local Government Board and some of those of the Treasury. The miscellany ranged from the police to fisheries, and from wild birds' protection to prisons. The office, set up in Whitehall, got off to an inauspicious start with five secretaries in sixteen months. Growth of the Scottish Office and extension of power over succeeding decades has been partly a response to the continuing pressures of nationalist sentiment and partly utilisation of an administrative convenience.

The Scottish Office is now responsible for agriculture and fisheries, local government and associated services, electricity, education, law and order, health and welfare as well as a variety of cultural and general service institutions (e.g. National Library, Register Office, Law Commission). Its range of administrative responsibility, however, should not be allowed to mask the absence of fiscal autonomy. It is subject, like any other department, to the Treasury in the battle for resources. Increasingly it has come to be a pressure group for Scottish interests in Whitehall, the Secretary of State representing them in the Cabinet, the staff of Dover House in negotiation with other departments. While retaining administrative control of its various services, it is of course subject to the political pressures of London – usually in the direction of overall uniformity.

The strength of London's demand for uniformity and its lack of faith in this kind of administrative deconcentration is witnessed by the extent to which Great Britain departments hold sway in Scotland. It is not just that a Treasury retains financial control: the Department of Trade and Industry retain controlling interest in regional/industrial development (the saga of shipbuilding on the Clyde and all that stems from it highlights the DTI and its predecessor and not the Scottish Office; oil and related developments under the nominal direction of a Scottish Office Minister were increasingly seen to be central to the DTIs interests before passing to the new Energy Ministry). The departments of Employment and of Health and Social Security have full responsibility for Scotland; the Department of the Environment, like the DTI, finds itself with shared and often overlapping powers. And so the list continues. Contrary to the wishful thinking of many people there is only partial administrative deconcentration. The extension of the idea to Wales is even more limited. A Welsh Office to deal with the responsibilities of the Ministry of Housing and Local Government was established in 1951; a Minister of State was appointed shortly afterwards and a Secretary of State in 1964. With this last appointment goes charge over housing, local government, roads, primary and secondary education, health and welfare services and some shared functions with the Ministry of Agriculture. The publication of the Hardman (1973) report on the dispersal of civil servants from London is again witness to Whitehall's wooly attitude. It did no more than make a token gesture. There is a mentality wedded not only to central control but to the necessity of living within easy reach of St James' Park.

Before leaving the 'Celtic fringes', one more regional or sub-regional institution is worthy of note. The Highlands and Islands Development Board was set up to deal with an area of depopulation and economic decay. What is unique about the Board is that it has executive powers so that it is charged with developing a regional strategy and with pursuing it. It has a budget of about £1 million per annum, the power to borrow, acquire land or business by compulsory purchase and to run its own enterprises. The meagre financial provision ensures operations on a modest scale but the experiment is exceptional in the British context. The Board of officials are appointed by the Scottish Secretary and responsible to him in a general way. Power of appointment and over the purse strings can ensure such a body does not step too far out of line but this does not dull the contrast with the English Planning Boards. The cynic doubtless finds it significant that the Board is tucked away in Inverness and responsible for the most distant (from London) and under-developed region in Britain.

The pressures for regional deconcentration have had strong economic motive, occasionally being given added voice by academic commentators. There is a general consensus that the prime objective of economic policy is growth and the increase of private wealth; that there are regional disparities is unfortunate and they should be ironed out in the progress toward the greater end. However the impetus of technology and the increasing irrelevance of 'natural' location (so important to the capital industries on which early development was founded) to much of modern industry has resulted in increasing concentration on the London-Birmingham axis, itself a clear extension of the European industrial belt. Proximity to major markets, export outlets and to suppliers has further increased the momentum. The consequence is a centralisation of economic power and relatively little concern about the disparities on the part of private capital. The battle has been waged primarily by those who see themselves as under-privileged. Politicians have responded with concern when worried about the electoral consequences of inaction. The response has been in terms of centrally directed aid and toothless advisory bodies.

In recent years there have been occasional manifestations of popular feeling and constant below-surface rumblings about the problems of a centralised political system. The successes of Scottish and Welsh nationalists during the 1964-70 Wilson administration are a case in point. Feelings of underprivilege strengthened by distance from the centre and hasty attempts to reawaken 'national' cultural consciousness raised the spectre of a more far-reaching political and administrative devolution. Mr Wilson set up a Royal Commission on the Constitution and Mr Heath, not to be outdone, his own committee on the Scottish situation. However, sustained pressure for an increase in the number or scope of democratic institutions is weak. Ther is little consensus in Scotland and Wales, let alone in the English regions.

The publication of the Kilbrandon Report (1973) and the reaction to it has demonstrated this well. Seldom can there have been a Royal Commission report with so many minuted reservations by members. Seldom, too, can there have been such determination by a national political elite to give a report so quick and public a burial. The Commission recommended separate Parliaments for Scotland and Wales (with a power of veto given to Westminster) responsible for the sort of functions now in the hands of the Scottish Office and gave lukewarm support to Englishregional councils with no teeth. Devolution to Scotland and Wales would be underpinned by a Treasury grant negotiated with an 'independent' Treasury Board. This, like much of the report, is ill-thought out and badly argued with precious little understanding of the constitutional (e.g. the relationship of subnational and Westminster Parliaments) and political (e.g. party) problems involved. Two members of the Commission refused association with the majority and produced a Memorandum of Dissent arguing for a much more extensive administrative — but not legislative — devolution. More of this later.

Mr Heath remains committed to some kind of legislative Assembly for Scotland, apparently unaware of his Scottish party's appreciation that there would be a permanent anti-Conservative majority and uncertain about the constitutional implications of its relationship with the UK Parliament. Despite immediate electoral benefit, the Labour Party remain unmoved, all too conscious of the potential embarrassments. Neither party shows any concern even for bringing the variety of *ad hoc* agencies at national or regional level within the purview of elected assemblies. Whatever the decoys, there is little consensus about regionalism as an antidote to centralisation in the UK.

It is true that pressure for local government reform came from both Whitehall and the town and county halls. We have already suggested that Whitehall saw the whole thing in terms of improving the inefficiency of their agents. Why then was local government itself eager for change? Undoubtedly the movement of population without changes in boundary, the multiplicity of authorities, the consequent shortage of personnel, etc. made change essential. Local government had been suffering from these problems for some time and the increasing incursion of central government was thought to be no coincidence. Officials and councillors saw the opportunity as one of putting their own house in order with the hope that this would keep Whitehall at bay. They too were concerned with their efficiency, though from a different standpoint.

In Britain inefficiency in administration is taken to be a major source of frustration with bureaucracy, public or private. Consequently many of the more significant administrative reforms of recent years have been to do with improving internal efficiency. While geographical deconcentration has not been pursued very far, the crisis of confidence has been met by functional deconcentration in a number of forms and by the application of new administrative and decision-making techniques.

The most extreme recent attempts have been to do with hiving-off particular responsibilities from government and returning them to the market place. Proposals for this played an important part in the 1970 Conservative Party manifesto; the success of the policy has not been marked. The problem is that such services were moved into the public sector in the first place because of their strategic importance. The attractions of 'hiving-off' — reducing the number of personnel and the overall size and scope of the machine — are outweighed by the disadvantages of diminishing political control. The idea is ideologically important to the Right but has been limited to such institutions as the State Brewery in Carlisle (nationalised to curb drunkenness at at armaments factories in the First World War) and Thos. Cook, (the travel agents taken over because of threat of subversion in the Second World War).

A less extreme version of the 'hiving-off' strategy is the one discussed by the Fulton Report on the Civil Service. This concerns the removal of areas of work from the central government machine to autonomous public boards and corporations. The Post Office is a good example of a commercial activity formerly a departmental responsibility and now an autonomous corporation; the Atomic Energy Authority an example of a non-commercial operation similarly organised. The Fulton Committee drew attention to the problems of the boundary lines of Ministerial and Board responsibilities and to the constitutional issues in the relationship with Parliament. They have been taken to heart.

The creation of specialised agencies to deal with problems *as they arise* is a well entrenched feature of British public administration. There is great variety in their size, function and relationship to departments and Ministers. Some of these are the providers of services (e.g. the BBC), some regulatory (Air Transport Licensing Board, White Fish Authority), some commercial (National Airports Authority, Transport Holding Company) or promotional (research councils), others concerned with economic control or development (Pay and Prices Boards, NEDC) and yet others with varieties of function (River Authorities, Community Relations Commission). It would be wrong to see the use of *ad hoc* agencies only as a response to the contemporary problems of centralisation: it has been going on for too long. However, it continues to remain an important way of dealing with a new problem or responsibility without further encumbering central departments.

Such agencies have the advantage of appearing separate from the rest of government and free of political control even if they are not. There is a strange mythology which surrounds the relation of a Minister to the agencies which are his responsibility. Channels of influence are curiously hidden as indeed is agency accountability to the public. An extraordinary convention that a controlling board or council appointed by a Minister acts as representative of the public is perpetuated. This body is the instrument of accountability, of overall supervision and, maybe, the government's will. A research project at Glasgow University uncovered some seven hundred organisations which were not government departments but were funded by government with specific public functions. Their number and scope makes it likely that most people will come into contact with them at some time or other. Their clouded relationship to both public and government makes it likely the frustrations with bureaucracy are increased not relieved.

The advantage of autonomous agencies whether hived-off or

purpose-built is that they lie outside the ordinary hierarchy of central departments and are not subject to departmental financial accountability. Executive authority lies where the job is being done and not with departmental superiors. The Fulton Committee recommended:

> 'In the interests of efficiency, the principles of accountable management should be applied to the organisation of departments. This means that clear allocation of responsibility and authority to accountable units with defined objectives. It also means a corresponding addition to the system of government accounting.'

Correctly the Committee had concluded that one of the major problems of the central departments was their rigidity arising from a reluctance to delegate authority. This reluctance was itself derived from the system of vote-accounting to Parliament. In recommending the need to experiment with new forms of organisation, the Committee was characteristically underlining a train of thought which had been gaining support through the 1960s. Accountabe management, it should be said, means not only holding people responsible for performance but also measuring it as objectively as possible. In the words of Fulton, it should be used whenever 'output can be measured against cost or other criteria, and where individuals can be held responsible for their performance'. The full significance of this will be apparent later.

Slowly the machinery responded. Derek Rayner of Shell (appointed by Mr Heath to look at the problems of Defence Procurement and Civil Aerospace) reported in spring 1971 on the desirability of creating a Defence Procurement Executive as just such a unit. Commenting on the Fulton proposal quoted above he was able to say,

> '... we have looked in vain in the existing organisations for managers who have clearcut responsibilities for a whole task and who have the necessary authority to influence events across the range of functions necessary for this.'

The argument Rayner pursued in favour of the Executive was that the procurement of weaponry was a large-scale undertaking (involving around 52,000 people) operating on the fringes of the commercial world and in an area where the skills of the professional accountant are at a premium and where there should be full managerial authority vested in people on the job. Existing only to meet consumer needs and in a non-competitive market prevents operation on full commercial principles and so made any suggestion of 'hiving-off' to the market place unthinkable. It was recommended that a unit be set up under the executive authority of the Secretary of State for Defence but outside the usual departmental structure. It would be headed by a Chief Executive with subordinate Controllers each responsible for a principal area of activity. The Chief Executive and four controllers would be Accounting Officers, each responsible for their Parliamentary Vote. The remaining controllers would answer directly to the Chief Executive. Line management within the area of defence procurement would also be strengthened. Full authority and responsibility, financial and managerial, would be concentrated inside the Executive with no dependence on a parallel hierarchy in the Defence Ministry. The proposals were accepted by the government and the Executive created in April 1972.

In July 1971 another report — under the name of Sir John Mallabar — was published, this time on Government Industrial Establishments (Royal Ordnance Factories and Royal Dockyards). Once again it was argued that, although on the fringe of the commercial world, neither was a candidate for 'hiving-off'. In the case of the Ordnance Factories, for instance, it was stated that as suppliers of munitions to the forces they could not refuse an order, design the product or determine its quality; that before overseas orders could be taken government approval had to be sought; and that the ROFs had to provide the main national reserve of capacity for a substantial range of ministries. Combined, these factors prevented full commercial operation and made the law of the market place inappropriate. The need to move the establishment away from the restrictions of Vote financing were seen to be just as crucial here as in the Defence Procurement area and consequently a Trading Fund was recommended. It was proposed that the Controller, ROF, should be recognised as the accountable manager with maximum possible delegated authority for the purchase and disposal of materials, personnel management and industrial relations and control of building works and maintenance. The dichotomy of financial and technical control was thereby to be eliminated.

More recently the need to give the Labour Exchanges a brighter image and to move into the managerial/professional employment field led the Department of Employment to review its employment services. The upshot has been the creation of an Agency again outside the departmental hierarchy but under the executive aegis of the Secretary of State for Employment. In all cases the argument has been that the traditional hierarchy with financial responsibility located at the top (the Permanent Secretary is usually the officer accountable to Parliament for the spending of the Departments' Vote) has been the cause of inefficiency by stifling responsibility. The men doing the job have never had full authority for it. To overcome this, exceptions to the accepted pattern have been argued for and implemented.

Strangely enough, there has been little general discussion of financial Parliamentary accountability. This dates from the Gladstone reforms of the 1860s and is concerned to ensure regularity in expenditure: that money is spent on the things for which it is voted. This made sense in the context of putting the business of government on a more honest and responsible footing; it makes less sense today. The problem is that the fiscal model is the bulwark of centralisation and hierarchy; it also induces a concern for the *minutiae* of expenditure which can produce an incapacity to see the wood for the trees. Derek Rayner observed that although most senior people have a balanced view of the requirements of the Public Accounts Committee, at more junior levels fear of criticism from the Committee clearly causes the priority in work to be the avoidance of mistakes.

Parliament has already begun to experiment with alternative models of accountability in its concern for programmes (whether desired results are being achieved) and process (the making of decisions and so on) through the Expenditure Committee and the remaining specialist Select Committees. Government itself is showing the same concern: the Central Policy Review Staff and the institution of Programme Analysis and Review are witness to this. The need to continue experiment is important: not only would greater flexibility allow for changes within the government machine along the lines of the 'exceptions' already discussed but it might also reduce constraints to the point where government was seen by its public to be adaptive and capable of dealing with situations of complex change. It could well be the moment to bring the great variety of *ad hoc* agencies into the scope of Parliamentary accountability without threatening their financial freedom. But until programme or process models of accountability are more generally acceptable the problem will not be solved. Despite the flirtation by Parliament there is no real sign that the importance of the alternative models is recognised. Nor is there much indication that its central concern is shifting from financial regularity to an efficiency audit, taking up some of the lessons of the US General Accounting Office or the French *Cour des Comptes* (without its constitutional isolation). It is surprising that there has been so little discussion of accountability, given its importance and given that reformers have had to argue for continuing exceptions to the status quo.

Much more important has been the development of managerial efficiency. Local government reform appears to have been prompted by a desire for increased efficiency; autonomous agencies are used when it is the most efficient way of doing things; the emphasis on

accountable management is to do with improving efficiency. The
Fulton Committee Report is much concerned with the efficiency
of the government machine: this time in terms of its use of personnel.
Though an independent committee, it expresses the trend of
Whitehall thinking in the mid and late sixties stimulated by Plowden
(1961) rather than a set of original ideas or observations. The
Heath government came to power in 1970 dedicated to a new style
of government:

> 'More is involved than bringing forward new policies and
> programmes: it means resolving the issue of the proper
> sphere of government in a free society, and *improving the
> efficiency* of the machinery intended to achieve the aim it sets
> itself within that sphere.'

Although its policy committees had given the Conservative Party
a number of guidelines in opposition, these and the 1970 White Paper
again reflect the general progress of bureaucratic thinking. Juggling
with division of function, departmental boundaries were made more
all-encompassing; the threads of accountable management were picked
up; and considerable emphasis was placed on the need to improve the
analytic capability of government in policy-making.

Characteristic of the whole episode is an emphasis on managerialism:
the importation of ideas and techniques from management science and
the experience of private bureaucracy. This process started in the
United States with the Defense Department, in the first instance.
borrowing ideas from the management of some of the big corporations.
It was picked up on this side of the Atlantic in the mid and late sixties
with the Ministry of Defence often as the pioneer, (it is no coincidence
that the recommendations of Derek Rayner and Sir John Mallabar
were in the defence sphere).

It is reasonable to ask why the public administrators began to
look elsewhere for ways of putting their own house in order. The
complexity and technicality of many of the responsibilities assumed
by government in recent decades seemed to be defeating the capacities
of the administrative machine. More and more problems appeared as
the government sought to manage the economy, adapt the welfare
state and so on. In this situation of confusion the message of
management science seemed to provide many answers. The ideas of
corporate, accountable management; of cost-benefit and cost-
effectiveness analysis and of programme budgeting had become
fashionable in private administration and were being peddled by the
burgeoning business schools as certain panaceas for a
multitude of problems. In many cases they had their intellectual

origins in the theories and writings of the Scientific Management School of the early years of this century. As such they have a clarity and certainty which makes them appealing. That their basic assumptions of economic rationality and the like are open to question is easily ignored. As the nerve of the public administrator failed, here was something to restore confidence.

The influence of 'management' ideas has spread well beyond central departments: hand in hand with the reform of local government has gone a Department of the Environment sponsored blueprint for new management structures (Bains 1972). This is liberally splattered with the jargon and, significantly, ignores the role of politics in local government. The counterpart for Scotland (Patterson 1973) tells a similar story and is largely the work of a seconded management consultant. The reshaping of the Health Service has been accompanied by similar moves: a report by McKinsey (the American management consultancy firm) has been used for an outline of Management Arrangements (1972). A new set of Water Authorities are busy adopting a management report. Up and down the country public officials in a great variety of agencies are learning the language.

This seems harmless enough. Who wants inefficient administration? The rub comes in what is meant by efficiency. The public and private sectors are not analogous. The private world of business is dominated by the market place: its objectives are, put crudely, the maximisation of profit. The tests of whether these objectives are being attained are those of market efficiency. Efficiency refers to an input-output relationship: the obtaining of maximum satisfaction for any outlay of resources. There is market competition for resources; and firms which are most efficient in utilisation attract more. The public sector is rather different. It is dominated by political and not market influences. It has to respond not to market demand but to a complex — and often conflicting — set of pressures articulated through the political system. Its objectives are not so readily discernible and there may not even be common agreement about which are most important. Tests of profit for efficiency and the attainment of objectives are lacking and, rather than a market competition for resources, there is political conflict about which demands are to be curtailed in the interests of economy. The battle for *limited* resources is a real one.

Simplified though this picture may be, it does underline the danger of public administration using the private sector as a paradigm. Any attempt to value the output of government in monetary terms, for instance, must be treated with great suspicion. Business can be concerned with resource efficiency; government must be concerned with general social welfare. However the direct and indirect social

social effects of almost any policy (both costs and benefits) are of such magnitude and of such a kind that they defy measurement.

And so we should be aware of different kinds of 'efficiency'. Where business or 'managerial' efficiency is the maxim, it is incompatible with much of the political world. That is not to deny any sort of efficiency. What is needed is an administrative system which is both responsible to its public, and processes the demands made upon it in such a way that the politicians can make the decisions most clearly in line with their declared intentions. This we might call 'political' efficiency. The Public Expenditure Survey Committee and Programme Analysis and Review are administrative devices which probably fulfil this last criterion. Both are designed to ensure that resources are distributed in such a way that money is well spent and objectives achieved. In practice PESC appears to be used often as an administrative device by the Treasury in order to get its own way and control public spending. There is no reason, however, why both devices could not be more overtly political – as the Central Policy Review Staff is with its roving brief across the whole range of policy objectives.

The fact of the matter is that any government has difficulty in doing either all the things it promised or all the things that are demanded of it. New resources are limited; reallocation is a slow process and each day throws up new demands and perspectives. Qualitative judgements have to be made: they need to be based on a real understanding of the problems involved. In the age of the professional manager it is unfashionable to argue the politician's case; this is a sad reflection of our state of mind for the decisions that have to be made are choices of value and are concerned with the kind of society we want to live in.

The demands for administrative change have come sometimes from the practitioners themselves and sometimes from the outside world (e.g. the Conservative Government's advisers from business firms). Enthusiasm for new devices must be tempered by an assessment of their suitability for the political world. Quite apart from the more fundamental problems, it is easy to begin to talk a technical language which hides the issues, misleads the politician and becomes an excuse to diminish his role in the name of expertise. This in its turn enlarges the distance of bureaucracy and government from their public bringing more frustration and making communication more difficult.

The refusal to take seriously the possibility of geographical deconcentration or devolution – and the emphasis on central administrative reform – are predicated on the assumption that the centre must and will remain dominant, in the interests of economic growth and management, social planning and so on. Consequently operational efficiency must be improved. The fact that central economic planning has not been noted for its success and that social planning has had its pitfalls, not least the continuing failure to deal adequately with urban social deprivation, does not seem to be taken into account. The pressures for uniformity, which dictate central government intervention in local authorities, operate persuasively in favour of strong central control. Those which argue for the necessity of coordination and control of policy, resources and expertise in the public sector ensure not only strong central government with fewer, larger departments but also a strengthening of the key departments of central government (Treasury, Civil Service Department and Cabinet Office).

The obvious question at issue is whether this orthodoxy is as much beyond question as it is made out. Is the only way of dealing with public frustration and disillusion that of tampering with the central machine? Indeed, is the only cause of frustration and disillusion the supposed inefficiency of central bureaucracy? Certainly its incapacities are marked, but might they not be compounded by the pressures of centralisation themselves? There is little doubt that the time will come when more radical measures are needed. As a start, there are three areas where progress could be made, even if the signs of the moment suggest change will be slow. First of all, membership of the European Community must lead to serious thought about the kind of government responsibilities which can be moved upwards to an international level. This is discussed elsewhere in this book and is an immediate problem.

Secondly, at the level of national government, there is a need to improve public accountability. Confidence in the complex machinery of Whitehall would come more easily were it really seen to be responsible to its public. This means much more than lifting the heavy cloak of secrecy which surrounds its day-to-day activities. It means rethinking both the relationship to Parliament and the root concerns of accountability. Often discussion begins to assume separation of power between Parliament and Government and to ignore the continuing dependence of the latter on the former. That is not going to change, but there is no reason why Parliament should not be concerned less with financial regularity and rather more with the broader questions of *how* money is spent and whether it is being spent in the best way. A move to 'process' and 'programme' accountability and away from the fiscal model would probably give Parliament more influence over policy; it would certainly yield more information about what happens inside the government machine (and induce a visible sense of responsibility). Such a development would also allow for greater flexibility within departments, by removing the burden of hierarchy which supports financial control concentrates authority at the top and induces too much concern for detail. For the first time there would also be the possibility of bringing within its ambit the host of *ad hoc* agencies, without interfering with their financial autonomy.

Thirdly, more radical and with consequences for the accountability problem, there is a strong case for moving responsibilities downwards to subnational units. This means more than another set of administrative agencies: it means abdication of political power from the centre, and real fiscal autonomy. Functional deoncentration may have its uses but it does not necessarily lessen the problems of centralisation: services do not necessarily become more adaptable to regional or local need, nor their providers closer to the people; and there is little evidence to suggest that they coordinate any better with related public services. While the Kilbrandon Report may have been a damp squib, there was published with it a dissenting memorandum which is, at least, a coherent alternative scheme as an antidote to centralisation. Not only this, but an argument supported by a more sophisticated analysis of the contemporary situation and realistic appraisal of the problems involved.

The enormous expansion of central government and its apparent rigidity, the decline of Parliament and local government, the growth of nominated *ad hoc* authorities and the disparate regional offices of central departments led Lord Crowther-Hunt and Professor Alan Peacock to argue for extensive administrative devolution to a system of subnational governments covering the whole of Great Britain. Their intention is to reduce the excessive burdens of the centre, increase the influence of the elected politician, provide greater accessibility for the public and adequate means for the redress of grievances. While appreciating the special position of Scotland and Wales they argue that it is just as important to achieve these objectives for the people of England. They divide the latter into five regions one of which (the South-East) is probably too big and needs dividing into two or three.

Seven elected Assemblies and Governments would take responsibility for the outposts of central government and noncommercial, non-industrial *ad hoc* authorities (e.g. Health and Water Authorities) in their area. They would also be given supervising responsibility in respect of the public corporations and would be 'responsible for devising policies for the general welfare and good government of their respective areas' within the framework of the UK Government and Parliament and the EEC. Each intermediate government would have its own civil service; and, while the framework of local government would remain, it would deal with intermediate and not central government.

Independent revenue-raising powers and a negotiated Treasury grant (without strings attached) would provide the requisite degree of freedom.

The financial and economic proposals strike at the heart of the centralising creed. It is suggested that not only will they provide independence but, by initiating the business of resource allocation and planning at the intermediate level and then aggregating the plans at the centre, they will enhance the ability of central government to achieve its economic objectives. Planning from the top down is not the only way of managing national economic affairs. To use the Schon analogy again, dictation by the centre to the periphery is not conducive to adaptability, innovation and 'good government'. A network of 'intermediate' centres is likely to be much more successful.

The Scottish and Welsh Offices, as we have seen, have wide responsibilities in the education and housing areas and in the general field of social planning. The vesting of these responsibilities in all the intermediate governments in combination with control of *ad hoc* authorities should make for a situation of improved accessibility. It would take away from the centre an enormous burden of administration and bring it — together with the operation of things like the Health Service — under closer scrutiny from the politicians. At the same time it allows for greater political and administrative scope in adjusting services to local need without the constant demand for uniformity.

The authors of the memorandum recognise that were the scheme to be accepted as feasible it could only be implemented over a considerable period of time. Their hopes that it might be implemented, founder on the prevalent attitudes of a national political and administrative elite which we have already discussed. It is possible to envisage a motley coalition who might support the proposal for a variety of reasons but it is hard to see a general acceptance or a wide measure of support in the immediate future. The Hunt-Peacock arguments are persuasive however, and the problems of physical and psychological remoteness, rigidity and inefficiency remain.

POSTSCRIPT

Since this chapter was written there have been two general elections, one producing minority Labour government, the other a small overall majority for Mr Wilson. The force of the proceeding arguments still remains, except for the fact that some kind of constitutional change is more likely. The question is whether it will be cosmetic, arranged for electoral purposes, or whether the opportunity will be used to undertake far-reaching reform along the lines of the chapter's closing paragraphs.

In February 1974 a Parliament was elected containing 14 Liberal MPs (backed by 6 million votes) and nine nationalists (7 from Scotland and 2 from Wales). The Liberals were declared devolutionists and electoral reformers; the nationalists, challengers of constitutional orthodoxy. The quickly buried Kilbrandon Report was rescussitated and bandied about in political argument, usually without an understanding of the problems of the 'periphery'. The government, worried that the nationalists would not disappear, appointed Lord Crowther-Hunt as adviser and set up working parties to explore alternative courses of devolutionary action. Crowther-Hunt, with only lukewarm political support and treated with suspicion by the civil service (he was suspected of being the author of the Fulton Report's attack on 'amateurism'), failed to carry the argument for far-reaching administrative devolution.

Whitehall's senior officials, unwilling to abrogate power, persuaded the politicians that mild legislative devolution was the only realistic solution. A White Paper, published only weeks before the October election, proposed assemblies for Scotland and Wales, without financial autonomy or control over economic and industrial policy and activity (including oil) and without much attention being given to the complicated relations of national and sub-national Parliaments.

The second 1974 election saw the Welsh nationalist position maintained and the SNP emerge as the largest opposition party in Scotland (with a third of the popular vote). The new government may be tempted to argue that the economic crisis and the narrowness of their majority make large-scale reform inappropriate but the ballot box will be taken as demanding prompt action. Many of those wanting such action (and they are to be found in varying numbers in all parties) will argue that the White Paper was electoral gimmickry and that more radical measures are called for. In this they will be backed by the government's 'outside' advisers and a growing number of civil servants whose work keeps them in places other than London. Their difficulty will be a lack of agreement about precise proposals. Without one, it may be hard to counter the 'Treasury mentality' of the Whitehall elite, even though the time is ripe for change.

Appendix

Table 1   Local Government Receipts and Expenditure 1971   (£ million)

	Receipts Current	Capital		Expenditure Current	Capital
Rates	2,087	–	Education	2,185	352
Grants	2,858	183	Debt Interest	1,134	–
Trading surplus	121	–	Personal health & social services	539	51
Rent	1,076	–			
Interest, etc.	109	–	Environmental Services	466	336
Loans	–	1,398			
Other	–	533	Police & Admin. of of Justice	446	28
			Roads & Lighting	274	270
			Housing	126	719
			Other	1,081	358
	6,251	2,114		6,251	2,114

Table 2   Estimated Expenditure by Layer of Government
(£ million at current prices based on expenditures for 1968-9)

	Devolved system		Present system	
Central government	9,880	(46.1%)	15,660	(73.0%)
Intermediate government	5,780	(26.9%)	–	
Local government	5,790	(27.0%)	5,790	(27.0%)
Combined public authorities	21,450	(100.0%)	21,450	(100.0%)

Note: Figures quoted by Professor Alan Peacock based on research done for the Kilbrandon Commission by Dr David King. The figures show the pattern for 1968-9 if devolution of expenditure to regions had been in operation and there had been no incentive for regions to alter either its pattern or amount.

Select Bibliography

Royal Commission Reports: Local Government in England and Wales (Maud) Cmnd. 4040, 1969; Local Government in Scotland (Wheatley) Cmnd. 4150, 1969; The Constitution (Kilbrandon) Cmnd. 5460, 1973.

Government Reports: Management of Local Government (Maud) 1967; Government Industrial Establishments (Mallabar) Cmnd. 4713, 1971; Committee on the Civil Service (Fulton) Cmnd. 3638, 1968; New Local Authorities: management and structure (Bains) 1972; Management Arrangements for the Reorganised NHS, 1972; The New Scottish Local Authorities (Paterson) 1973; Dispensal of Government Work from London (Hardman) Cmnd. 5322, 1973; Children and their Primary Schools (Plowden) 1967; Local Authority and Allied Personal Social Services (Seebohm) 1968; Transport Planning: The Men for the Job (Sharpe) 1970.

White Papers: Control of Public Expenditure Cmnd. 1432, 1961; Reorganisation of Central Government Cmnd. 4506, 1970; Government Organisation for Defence Procurement and Civil Aerospace Cmnd. 4641, 1971.

Green Papers: Future Shape of Local Government Finance Cmnd. 4741, 1971.

Other Works Cited: D. Schon *Loss of the Stable State*, Temple Smith, London, 1972. J. Stewart and R. Greenwood 'Towards a Typology of English Local Authorities' *Political Studies*, Vol XXI, No.1, pp.64-9, 1973.

4. DECENTRALISATION OF POWER IN THE FEDERAL REPUBLIC OF GERMANY

John Holloway

Discussion of decentralisation of power in West Germany may help to throw light on the debate in some of the other countries treated in this book, because the goal of regional decentralisation aspired to in these countries has already been formally achieved in the Federal Republic, without very great social effect. Regional decentralisation of power has, to a very large extent, been digested by political debate in Germany and the main focus of interest has switched in recent years to attempts to decentralise, or deconcentrate, economic power.

Both forms of decentralisation (regional and economic) formed an important part of the Western Allies' 'struggle for democracy' in that part of Germany which they occupied after the war, of their attempt to build a state to their liking on the ruined 'Germany of the year Zero'. Both represent a reaction against what was seen as the overcentralisation of power under the Nazi regime.

The Nazi state had been a unitary state, in which the federal states (Länder) of the Weimar constitution, too weak to offer any opposition, were reduced to administrative districts under the direction of party Gauleiter. This concentration of political power in the hands of the central government was to be avoided in the future by firmly establishing federalism in the new constitution. The Potsdam Agreement of August 1945 had already stipulated that Germany should have a decentralised political structure and the administration of the Allied forces was organised not only on a zonal but also on a federal basis; each zone of occupation was subdivided into a number of Länder, and it was on the basis of these Länder that political and administrative life was first reorganised. When, in July 1948, the Western Allies asked German politicians to draw up a 'democratic constitution' which would 'establish for the participating states a government structure of federal type' for the part of Germany which they occupied, their main concern was to see that not too much power was given to the central government. The purpose behind this insistence on the federal element was threefold. It was hoped that the division of power between so many bodies would make the system of government more stable and prevent the emergence of someone like Hitler who might again 'lead the German people astray'.[1] Decentralisation of the political structure would also encourage the development of local responsibility and so help to solve 'the problem of democracy in Germany'. Finally, it was hoped that the division of power would make

Germany less effective politically and less of a threat to the security of her neighbours.

The attempts to break up the large concentrations of economic power also formed part of the reaction against the over-centralisation of the Nazi period. Concentration in banking and in industry had been promoted by the Nazis, and large concerns such as IG Farben had helped the Nazis come to power and had played an important part in the preparation for the war and in the exploitation of occupied territories. Because of this intimate association of the large concerns with National Socialism, the Postdam Agreement called for the rapid decentralisation of German economic life and the breaking up of all concentrations of economic power. This call for decentralisation corresponded in some measure to a feeling widespread among the German people at the time that the economic system should be radically reformed. The breaking up of concentrations of economic power was also one of the central themes proclaimed by the neo-liberal school in Germany, which, through the person of Ludwig Erhard, economics minister from 1949 to 1963, and then Chancellor until 1966, exercised an important influence on the development of post-war Germany.

The Freiburg school of 'Ordoliberalismus', which provided a model of reference for the post-war economic development of the Federal Republic, was one of the branches of the 'neo-liberalism' which developed in most capitalist countries after the First World War. Its particular characteristic was its insistence on the notion of a 'liberal order'. State intervention in the market should be kept to a minimum, and competition allowed to flourish freely. But, unlike the adherents of classical liberalism, the members of the Freiburg school did not think that a system of free competition could survive unprotected: it could flourish only within a framework created by law and maintained by the state. The most important element of such a framework would be the prohibition of monopolistic practices and agreements and the dismantling of existing monopolies. Some members of the school wanted an even more far-reaching economic decentralisation and advocated the creation of a 'people's capitalism' by the diffusion of property among all layers of the population.

The new economic order advocated by the Freiburg school would not be a restoration of capitalism, it would be something qualitatively new: the 'social market economy' *('Soziale Marktwirtschaft')* as it came to be called. As one of its apologists wrote in 1960:

'Nobody defends outmoded capitalism, and, as once Germany brought forth socialism, so, after the controlled economy of the Second World War, it has become the pioneer of an economic order which aims at being something different from a mere restoration of capitalism. Its central idea is competition, its fight is against restrictions of competition and the amassing of economic power, its name is Social Market Economy'.[2]

The doctrines of the school were not purely economic: the fight against the amassing of economic power was seen as but one aspect of the attempt to prevent any concentration of power which might again lead to the loss of political freedom.

Clearly there are close links between federalism and economic liberalism: not only do both aim at preventing a concentration of power, but both were supported most strongly by the same groups in West Germany, the Americans and the Christian Democrats. Both hark back to the romantic ideal of the small unit in which each individual plays his part and both treat West Germany as though it could be moulded at will and as though it really did exist in an a-historical year Zero, and not as part of the post-war capitalist economic system. There is also an important practical link between the two. The creation of a federal state gives support to the doctrines of liberalism by making state intervention in the economic process more difficult. This is why, in the discussions on the draft Basic Law in 1948 and 1949, the Social Democrats (SPD) strongly opposed weakening the financial powers of the central government. This also explains why, when, in the mid-1960s, liberal doctrine is shown to be inadequate to meet the needs of the West German economy and state intervention becomes more important, the structures of federalism also come under pressure.

Neo-liberalism may be described as the ideology of the post-war restoration in Western Germany. Despite popular demands after the war for radical measures of socialisation of industry, and the widespread association of capitalism with fascism in popular consciousness, the 'struggle for democracy', as carried through by the Western Allies, did not involve any major economic reform. The capitalist economy was restored, but, as it was presented by the Allies and by the German Christian Democrats, this was to be a healthy, democratic capitalism, in which totalitarian excesses would be prevented by the maintenance of free competition and the establishment of a federal system, i.e. by the decentralisation of economic and political power.

Yet, developments since the founding of the Federal Republic suggest that this liberalism, in so far as it was seriously held, was an illusion. The restoration of a capitalist economy expected to hold its own on the world market made effective economic deconcentration impracticable, and has led, on the contrary, to increasing concentration of economic power. This concentration has had the effect of putting the political decentralisation achieved in the Basic Law under great pressure.

Though the issues of federalism and economic deconcentration are intimately related, this essay will attempt to review some of the main features and problems of each in turn.

Federalism[3]

The fact that the Allies insisted that the new West German state should have a federal structure does not mean that federalism was simply foisted upon the Germans from outside.

Germany already had a tradition of federalism. The kingdoms, principalities and duchies of Germany were united into one state only in 1871, under the dominance of Prussia. The Constitution of 1871 created a federal state, with a federal legislature divided into two chambers, the popularly elected *Reichstag* and the *Bundesrat* (federal council) in which the various states had their representatives. The administration of federal laws was left in the hands of these states. Under the Weimar Constitution of 1919, a similar structure was preserved, but there was a significant shift in power away from the Länder. Both the powers of the federal Council *(Reichsrat,* as it was now called) and the area of competence of the Länder were considerably reduced. During the Weimar period the power of the Länder declined further until finally, under the rule of the Nazis, the Länder were reduced to administrative districts and the Reichsrat was dissolved.

With the exception of the Communist Party (KPD), all the political parties represented in the Parliamentary Council which was responsible for drawing up the new constitution after the War, the Basic Law, supported the restoration of federalism in Germany. They differed only in the degree to which they wanted to strengthen or weaken the powers of the Länder. Support for a greater decentralisation of power came mainly from liberal-conservative elements, notably from the Christian Democrats (the CDU and her Bavarian sister party, the CSU), the German Party (DP) and the most conservative business and agricultural interests who hoped to curtail the power of the state. The Social Democrats (SPD) wanted only a limited decentralisation of power, for converse reasons: to give too much power to the Länder would make economic planning very difficult. The Basic Law represents a compromise between the views of the various parties and those of the Allies. It was accepted by all parties except the Communists and the most extreme federalists (CSU and DP), and by the parliaments of all the

Länder except Bavaria, which nevertheless voted to join the new Federal Republic.

The social and economic structure of Western Germany provides conditions favourable to a federal system which are not present in most other countries of Western Europe. With the loss of the former capital, Berlin, and the choice of Bonn as a provisional seat of government pending reunification, there is no city which far exceeds the others in importance, in the manner of Paris or London, and there is a fairly even distribution of important cities throughout the whole territory of the Republic. Another consequence, no doubt, of the late unification of Germany, is that regional traditions have remained strong, particularly in the south. Yet the states which emerged as the Länder of the new Federation corresponded more to the administrative convenience and bargains of the occupying powers than to historical tradition. All had been created or revived by the Allies as political and administrative units before the founding of the Federal Republic. Consequently, their boundaries were greatly influenced by the configuration of the zones of occupation. Of the ten states[4] only three (Bavaria and the city states of Hamburg and Bremen) can claim a long historical tradition. Others, such as the Rhineland Palatinate or North-Rhine-Westphalia, were pieced together from parts of the pre-war German Länder, according to administrative convenience and the accidents of the Allied division of the defeated Germany. The Länder vary in size, from Bavaria (area 27,339 sq. miles; population ten and a half million) and North Rhine Westphalia (area 13,111 sq. miles; population seventeen million), on the one hand, to Bremen, on the other, with its area of only 156 square miles and its population of 750,000. They vary greatly in prosperity also, as is shown by Appendix 1.

Within the Federation, each Land has its own constitution providing for a legislature (which is bicameral in Bavaria), government, administration and judiciary. Legislative power is divided by the Basic Law into three areas: those matters on which the Federation *(Bund)* has exclusive power to legislate, those matters over which Bund and Länder have concurrent competence and those over which the Länder exercise exclusive control. The first category (Art.73 of the Basic Law) includes such things as foreign affairs (and, since 1954, defence), currency, money and coinage, customs, federal railways and air traffic, postal and telecommunication services. The list of matters covered by concurrent legislative power (Art. 74) is very long and covers, for example, civil law, criminal law, public relief, labour law and labour relations, economic law, expropriation and road traffic. To speak of concurrent legislative power in these areas is, however, deceptive, for the Länder may legislate on these matters only 'as long as, and to the extent that, the Federation does not use its legislative power' (Art. 72). Since the Federation is subject only to vague restrictions on the use of its power, and since indeed federal law on many of these topics already existed in 1949, the legislative competence of the Länder is, broadly speaking, limited to the area over which they exercise exclusive power. This includes all those topics not listed as part of the other two categories (Art. 70). In practice, this means that the state legislatures have competence in the domains of culture (including education and the mass media), local government and police. But even this area of competence was made subject to the Federation's power to enact outline or 'framework' legislation *(Rahmengesetze)* in certain areas, covering, for example, the status of the press and motion pictures, the care of the countryside and regional planning (Art. 75).

The legislative influence of the Länder is greatly increased by the existence of the Bundesrat. This is the revised second chamber of the federal legislature, in which the representatives (three, four or five, according to the population of the Land) of the governments of the various Länder sit. The Bundesrat has more power than most European second chambers, for any law affecting the interests of the Länder (or, more accurately, any law for which the Basic Law requires the acceptance of the Bundesrat) can be passed only with the assent of that body. Since such laws *(Zustimmungsgesetze)* have proved to be the rule rather than the exception, the votes of the Land governments acquire considerable national importance.

Administrative devolution to the Länder is far more extensive than the decentralisation of legislative power. In general, the Länder are responsible for the execution of all federal legislation. They normally administer federal laws 'as their own affair' (Art. 83), in which case the Federal administration may intervene only if it considers that the Land administration is not complying with the law; exceptionally, Länder are required to administer federal laws as agents of the Federation, in which case their administration is subject to supervision by the federal authorities both as to its legality and as to its merits. Federal administration (except in special areas such as defence, railways and postal services), does not exist at field level.[5]

Of central importance to the autonomy of the Länder are the financial arrangements of the Federation. When the Basic Law was drawn up, the Allies, fearful for the independence of the Länder, insisted that separate taxes should be attributed to the Federation and the Länder. Income tax, corporation tax, taxes on transactions with the exception of the transport tax and turnover tax, property and inheritance taxes, taxes on beer, real estate and businesses *(Realsteuern)* and taxes of local application were to accrue to the Länder. The Federation was given turnover tax, customs duties, the yield of monopolies, the excise taxes with the exception of the beer tax, the transportation tax and capital levies for non-recurrent purposes. An important exception was made, however, to the principle of the separation of taxes by allowing the Federation (by means of a federal law requiring the assent of the Bundesrat) to claim a part of the revenue from income tax and corporation tax to meet its needs. The same article of the Basic Law (Art. 106) also provided[6] for financial equalisation between the richer and poorer Länder; this is also to be executed by a federal law requiring the consent of the Bundesrat.

Development of Federalism

Since 1949, the federal structure outlined above has come under considerable pressures. In so far as these pressures reflect trends which are common to all advanced capitalist societies, the development raises problems relevant to the discussion in the other countries treated in this book. It is true that the federalism of the Basic Law of 1949 posed special problems in so far as it was imposed by the Allies and the Länder were not formed on the basis of German tradition, but the discussion has been concerned less with restoring traditional boundaries and allegiances than with achieving economic efficiency. It is primarily the conflict between political decentralisation and economic efficiency which has led to the gradual erosion of the federal structure, particularly in the last ten years.

The principal force tending to reduce the autonomy of the Länder is the increasing need for the central control of the economy. The links between federalism and economic liberalism have been mentioned above. As long as the Federal Government clung to its liberal ideology, the federal structure came under little strain. But since the mid-1960s, the economic development of Western Germany has made state intervention increasingly necessary and this has led to significant changes in the federal system.

During the early post-war years, the role of the Government was limited to stimulating investment by means of tax concessions, subsidies, contracts etc. In accordance with its liberal principles, no attempt was made at global planning or at controlling public expenditure in the interests of short-term economic policy. As long as objective conditions (such as Marshall Aid, the Korean War boom, the absence of a defence burden on the budget, the existence of a plentiful labour supply) favoured the rapid revival of the German economy, no great economic strain was put on relations between Federation and Länder.

But in the late 1950s and early 1960s conditions changed. Public expenditure rose rapidly, especially after rearmament in 1955 and the improvement of the pension system in 1957; this meant a corresponding increase in the economic significance of public expenditure. The boom period of the 1950s had stimulated over-production and led to a shortage of labour (particularly after the building of the Berlin Wall in 1961 had cut off the supply of refugees from the German Democratic Republic). This led to a fall in profits and in investment which, together with increasing inflation and structural difficulties in important sectors such as coal, steel, textiles and ship building, made state intervention increasingly necessary. Because of the liberalisation of the international capital market and the growing measure of self-financing of the big companies and their ability to pass higher rates of interest on to prices, action by the Federal Bank (the traditional means of anticyclical policy) was insufficient, and an active anticyclical policy by the state involving control of all public expenditure became indispensable. The Erhard government was too slow to abandon its economic liberalism and the beginning crisis of 1966 led to its downfall.

One of the first measures to restore the economy taken by the Grand Coalition, the CDU/CSU-SPD coalition which replaced the Erhard government, was to pass the *Stabilitätsgesetz* (Stability Act), which augmented the economic powers of the government and greatly increased federal control over the Länder.

One of the most important guarantees of the autonomy of the Länder had been Art. 109 of the Basic Law, which said:

'The Federation and the Länder are autonomous and independent of each other as regards their budgets.'

Under the changed conditions of the mid-1960s, it was no longer possible to maintain this principle intact. The expenditure of the Länder and communes accounts for fifty per cent of all public expenditure, and it was partly the continued increase in local expenditure in 1965-6 which precipitated the recession of 1966-7. Consequently, the fifteenth amendment to the Constitution, which paved the way for the Stability Act, enlarged Art. 109 to give the Federation some control over the expenditure of Länder. The article now obliges Länder 'to take due account in their fiscal administration of the requirements of overall economic equilibrium'. An amendment of 1969 goes further by providing that federal legislation (requiring the consent of the Bundesrat) may establish 'principles common to the Federation and the Länder ... governing budget law, responsiveness of the fiscal administration to economic fluctuations, and pluriannual planning'. Under another new provision of Art. 109, legislation may now set limits to the debts which may be incurred by public administrative bodies, and oblige Federation and Länder to maintain interest-free deposits, known as anticyclical reserves, in the Federal Bank.

The Stability Act enlarges the economic power of the Federation in accordance with the new constitutional provisions. Section 1 lays down principles to guide economic and fiscal measures taken by the Federation and Länder, the so-called 'magic square' of stable prices, a high level of employment, a healthy balance of payments and steady and adequate economic growth. In support of these aims, the Act provides for what is known as 'concerted action' *(konzertierte Aktion)*: 'if any of the aims . . . are in jeopardy, the Federal Government shall provide data as a guide for simultaneous and mutually adjusted policy of the Federation, the Länder, the municipal corporations, trade unions and employers' associations in order to achieve the aims set out in s.1'. To back these provisions up, the Act establishes a Council for Cyclical Policy *(Konjunkturrat für die öffentliche Hand)*,[7] consisting of the Federal Minister for Economic Affairs (as Chairman), the Federal Minister of Finance, one representative for each Land and four representatives for the municipal corporations. The aim of this Council (which meets at regular intervals) is to coordinate policy in order to achieve the four goals set out by the Stability Act. Although it makes recommendations only, the influence of these recommendations is considerable. Finally, the Act gives the Federal Government power, with the consent of the Bundesrat, to oblige Federation and Länder to pay up to three per cent of their tax receipts for the previous year into an anti-cyclical reserve fund, and to fix a limit to the debts which Federation, Länder and other public bodies may incur. Frequent use has been made of these powers, most recently as part of the Federal Government's current 'stability programme' directed against inflation.

The bundle of measures known as the Finance Reform of 1969, said by the President of the Bundesrat to be the 'deepest and most extensive reform of our Basic Law in the twenty years of its existence',[8] took a step further in the direction of increasing federal control over the finances of the Länder. Apart from the amendment to Art. 109 of the Basic Law, the measures taken under the Finance Reform, which followed on the recommendations made by the Troeger Commission in 1966, included the establishment of a Council for Financial Planning *(Finanzplanungsrat)*[9] to coordinate the medium-term planning of Federation and Länder according to principles laid down by the Budget Principles Act, which also formed part of the Finance Reform. Like the Council for Cyclical Policy, this Council has power only to make 'recommendations' and thus formally respects the autonomy of the Länder, but the recommendations exercise in practice a decisive influence on the budgets and financial plans of the Länder.

Another part of the Finance Reform which affected the financial autonomy of the Länder was the institutionalisation of the so-called *Gemeinschaftsaufgaben* ('common tasks'). The Troeger Commission felt that there were certain investments (such as those involving the improvement of the regional economic structure, the improvement of the agrarian structure, the protection of the coast and the building of universities), which, although they fell within the competence of the Länder, often entailed costs which the individual Länder could not support and involved decisions which were important for the economy of the whole country. It had already become practice for the Federation and Länder to collaborate on such investments, but the constitutionality of such collaboration had been questioned. Following the suggestion of the Troeger Commission, the Finance Reform institutionalised this practice. Under the new Art. 91 of the Basic Law, such collaboration is now obligatory in the areas mentioned above. Such investments may now take place only within the framework of a federal plan. With regard to investments which do not come within the scope of Art. 91, but which are nevertheless of significance for the national economy, another amendment to the Basic Law (Art. 104) allows the Federation to give grants to the Länder. Granting aid in such cases naturally gives the Federation some control over the investments.

It seems likely that the erosion of the financial autonomy of the Länder has not yet come to an end. The Federal Minister of Finance has recently hinted[10] that the expenditure of the Länder is weakening the effect of the federal stability programme and that it may be necessary to alter Art. 109(1)[11], upon which the financial autonomy (or what remains of it) of the Länder is founded. This suggestion has provoked a sharp reply[12] from the Finance Ministers of the Länder. Although it is unlikely that any further change will be made in the near future, it is clear that, as the need grows for an effective governmental policy to combat the difficulties of the economy, the need for a tighter central control of all public expenditure will also grow.

The centralising forces inherent in the development of the economy have affected not only the financial autonomy of the Länder but the whole sphere of their competence. The possibilities for a distinctive and separate development by individual Länder have been restricted by various pressures, all arising directly or indirectly from the economic development of the country. The Federation's responsibility for the economy as a whole means that it must be concerned with all areas which have a significant impact on the labour market and has led, most notably, to its encroachment into the field of education, traditionally a well-guarded preserve of the Länder. The mobility of the labour force has led to pressure on the Länder to find a uniform solution to such problems as school holidays and the time when the school year begins. This mobility, together with improved communications, creates a demand for similar social standards throughout the Republic.

The result of these pressures has been a constant drain of legislative power from the Länder to the Federation and the growth of institutionalised cooperation between Federation and Länder, or between the Länder themselves.

The shift in legislative power has taken two forms. The legislative power of the Länder has been restricted, on the one hand, by the exercise by the Federation of its concurrent legislative power under Art. 74 of the Basic Law. Federal legislation on the consequences of the war (reparations, pensions, etc.), on the rebuilding of cities and on rents, on transport, on economic and a wide range of social matters has excluded the Länder from these areas. On the other hand, and going beyond this, there have been a number of amendments to the Basic Law, giving to the Federation powers which it did not originally possess. The Federation now has legislative powers in the areas of defence and nuclear energy, as well as under the Emergency Law *(Notstandsgesetz)* of 1968. An amendment passed in 1969, at the same time as the Finance Reform, gave the Federation concurrent competence (under Art. 74) in relation to training grants, the financing of hospitals and the levying of road taxes. It also gave the Federation power to pass a general or framework law *(Rahmengesetz)* under Art. 75 on 'the general principles of the system of higher education' and the establishment of uniform criteria for the payment of civil servants. In the field of higher education, which has until now been subject to the sole competence of the Länder, there is at the time of writing a federal bill *(Hochschulrahmengesetz)* under discussion, which seeks to reduce periods of study, regulate university entry and the composition of university decision-making bodies and to integrate the whole system of higher education. The bill has, however, encountered strong opposition from the governments of the Länder who feel that the Federation is encroaching too far into this area of Land sovereignty.

The drain of legislative power from Länder to Federation has not been accompanied by a similar transfer of administrative competence. Although the number of civil servants employed at federal level has grown more quickly, the general principle that the Länder are responsible for the execution of Federal laws remains valid.[13] Indeed, as the legislative powers of the Länder are eroded, the German federal system is coming closer to one of mere administrative devolution.[14]

If there has been little change in the division of administrative competence, the Federal budget has nevertheless grown more rapidly than that of the Länder. Even leaving aside expenditure on foreign relations and the important item of defence (which plays a part only after 1955 and is under the exclusive control of the Federation), it has been calculated[15] that the Federal expenditure per head of population was 221.90 DM in 1950, 656.43 DM in 1965 and 839.43 DM in 1968. The corresponding figures for the Land of North Rhine Westphalia were 228.53 DM (1950), 576.67 DM (1965) and 680.00 DM (1968). The system by which tax revenues are divided between Federation and Länder has had to be revised several times. As we have seen above (p.112), the principle originally adopted by the Basic Law was that of the separation of taxes. Of the most important taxes, the turnover tax was to go to the Federation and income tax and corporation tax were given to the Länder. An exception was made, it will be recalled, to the general principle by allowing the Federation to claim a part of the revenue from income tax and corporation tax to meet its needs. From 1951, the Federation did claim a proportion of this revenue, first twenty seven per cent, then thirty seven per cent for 1952 and thirty eight per cent for 1953. A constitutional amendment of 1955 fixed the apportionment of these direct taxes between Federation and Länder, attributing first thirty three and a third per cent to the Federation and sixty six and two-thirds to the Länder, but providing that the proportions should be thirty five per cent and sixty five per cent from April 1st, 1958 and that they should be subject to subsequent review. The Troeger Commission recommended that, in the interests of fiscal stability, turnover tax should be added to the taxes divided between Federation and Länder and that the three taxes should be apportioned between Federation and Länder by an annual Federal law. Because of opposition from some of the Länder, the solution adopted by the Finance Reform is not as flexible as that suggested by the Commission: the Basic Law (Art. 106) now provides that Federation and Länder should each receive half of the revenue from income and corporation taxes, and the revenue from the turnover tax is divided annually between the Federation and the Länder, by a Federal law requiring the assent of the Bundesrat.[16] As far as the division of the taxes attributed to the Länder is concerned, Art. 107 now provides that the revenue from taxes which go exclusively to the Länder and the Länder's share of income and corporation taxes should go to the Länder in which they are raised. In order to help the poorer Länder, turnover tax is divided among the Länder according to population. On top of this, a Federal law may attribute up to twenty five per cent of the revenue from turnover tax to the poorer states.[17] In addition to the revenue they receive from this apportionment of taxes, Länder receive subsidies from the Federation in various forms, mainly as contributions towards particular investments or to help with the administration of particular laws.

The need for uniformity has been met not only by a direct centralisation of financial and legislative control, but also by the growth of many forms of cooperation between the Länder themselves and between the Federation and the Länder. An enormous number of regular or occasional meetings, conferences and committees bring representatives of the Länder into contact with one another at all levels, to discuss common problems and, in some cases, to seek common solutions, or a common front against the Federation. A similar network of meetings at all levels aims at promoting cooperation between Federation and Länder.[18] Agreements are common between individual Länder, as between the Federation and individual Länder, to undertake together certain investments which would be too great a burden for the individual Land to bear on its own. One of the disadvantages of this system of 'cooperative federalism', as it is called, is that, increasingly, decisions which affect the area of sovereignty still remaining to the Länder are taken, not by the Parliaments of the Länder, but by committees over which they have no real control.

The loss in power of the Parliaments, and indeed the loss in power of the Länder as a whole, has no doubt contributed to the general subordination of Land politics to Federal politics. Ironically, the influence of the Bundesrat has also contributed to this. This institution, which is supposed to guarantee the influence of the Länder in Federal legislation, has also had the inverse effect of greatly increasing Federal influence over Land politics. The very fact that the Bundesrat has such power and that the members of the Bundesrat are bound by the instructions of their Land governments, means that the composition of the Land governments may be of great importance in federal politics. Since Bundesrat members often vote along party lines for or against the government, Landtag election have tended to become indirect elections to the Bundesrat, with the intervention of federal politicians and campaigns fought on federal rather than on local issues.[19] Because not only the outcome of the election but the composition of the Land government is important, national parties have put pressure on Land parties to form coalitions which mirror the coalitions in Bonn.

Partly to halt the general drift of power from the Länder, partly because it is felt that the massive structure of 'cooperative federalism' is an inadequate solution to the difficulties which arise from the division of the federal territory into unsatisfactory units, there has been mounting pressure in recent years for a reorganisation

of the Federation. Under the present organisation, it is argued, many of
the Länder are too small to perform their constitutional tasks
unaided: this leads to the need for federal intervention and thus to a
loss of Land autonomy. Moreover, many of the present frontiers cut
across economically coherent units: the cities of Hamburg and
Bremen, for example, are separated by a state frontier from the
surrounding countryside. This contributes to the great disparities
in prosperity which exist between some of the present states, most
strikingly between Hamburg and the neighbouring Schleswig-Holstein.
Any reorganisation of the Länder would take place under Art. 29
of the Basic Law. This provision was inserted in the Basic Law
both because of the great variation in the size and prosperity of the
Länder and because many of them lacked any historical tradition.
Hence, Art. 29(1) is rather contradictory:

> 'The division of the Federal territory into Länder is to be
> revised by a Federal law with due regard to regional ties,
> historical and cultural connections, economic expediency and
> social structure. Such reorganisation should create Länder
> which by their size and capacity are able effectively to fulfil the
> functions incumbent upon them.'

While some of the guidelines in the first sentence would lead to the
creation of smaller Länder, the creation of larger Länder would be
necessary to fulfil the provisions of the second sentence. The
commission established to consider the reorganisation of the
Länder in the 1950s, the Luther Commission, decided to give the
two sentences equal priority and came up with a whole range of
alternative proposals, none of which had any effect. The Troeger
Commission, which published its proposals for a financial reform in
1966, again urged the reorganisation of the Länder as a pressing
economic need, and in 1970 the Government established a new
Commission, known as the Ernst Commission, to consider the matter
again. This Commission recognised the incompatibility of the two
sentences of Art. 29(1) and gave priority to the second; their aim was
to create states which would be 'efficient' *(leistungsfähig)*,
economically, administratively and politically. The Commission's report,
published in the spring of 1973, proposed that the number of Länder
should be reduced to either five or six, each with at least five million
inhabitants, according to one of four different models. This
proposal gave rise to widespread discussion, which soon died down.
The government has not yet decided on any action.

 There is, of course, opposition from all the established interests
which have prevented the execution of Art. 29 till now.[20] Opposition

is particularly strong from the small, prosperous and SPD-controlled[21] city states of Bremen and Hamburg which would disappear. That reorganisation is against the interests of the poorer small states (such as Schleswig-Holstein and the Rhineland Palatinate), or against those of the large states is not so clear.

Under Art. 29 of the Basic Law, the decision lies not with the individual Länder, but with the Federation as a whole. The alterations may be made by a simple law, not requiring the assent of the Bundesrat. In so far as particular areas are moved from one Land to another, it is required, however, to hold a referendum in those areas. If the result of this referendum does not correspond to the Federal proposal, the Federal parliament (or rather the first chamber, the Bundestag) must reconsider its proposal and, if it decides to continue with it, must submit the question to a Federal referendum. The final decision thus lies, not with the inhabitants of the area directly affected, but with the citizens of the whole Federation. The initiative lies basically with the Federal Government.

There is one constitutional anomaly which may force the Government to act. In the 1950s, popular initiatives were conducted successfully in a number of regions, demanding either that the regions before 31 March 1975, to decide on the issues raised by be transferred to other Länder. According to the present provisions of Art. 29(3) of the Basic Law, referenda must be held in those regions before the 31 March 1975, to decide on the issues raised by the popular initiatives. The Federal legislature is then obliged to give effect to the results of these referenda (which might, for example, recommend the revival of the pre-war Länder of Oldenburg and Schaumburg-Lippe), unless it can show that the result would be contrary to the aim of Art. 29. In order to do this, it is argued, the legislature, or the government, would have to propose some plan for the reorganisation of the Länder. It may be, however, that the Federal Government will prefer to avoid political difficulties by postponing the date by which the popular initiatives must be implemented. In the Federal Chancellor's recent speech[22] to the Bundesrat, in which it is traditional, as he put it, 'to reflect on the basic principles of the relationship between Federation and Länder', no mention was made of a reorganisation of the Länder.

Reorganisation of the Länder is seen by many as being necessary to save the federal system, to halt the drain of power from Länder to Federation. The period since the founding of the Federal Republic has witnessed the undermining of the budgetary autonomy of the Länder, a marked shift in legislative and financial power to the Federation, and the growth of the elaborate machinery of 'cooperative federalism' to cope with the inadequacies of the Länder. The purpose of the reorganisation would be adapt the Länder to the new economic realities. Whereas the liberal view of twenty years ago linked federalism, or regional decentralisation, with local participation and the maintenance of historical traditions, the discussion today is primarily concerned with economic efficiency. Because there is a conflict between economic efficiency and the autonomy of the Länder, it is necessary to reorganise the Länder to make them more efficient. This explains perhaps why the whole question of federal organisation arouses very little popular interest.[23] The whole question of regional decentralisation plays little part in political debate and almost none in the programmes of those movements (such as the *Jungsozialisten*) which aim at a greater democratisation of German political life. Political discussion has come to focus increasingly not on the regional decentralisation of political power but on the problems of decentralising or deconcentrating economic power, and it is to these problems that we shall turn our attention in the second half of this essay.

Economic Deconcentration

Discussion of the increasing concentration of property is concerned not so much with the direct effects of wealth and poverty as with the social power wielded by those who own or control property and the problems of how to distribute this power more fairly. The power of what is known as the 'private' sector, is, it is argued, of great social importance. The annual turnover of the larger concerns such as Volkswagen or Siemens, or the Krupp or Flick groups, is larger than the annual budget of individual Länder. Decisions taken by the leaders of such firms directly affect clients, competitors, workers and consumers, as well as the environment and economy of whole areas. They are also of enormous importance to government, the traditional 'public' sphere of decision: not only do these firms exercise direct influence on government, through pressure groups which are consulted regularly before legislation, but the whole success or failure of a government depends on its ability to manage the economy, maintain stable growth and full employment, which means, in an economy which depends largely on private investment, that the government must maintain conditions favourable to those with the power of investment.

The issues which are at the centre of political discussion in Germany today are concerned with attempts to control or democratise the social power of the 'private sphere'. These issues are, principally: competition policy, capital formation and codetermination.

The pre-war German economy had been heavily concentrated with the market dominated by a small number of enormous cartels. Many of the cartels were associated with the rise of the Nazis to power and the latter had, after 1933, sought to 'rationalise' the economy by giving cartels a compulsory and quasi-official character.

Consequently, decentralisation of the economy by the Allies, as provided for in the Potsdam Agreement, was seen as an attempt to democratise the economy. Although much discussion was devoted to the problem of breaking up the monopolies and cartels, the effects were very limited. In the coal and steel industries, measures taken by the Allies were quickly overtaken by the industry's own reorganisation of itself into larger units again. The Allies' attempt to break up the Big Three banks (the Dresdner Bank, the Commerzbank and the Deutsche Bank) in Western Germany into thirty smaller banks was an even greater failure: by 1950 the three banks had all emerged again with their former power. The greatest effect of the policy was in the chemical industry, where the giant IG Farben was broken up into the three smaller giants, Farbwerke Hoechst, Badische Anilin und Soda Fabrik (BASF) and Bayer. The general failure of the policy may be attributed to a number of causes: the organisation of industrialists to protect their own interests, the disagreement among the Allies as to the desirable degree of deconcentration, the general lack of enthusiasm on the part of the Allies for the policy and, above all, the need to make the German economy viable in a world market. If German firms were to withstand international competition, they should not be too small: in this sense liberalism was, from the start, an illusion.

Despite the liberal, free market, antimonopoly ideology of the Christian Democrats, their economic policy, especially during the 1950s, encouraged concentration, principally by means of granting tax advantages to large concerns. The very favourable amortisation provisions under the law on income tax helped self-financing and were of particular advantage to already existing firms, with the result that many of the old names were able to maintain their position. Of the fifteen largest firms in the late 1950s, eleven had already belonged to this group before the war. Measures which contributed even more directly to industrial concentration were the exoneration of non-distributed profits and the exemption from turnover tax of transactions between legally autonomous companies which were closely affiliated. For 1965 alone, it has been calculated that this latter concession cost the government 600 million DM, and that one company, the August-Thyssen Foundry, saved 40 million DM. This provision naturally encouraged large firms to buy up clients, suppliers, etc.

The inevitable price of the 'economic miracle', of boosting profits in order to stimulate private investment and of making German industry internationally competitive, was to create large inequalities of wealth and a great concentration of economic power. An inquiry ordered by the government in 1960 and published in 1964 showed that concentration had increased considerably since 1954. In that period, the share of the fifty largest industrial enterprises in the total industrial turnover had increased from 17.7 per cent to 22.8 per cent. The influence of banks in the control of industry is enormous: although the banks themselves held at the time of the report only 4.9 per cent of the capital of companies quoted on the stock exchange this masks their true power, for they are allowed by German law to represent clients in general meetings of the companies of which they are shareholders. The report revealed that 75 per cent of the capital of 427 companies (representing three quarters of the capital of companies quoted on the stock exchange) was controlled by the banks in 1960; of this, the share of the Big Three banks was 70 per cent. There is nothing to suggest that the process of concentration has slowed down. On the contrary, all the available data suggest that the process of concentration is continuing, even accelerating. The following table shows how the concentration developed in some of the leading branches of German industry:

Table 1 Development of the Degree of Concentration in leading branches of industry in the FRG (in percentages)

Concerns per branch	Share of turnover		Share of the number of people employed in the branch	
	1961	1969	1961	1969
3 concerns of the chemical industry [a]	38	49	41	46
8 concerns of the electrical industry [b]	60	68	62	68
4 concerns of the steel industry [c]	61	65	66	60
5 concerns of the car industry [d]	76	92	61	76

(a) Farbenfabriken Bayer AG, Farbwerke Hoechst AG, Badische Anilin- und Soda Fabrik AG.
(b) Siemens AG, AEG Telefunken, Robert Bosch GmbH, Grundigwerke GmbH, IBM Deutschland Internationale Büromaschinen GmbH, Brown Boveri & Cie, AG, Standard Elektrik Lorenz AG, Felten Guilleaume Carlswerke AG.
(c) Thyssen, Mannesmann, Hoesch, Krupp.
(d) Volkswagen Werk AG, Dainler-Benz AG, Adam Opel AG, Ford Werke AG, Bayerische Motoren Werke AG.[25]

In 1969, although there were 71,842 registered companies, with a nominal capital of 91,040 million DM, 304 (or 0.42 per cent) of these companies had at their disposal 58.5 per cent of this capital.[26] A similar process of concentration is, of course, common to all capitalist countries, but concern with economic power or 'economic democracy' is a particularly important issue in German politics.

The measures taken by the government to meet the dissatisfaction caused by this concentration of economic power are of two kinds. Cartel laws seek to prevent the formation of such large units and to check abuses of their power. Other measures purportedly aim, not at breaking up these units, but at democratising them from within. The most important of these measures are those concerning codetermination *(Mitbestimmung)* in industry and the formation of capital in the hands of the workers *(Vermögensbildung in Arbeitnehmerhand)*.

The first project for a Cartel Law to control and promote competition in the Federal Republic was presented by the Federal Economics Ministry as early as 1949. The original draft reflected the ideas of the Freiburg School which held cartels and monopolistic concentrations to be dangerous and incompatible with a market economy, and proposed that cartels should be prohibited. This also reflected the wishes of the Allies (who had already prohibited cartels by a law of 1947) and no doubt the interests of American firms eager to capture the European market.[27] The German employers' associations, however, opposed this plan, arguing that concentrations and cartels are not bad in themselves, but, on the contrary, indispensable to economic rationalisation and progress, and that consequently only abuses should be controlled. Negotiations between the government and the employers continued for more than seven years — the 'seven years war' it has been called — and the outcome, the Cartel Law *(Gesetz gegen Wettbewerbsbeschränkungen)* of 1957, has been hailed as a victory by the employers.[28] The 1957 Law does not prohibit fusions or other forms of concentration, but merely requires that the most important mergers should be notified to the Federal Cartel Office established by the Law, which is empowered only to require a public explanation of the conduct of the parties concerned. Unlike the position in the United States and in Britain, the federal authorities have no power under the 1957 law to prohibit a merger judged detrimental to the public interest. Restrictive agreements between firms or groups of firms are forbidden, but there are many exceptions provided to this rule and there is only a limited restriction of price-fixing.

The Cartel Law has been applied with moderation. In the first ten years of the Law's operation, 4,546 proceedings were initiated concerning suspected infringements of the Law. Of these, 3,842 were abandoned, 1,482 because there was a change in the conduct under investigation, 2,421 'for other reasons'. In only five of the cases was a fine actually enforced. As we have seen, concentration has continued unabated. The attitude of the authorities — of the Cartel Office and particularly of the Bonn government — towards competition has changed since the mid-1950s. The model of perfect competition has now been replaced as the ideal by that of 'oligopolistic competition'. The trend towards concentration has come to be regarded as inevitable and indeed, in view of increased international competition, especially since the formation of the EEC, as beneficial. The state has come to encourage, and even to subsidise, the creation of larger units in some branches of industry. Some indication of the rate at which concentration is proceeding is given by the fact that the number of mergers notified to the Federal Cartel Office (and only the biggest mergers have to be so notified) rose from 15 in 1958, to 38 in 1962, 50 in 1965, 65 in 1968, 168 in 1969 and 305 in 1970.[29]

It is unlikely that the new Cartel Law, enacted in June 1973, will have any great effect on this trend. This law prohibits price-fixing, but does nothing to hinder price recommendation by producers, which has grown greatly in importance in the past year, and has an effect similar to that of price-fixing. A limited control of mergers is also introduced for the first time: mergers between firms with an annual turnover of 500 million DM or more must in future be notified to the Cartel Office. The Cartel Office will then examine whether the fusion will give the new firm a dominant position on the market and thus limit competition. If this is the case, then the Cartel Office has power to forbid the merger or break up the new firm, or to impose conditions on the merging firms. It remains to be seen what the policy of the Cartel Office will be in deciding whether to make use of its powers. Both present trends and the fact that the Law was supported by all the parties in the Federal Parliament suggest that the Law will do no more to halt concentration than did its predecessor.

The reason why the effect of any Cartel Law of this type must be extremely limited is surely that it is essential for the economy of any country that the industry based in that country should be able to withstand international competition; any government which seriously strikes at the power of its industry will damage the economic prosperity of the country and so undermine its own popularity.

The policy of diffusing property, or encouraging the formation of capital in the hands of the workers, is the other keystone of the liberal policy to combat the increasing concentration of property. According to Röpke, one of the leaders of the Freiburg school, it was not enough to dismantle the monopolies and so reduce the size of economic units, it was necessary also to create a 'people's capitalism' by diffusing the property in these units throughout all layers of society. This was adopted as the policy of the CDU about 1949, as a concession given

to the workers' wing of the party in return for their abandoning
demands for nationalisation. The model held up as a goal and opposed to
monopoly capitalism, was that of a 'people's capitalism', in which the
workers would also be property-owners and, as such, have a share in
the wealth, independence and responsibility which property brings with
it. This idea has played an important part in German social policy since
the founding of the Federal Republic, not only under CDU-dominated,
but also, with a different emphasis, under SPD-dominated governments.

Among the measures taken under this policy there has been a
series of laws, the so-called '312DM' and '624DM' laws, designed
to promote the distribution of companies' shares among their
employees. These laws encourage companies, by means of fiscal and
parafiscal advantages, to pay their employees a premium of up to
624 DM a year, a sum which must be saved in some way, either
by investment in the shares of the company or otherwise. Although
two-thirds of all employees have 'benefited' from these provisions,
the average amount per worker involved has been rather small and
the laws have made little impact on the economic structure of the
companies affected.

The other major series of measures taken to make the dream
of a 'people's capitalism' come true aimed not at the workers of a
particular company but at the population as a whole. This was the
series of denationalisations or 'privatisations' undertaken between
1959 and 1965. The CDU/CSU government had inherited from its
predecessors a large amount of state-controlled industry. Partly as an
expression of liberal faith, partly to meet growing disquiet caused by
the increasing concentration of economic power and partly to protect
the people against the temptations of communism,[30] it was decided
to denationalise, at least in part, three state-owned firms, Volkswagen,
Preussag and the Vereinigte Elektrizitäts und Bergwerke A.G. (VEBA).
Since the aim was to promote a wide distribution of property, the
shares of the companies could be bought only by those with annual
incomes below a fairly modest limit (8000 DM for single people,
16000 DM for a couple), and only in a very limited quantity. To prevent
the shares being bought up subsequently by someone interested in
gaining control of the company, it was decided that nobody could
dispose, in a general meeting, of a number of votes greater than
one thousandth of the subscribed capital. The sale of the three
companies was a limited success, in that it increased several-fold the
number of shareholders in the Federal Republic: thus Volkswagen, the
largest company in Germany, is now owned by about one and a half
million shareholders.

But, although these various measures may have increased the
number of shareholders, they have not brought about any significant

change in the structure of economic power. The fact that a person holds a small number of shares in a company does not give him any say in the running of the company. The main effect is rather to place his capital at the disposal of the big shareholders or managers who control the company. This is true whether the small shareholders are employees of the company (as under the 312DM and 624DM laws) or not. The powerlessness of small shareholders is illustrated by the first general meeting of Volkswagen, in which six thousand shareholders took part:[31] after various proposals from those present had been rejected, the proposals put forward by the management were accepted by massive majorities.

That the impact of measures taken in this field has been little more than ideological is demonstrated by a study published in 1971.[32] This showed that in 1960, 1.7 per cent of the households of the Federal Republic possessed 70 per cent of the productive property. In 1966, after the denationalisation of Volkswagen and VEBA had intervened and the first two '312DM' laws had been passed, the same proportion of households possessed 74 per cent of the productive property of the country.

The new 'capital formation' plan put forward by the SPD and accepted by a large majority at the party conference at Hanover in April 1973, recognises the futility of earlier plans. According to this plan, all enterprises with a taxable profit of 400,000 DM or more would have to contribute each year a certain (not yet fixed) percentage of their profits into a central fund, in the form of shares. In the first year, the income of this fund would be 5,000 million DM. All workers in the country with an annual income of less than 36,000 DM (48,000 DM for married workers) would receive a certificate each year giving them drawing rights on the Fund to the value of 200 DM; these certificates could be cashed only after seven years. The capital of the Fund would be used to grant loans to finance social investment.

The plan abandons the liberalism of earlier plans in that it aims not so much at increasing the power of wealth of the individual worker as at increasing collective power over the economy. The plan would indeed do little for the individual worker: 200 DM is little more than half the average weekly wage, and it is quite likely that the amount gained in this manner would be compensated for by lower wages. But it would give considerable power to the controllers of the central fund. It is calculated that after ten years the Fund would own about 25 per cent of the capital of all the larger companies in Germany, and that in thirty to forty years' time, the Fund would own virtually all German industry. Two-thirds of the board administering the Fund would be elected by the 20 million workers with certificate rights: each member would, according to the plan, represent about 50,000 certificate holders. The other third of the board would be representatives of the public interest. In practice, it is expected that the Fund would be controlled by the trade unions.

The fact that this plan has been accepted by the party conference of the principal government party does not mean that it will be put into effect. The SPDs coalition partner, the FDP, has its own capital-formation plan. This is somewhat similar in form, but it would benefit not only employed persons, but all residents in the Federal Republic. What is more important, there is no attempt to create a new central power in the economy: the funds created would be decentralised and administered not by the trade unions, but principally by the banks. Although both government parties are thus pledged to bring in a major reform in this area, they have so far been unable to reach a compromise.

These plans pose many interesting questions, but their full implications are best appreciated when related to the current discussion on codetermination *(Mitbestimmung)*. Like capital-formation plans, plans for codetermination[33] aim at democratising economic enterprises from within. But unlike the other two policies already outlined, the policy of codetermination did not spring directly from post-war liberal ideology. Rather, its adoption by the Federal government was originally a concession granted to the trade unions by the CDU. In view of the delicate state of the economy at the end of the 1940s, Adenauer agreed with the leader of the trade union federation (DGB), Boeckler, that if the unions were moderate in their wage demands and cooperative in their general approach, he, Adenauer, would see that a law was passed granting their demands for codetermination. In fact, the unions' wishes were met only in relation to the coal and steel industries: the codetermination they demanded was implemented in this area by a law of 1951, the *Montanmitbestimmungsgesetz* (MBG). By the time the law relating to the rest of the economy (the *Betriebsverfassungsgesetz)* was passed in October 1952, the position of the unions was no longer so strong and they were forced to accept a compromise.

The 1951 law, which applies to coal and steel firms with more than 1000 employees (originally about a hundred in number, now about sixty), provides for equal representation of workers and shareholders on the 'supervisory board' *(Aufsichtsrat)* of these companies. Of the eleven members who normally sit on the board, five are chosen by the shareholders and five represent the employees of the company; a 'neutral' eleventh man is then chosen by the other ten. Of the five workers' delegates, three are chosen directly by the unions and two, who may of course be also members of the union, by the workers themselves. The equal representation of shareholders and workers applies only to the supervisory board, and not to the board of management *(Vorstand)* which is responsible for the day-to-day running of the firm. With regard to this board, the law provides only that one of its members, the work director *(Arbeitsdirektor)* may be appointed by the supervisory board only with the agreement of the workers' delegates. Nor are the workers represented at the general meetings of the shareholders of the company, which retain the ultimate] power of decision.

The later law applies to all companies employing more than 500 people, but the representation of the workers on the supervisory board is limited to one-third, and there is no equivalent to the work director of the MBG. This general law has not worked well: many companies have taken steps to reduce the powers of the supervisory board, and the unions, dissatisfied with their representation, have done little to make the law work effectively.

Since their congress in Düsseldorf in 1963, the trade unions, after a period of disenchantment with the whole notion of codetermination, have been demanding the extension to all large companies (between 400 and 600 in all) of a model similar to that which now applies to coal and steel enterprises. A modified version of the DGB plan was adopted by the SPD in 1968. Although the present Government has promised to legislate on this issue during the current session of Parliament, the same difficulty has arisen as in the case of property formation. The coalition partners, the SPD and the FDP, have so far been unable to reach any agreement. The FDP has put forward two plans of its own, one of which maintains majority representation for shareholders, while the other accepts parity for shareholders and workers, but insists that, in addition, a special position should be given to representatives of the senior salaried staff *(leitende Angestellte)*.[34] The SPD and the unions object to this on the grounds that such representatives would tend to support the interests of the shareholders.

Given the influence of the FDP within the coalition, and given the fact that the SPD appear to be losing popularity to the FDP and to the CDU/CSU opposition, it is clear that the SPD plans on codetermination and property formation will have to be significantly modified if legislation is to be passed in this session. If, as a result of the strength of the unions and the left wing within the SPD, no compromise is reached before the next elections, then all one can say is that the present leadership of the SPD is unlikely to try to win an absolute majority in Parliament by basing its electoral campaign on a radical call for economic democracy.[35]

Nevertheless, the reforms planned by the SPD raise many interesting questions. Even if they became law without being modified, would they radically alter the structure of socioeconomic power? If both plans came into force, it would mean that within a few years, trade unionists and other representatives of the workers would form a majority on the supervisory boards of all large public companies, for, in addition to the seats which they would acquire under the codetermination law, they would soon be entitled to representation as shareholders under the capital formation law.

In so far as these measures would allow the representatives of the workers to participate in the wielding of economic power, they would indeed represent a step towards the goal of 'economic democracy'. That such a step would be very limited and that it would make very little difference to the way in which this power is used, is suggested by the experience with the MBG in the coal and steel industries.

Experience in this sector has shown that workers' representatives on supervisory boards have acted very much like any other members of those boards. The system has generally worked to the satisfaction of the shareholders in the enterprises effected. Thus, Herman J. Abs, the banker, was able to say at the CDU Party Conference in 1954:

> 'On the basis of the experience with it [codetermination] so far, I see it as a real success. It will, I believe stay with us in the future, so long as the social partners continue to strive for loyal cooperation and each is ready to give the other his due'[36]

The experience is even seen as making a positive contribution to management in so far as it promotes better industrial relations within the firm. Indeed one of the arguments on which the DGB has based its demand for an extension of codetermination is that it is in the interests of economic efficiency. As a leading industrialist put it:

> 'The trust between management and workers is made stronger and firmer, and that mutual mistrust which, under the slogan of the class struggle, has for so long burdened and, in part, poisoned the relations between the social partners, shall once and for all be overcome in an honest partnership between management, workers and shareholders'.[37]

The 'improvement of industrial relations' is perhaps the principal effect which the MBG has had. There has been no effect on the rate of concentration in the coal and steel industries. There has been no effect on the large number of pit closures in the coal industry, nor on the number of redundancies: at most one can say that the process of redundancy has been carried out more 'humanely'. There has been no effect on wage policies, nor on authoritarian and hierarchical structures within factories.

It may be argued that all this is due to the particular shortcomings of the MBG. Thus, the workers' representatives on the supervisory board are not protected against dismissal. Nor is there any possibility of making these representatives accountable to the workers, for they are obliged not to divulge confidential information disclosed in the meetings of the supervisory board. Most important of all, s.6 of the MBG obliges all members of the supervisory board, including the representatives of the workers, to work for the 'good of the enterprise'. But to place too great an emphasis on these provisions,[38] important though they are, is perhaps misleading. In a competitive market economy, it is not the law, but the necessity to survive which compels directors and managers, whoever they may be, to act in the interests of the enterprise, to compete for profits, to withhold information from their competitors and therefore from their workers, to hold down wages and to 'rationalise' their production and make men redundant when it is necessary. The achievement of codetermination or indeed of 'workers' control' will not make very much difference to this unless it is accompanied by other, more far-reaching measures.

The creation of a central fund controlled by the trade unions is unlikely to be any more effective in bringing about radical change. The effect of such a fund would depend on how the fund was managed. If the fund were invested in the most profitable manner, the social effect would be no greater than that of the creation of a large unit trust. If, on the other hand, the investment of the fund were inspired by social objectives, then the scheme would be less profitable to the individual worker and the general effect would be similar to that of a state subsidy in the area concerned.[39] There would also be considerable problems in the coordination of the social activity of the fund with that of the state. It may be argued that the long-term implication – the acquisition by the fund of almost all German industry in about forty years time – is revolutionary. This may be so, but it is clear that such a long-term socialisation of German industry could not take place without provoking considerable opposition, and it is hard now to say how the governments in the intervening period would react to such opposition.

This is not to dismiss the reforms proposed by the SPD as meaningless. Clearly, they do mark a reaction to dissatisfaction caused by the existing property relationships and they would mark a real shift in power to the trade unions. But it is only if such reforms were seen as being steps towards a much more fundamental change that this power could be wielded in a manner which would transcend the constraints imposed by competition in a market economy. It is much more likely, however, that such reforms would have the effect of further integrating the unions into the capitalist system and hinder them in their task of representing the interests of the workers. Whether the workers are made small shareholders, as under CDU plans, or the trade unions gain control of large amounts of capital, as under the SPD plan, the effect is the same: to blur the fundamental conflict between the interests of labour and those of capital.

Despite the cartel laws and despite the SPD's pledge to achieve a greater measure of economic democracy, the period since the War has seen the formation of ever larger units of economic power. Although the proposed reforms aim at democratising these units from within, such a reform, if it does come about, would make little difference to the fact that the power of these large units is wielded in the pursuit of private interests, in the pursuit of profits.

Conclusion

Stimulated by the discussion on the decentralisation of power which has become fashionable in most countries of Western Europe in recent years, this chapter has sought to illustrate some of the limitations of many of the arguments used by tracing some aspects of the failure of liberalism[40](or the hollowness of the appeal to liberal principles) in the Federal Republic of Germany. To trace this failure is not to lament it. Rather, the suggestion is that the trend towards the concentration of economic and political power is inevitable in an advanced capitalist society, and that the West German experience provides but one illustration of the forces at work in all such societies.

The same process of economic concentration is common to all advanced capitalist countries (and takes place, of course, not only within those countries but at an international level). This is inevitable in a competitive economy. The competition is most likely to be won by those enterprises which are the most highly and efficiently mechanised and which possess the largest funds for technological research and for marketing their products. Thus, 'the average size of enterprises increases uninterruptedly; a large number of small enterprises are beaten in the competitive struggle by a small number of big enterprises which command an increasing share of capital, labour, funds and production in entire branches of industry'.[41] In no country has this process been halted by antitrust legislation. Competition is increasingly international and, even leaving aside the direct influence of big business on government, no government is likely to take action which would damage the competitiveness of its industry.

The growth in the size of enterprises, or, more specifically, the increase in the scale of the investments undertaken by these enterprises, has contributed to that other phenomenon of modern capitalism, the growth of economic planning by the state and of state intervention in the economy. The scale of these private investments, and the risk involved as a result of the high rate of technological innovation, compels large enterprises to plan their production, marketing, research etc. on a long-term basis. This in turn leads to pressure on the state to stabilise those conditions (labour costs, consumption, etc.) which play an essential part in the internal planning of the large enterprises, in other words to plan itself and to take action to avoid the conjunctural fluctuations of the economy. This, together with other social and economic pressures,[42] has led to attempts by all Western governments systematically to 'manage the economy'.

Such management can, however, only take place on the national (or, increasingly, on the supranational) level. But as we have seen already, the necessity for such management imposes strict limitations on the extent to which 'political' and particularly legislative and budgetary power can effectively be developed to regions. It would seem from this that the concentration of political power, in the Federal Republic and elsewhere, is, to some extent, an indirect consequence of economic concentration. It seems likely that in the future the process of economic concentration will continue, that the need for state management of the economy will increase and that therefore the area of autonomy which can be given to regional subdivisions will further diminish.[43]

Appendix

Table 1 Länder of the FRG

	Schleswig-Holstein	Hamburg	Lower Saxony	Bremen	North Rhine Westphalia	Hesse	Rhineland Palatinate	Baden-Württemberg	Bavaria	Saarland	West Berlin
Area (sq. km.) 31-12-71	15,678	753	47,405	404	34,054	21,112	19,838	35,750	70,547	2,567	480
Population '000 31-12-72	2,567	1,766	7,215	734	17,193	5,533	3,690	9,154	10,779	1,119	2,063
GDP 1971 (Million DM)	25,763	36,719	74,489	11,864	217,084	71,188	42,127	114,985	125,623	12,025	27,871
%	3.4	4.8	9.8	1.6	28.6	9.4	5.5	15.1	16.5	1.6	3.7
Total Expenditure 1970 (Million DM)	3,171	5,038	8,085	1,719	18,099	7,058	4,429	10,866	11,860	1,312	6,800
Government 1-1-73	CDU	SPD/FDP	SPD	SPD	SPD/FDP	SPD/FDP	CDU	CDU	CSU	CDU	SPD
Number of votes in Bundesrat	4	3	5	3	5	4	4	5	5	3	4

Source: *Statistisches Jahrbuch für die BRD*, 1973, pp. 22, 30, 130, 526.

Table 2 Total Tax Revenues of the Federation, Länder and Communes
(in Million DM)

	1968(1)	1969(1)	1970(2)	1971(2)	1972(3)
Federation	66,180	81,415	83,597	92,060	101,706
Länder	39,404	46,684	50,482	56,606	66,945
Communes	14,794	18,829	18,240	21,131	25,319

(1) Before the Finance Reform of 1969 came into effect.
(2) Turnover tax: 70 per cent given to Federation, 30 per cent to Länder.
(3) Turnover tax: 65 per cent given to Federation, 35 per cent to Länder.

Source: Statistisches Jahrbuch für die Bundesrepublik Deutschland,
1969, p.400; 1970, p.382; 1971, p.404; 1972, p.408; 1973, p.422.

Notes

1. Cf. Zink (1957), p.98.
2. Erich Preiser, *Die Zukunft unserer Wirtschaftsordnung*, 3rd. ed., Göttingen, p.9; quoted in Jaeggi (1973), p.59.
3. For a clear and comprehensive description of the institutions of West German federalism, see Johnson (1973).
4. This does not include West Berlin, which, strictly speaking, is not an integral part of the Federal Republic. The people of West Berlin are represented in both the Bundestag and the Bundesrat, but their representatives do not have full voting rights.
5. For a fuller account of administrative decentralisation, see Johnson (1973), esp. pp.16-30.
6. This is now covered by Art. 107 of the Basic Law: below see p.118.
7. Translated by Johnson as 'Trade Cycle Commission'.
8. *Frankfurter Rundschau*, 10-5-1969, p.1: quoted in Huffschmid (1972), p.180.
9. Translated by Johnson as 'Financial Plannning Commission,
10. Helmut Schmidt in *Handelsblatt*, 3-9-1973.
11. The original Art. 109, quoted above, p.12.
12. *Handelsblatt*, 20-9-1973.
13. There has been a tendency, however, to increase the area of legislation administered by the Länder as agents of the Federation, rather than 'as their own affair'. Cf. 1969 amendment to Art. 104 of the Basic Law; Johnson (1973), p.18.
14. On the importance of this administrative devolution, see Johnson (1973)
15. Thieme (1970), 67ff.
16. That this amendment made little difference to the distribution of tax revenues between the Federation and Länder is made clear by Appendix 2.
17. In addition to this 'vertical equalisation', there is also a complex system of 'horizontal equalisation' between the Länder themselves. Cf. Johnson (1973), p.35.
18. Cf. Kunze (1968).

19. The fact that there are no by-elections in the German system means that Land elections are also regarded as the principal indicator of the popularity of the Federal Government between federal elections.
20. The unification in 1952 of the three south-western Länder of Baden-Württemberg took place under a separate provision (Art. 118) which was included in the Basic Law in order to facilitate the successful conclusion of negotiations which had already begun between the three Länder.
21. It should be noted, however, that the Ernst Commission took care to see that its proposals would not disturb the existing political balance. Cf. Reschke (1973).
22. 10 Nov. 1973. Printed in 'Press- und Informationsamt der Bundesregierung', *Bulletin*, nr.144, p.1426.
23. Cf. Johnson (1973), p.42: 'Opinion surveys carried out in 1952 showed that only 21 per cent of those questioned wanted the Länder governments to be retained and 49 per cent favoured their abolition. But by 1960 the respective proportions were 42 per cent and 24 per cent, with 34 per cent 'Don't Knows' *(Jahrbuch der öffentlichen Meinung,* 1958-64, Allensbach 1965)'. Despite the obvious swing in favour of federalism, these figures nevertheless indicate a considerable lack of enthusiasm for the system.
24. Cf. Huffschmid (1972), p.137; Jaeggi (1973), p.71.
25. From: *Imperialismus der BRD,* Frankfurt 1971, p.145. Cf. Jaeggi (1973), p.71.
26. The figures relating to the legal control of capital give, of course, only a vague impression of the economic power of the large companies. Small companies which are legally independent will in fact often depend totally on the favour of the big companies for their continued existence. This is probably true, for example, of many of the 30,000 firms which supply goods to Siemens, or the 23,000 suppliers of Krupp, or 17,000 suppliers of Daimler-Benz. Cf. Schäfer/Nedelmann (1969), vol.1, p.54.
27. Cf. Huffschmid (1972), p.144.
28. Ibid., p.146ff.
29. Cf. François-Poncet (1970), p.177; Stamokap (1973), p.58; *Jahresgutachten* 1971, ch.IV.
30. As the banker, Hermann Josef Abs, the man who, above all others, personifies the post-war concentration of economic power in the hands of the few, put it (on a different occasion): 'it will be impossible in the long run to maintain the private economic system of the Federal Republic close to the Iron Curtain, unless we succeed in binding a few million West Germans, as shareholders, more closely to this system'; *Der Spiegel,* 18-2-1959, quoted by Müller in Schäfer/Nedelmann (1969), vol.1, p.35.
31. The largest general meeting of shareholders ever held in Europe. Cf. François-Poncet (1970), p.150.
32. Siebke J., *Die Vermögensbildung der privaten Haushalte in der Bundesrepublik Deutschland.* Cited in Jaeggi (1973), p.69.
33. There has also been a movement for codetermination, or 'participation' in other spheres, particularly in the universities, where the question is one of the controversial points in the proposed *Hochschulrahmengesetz.* But our main concern here is with economic power.
34. The definition of this term is to be that given in the *Betriebsverfassungsgesetz* of 1972 *(Bundesgesetzblatt* 1972, *Teil* 1, pp.13ff.); according to this law ($5(3)) '*leitende Angestellte* are those who (1) 'have the right to employ or dismiss workers working in the firm or department of the firm, or (2) have plenipotentiary powers or power of attorney, or (3) are themselves responsible for duties, which, because of their importance for the running

and development of the firm, are regularly entrusted to them on the basis of their special experience and knowledge'.

35. An agreement between the coalition partners on both codetermination and capital formation policy was announced in January, 1974 (published in 'Presse- und Informationsamt der Bundesregierung', *Bulletin*, 30 January 1974). In both areas, but especially in the capital formation plan, the SPD have made significant concessions to the FDP.

In the field of capital formation, the most important concession made by the SPD is that the funds raised will not be administered centrally. Instead, they will be administered by a number of companies *(Vermögensanlagegesellschaften)* which will be specially created by public and private credit institutes in the form of private companies *(Gesellschaften mit beschränkter Haftung)*. Each certificate holder will have the right to choose which of these companies is to administer his share of the fund: thus the companies will have to compete with one another for funds. The resulting need to invest profitably will presumably be of decisive importance in the administration of the fund. Of the investment policy of these companies, it is said only that it should not lead to distortions of competition on the capital market. Their cash is to be invested in shares and, beyond that, they may finance public or private investments by means of fixed-interest bonds. Two-thirds of the seats of the supervisory boards of these companies are to be given to representatives elected indirectly by the certificate holders. It should be clear from the analysis in the text that the abandonment of the idea of a central fund deprives the proposed legislation of much of its interest.

The concessions made by the SPD on codetermination are not as far-reaching. It is proposed that the new law would apply to all companies with more than 2000 employees (the *Montanmitbestimmungsgesetz* would continue to apply to the coal and steel industry, and the *Betriebsverfassungsgesetz* to smaller firms). If the proposal is accepted, the Supervisory Board of these companies will have twenty members, ten representatives of the shareholders and ten representatives of the employees. Of the ten employees' representatives, seven will be employees of the company and three representatives of the trade unions. Of the seven – and this is the most important concession to the FDP – at least one must be a salaried employee *(Angestellter)* and one a member of the senior salaried staff *(leitender Angestellter)*. All the employees' representatives will be elected by a committee of electors, themselves elected separately by the workers, the salaried and the senior salaried staff. There will be no 'neutral member' in the Supervisory Board. In the event of an equal division of votes, the chairman could be given the casting vote if the majority of both sides agree. Unless otherwise agreed by two-thirds of the members, the Chairmanship of the Board will alternate between the two groups. There is no provision that any member of the Management should be appointed only with the agreement of the employees' representatives, i.e. there is no equivalent of the *Arbeitsdirektor* under the MBG. If one argues, as the SPD have in the past argued, that members of the senior salaried staff *(leitende Angestellte)* would identify with the interests of the shareholders, then it would seem that, notwithstanding the complex election procedures, the SPD have in fact abandoned the principle of 'parity', which was intended to be the basis of the whole reform. The argument in this essay, however, suggests that this will make little difference in practice.

The coalition compromise has, however, been strongly criticised by both

parliamentary parties, and especially by members of the SPD. It thus remains uncertain whether it will form the basis of eventual legislation.
36. Deppe *et al.* (1972), p.147.
37. Ibid., p.147.
38. Cf. Deppe (1972), ch. IV.
39. Probably the effect of such a fund would not be very different from the effect which IRI has on the Italian economy.
40. Though I have found it convenient to take liberal ideology as the starting point for this essay, it should not be assumed that this ideology has remained intact. In the mid-1960s the disparity between the liberal principles proclaimed by the government and the reality of economic concentration and increasing state intervention became too great. To justify the new turn which the economic policy of the government was taking, a new concept of a cooperative, indeed disciplined society (thus Erhard's *Formierte Gesellschaft* and the *konzertierte Aktion* of the Stability Act) was put forward, in which the key words were not 'competition' and 'individual enterprise' but 'growth', 'cooperation', 'general interest' Cf. Huffschmid (1972), ch.4.
41. Mandel (1971), p.163.
42. Some of which we have already mentioned above.
43. Does all this imply a 'failure of the state'? At least for the Federal Republic, the answer is: certainly not. Business has boomed and the masses have remained fairly quiescent: the state has been very successful.

Select Bibliography

P.D. Dagtoglou	'Fiscal Policy and Regional Autonomy: some constitutional aspects'. *New Atlantis*, no.3, vol. 2, 1971.
F. Deppe *et al.*	*Kritik der Mitbestimmung.* Suhrkamp, Frankfurt-am-Main, 3. Aufl. 1972.
J. François-Poncet	*La Politique économique de l'Allemagne Occidentale,* Sirey, Paris, 1970.
J. Huffschmid	*Die Politik des Kapitals; Konzentration und Wirtschaftspolitik in der Bundesrepublik.* Suhrkamp, Frnakfurt-am-Main, 8. Aufl. 1972.
U. Jaeggi	*Kapital und Arbeit in der Bundesrepublik,* Fischer Taschenbuch Verlag, Frankfurt-am-Main, 1973.
N. Johnson	'Federalism and Decentralisation in the Federal Republic of Germany' *(Commission on the Constitution, Research Papers, 1),* HMSO, London, 1973.
R. Kunze	*Kooperativer Föderalismus in der Bundesrepublik.* Gustav Fischer Verlag, Stuttgart, 1968.
E. Mandel	*Marxist Economic Theory.* Merlin Press, London, 2nd impression, 1971.
H. Reschke	'Die Neugliederung des Bundesgebietes', *in, Deutsches Verwaltungsblatt,* 1/15 Oktober 1973, pp.728-39.

G. Schäfer, C. Nedelmann (eds.)	*Der CDU - Staat, 2 Bde.* Suhrkamp, Frankfurt-am-Main, 1969.
Stamokap	*Der Thesenstreit um 'Stamokap': Die Dokumente zur Grundsatzdiskussion der Jungsozialisten.* Rowohlt, Reinbek bei Hamburg, 1973.
W. Thieme	*Föderalismus im Wandel.* Carl Heymanns Verlag, Köln, Berlin, Bonn, München, 1970.
H. Zink	*The United States in Germany, 1954-55.* Van Nostrand, Princeton, 1957.

POSTSCRIPT

The chapter was written before Chancellor Brandt's resignation in May 1974. One of the first decisions of the Schmidt government was to postpone the property formation plan: it is now hoped to inplement the plan by the beginning of 1978. It is still intended that the proposed legislation on codetermination should be passed by the spring of 1975.

5. MODELS OF REFORM IN EASTERN EUROPE

David Holloway

Decentralisation of power has been the main focus of political debate and reform in Eastern Europe in the post-Stalin period.[1] Economic reform has hinged on the decentralisation of economic decision-making, and has been inextricably bound up with attempts to democratise political power. The impetus to change has come from the search for efficiency in economic planning and administration, but this search has helped to create conditions in which different groups and classes have sought to wrest some degree of political power from the state. There exists therefore a complex and intricate relationship between economic and political decentralisation.

The debates and reforms have all taken place in the context of a move away from the Stalinist economic and political model, which was imposed by the Soviet Union on the societies of Eastern Europe in the late 1940s with little regard for national circumstances. Although there are important differences in the national patterns of development, the terms of the debate have a considerable unity. Decentralisation of economic decision-making has implied greater use of the market mechanism, and economic reform has moved away from the highly centralised planning system of the Stalinist type in two main directions: towards a system in which decision-making is devolved but the methods of administration are not fundamentally changed; and towards a decentralised system which makes extensive use of the market.

In a command economy, which allocates resources by administrative decision rather than through the market, economic power and political power are indistinguishable. Control over the central administrative apparatus gives control over resource allocation. Consequently a change in the arrangements for economic planning and administration cannot fail to affect political relationships. Many advocates of economic reform have seen in it an opportunity to bring state power under democratic control: decentralisation of economic decision-making would weaken the power of the central bureaucracy, and enterprise autonomy would open the way to workers' participation in industrial management. Opponents of the 'regulated market mechanism' have identified it as part of the anti-Marxist, revisionist concept of 'democratic' or 'human' socialism, on the grounds that it would undermine the party's leading and directing role in society.

To accept that economic reform has political consequences is not to accept that different systems of economic planning and administration will give birth directly to reform of the political system. Weakening the central bureaucracy and democratising industrial management do not constitute a political blueprint, and the adoption of a new model of the political system is itself a major political choice, one step at least removed from economic reform. Nevertheless, as the Hungarian sociologist Andras Hegedüs has argued, the experience of economic reform opens up the possibility of a conscious choice between different political models of socialism:

> 'the fundamental problem of Marxism today concerns the position to be taken regarding the theoretical or practical alternatives within the political structure, the power [structure?], the state, or — closer to reality — the administration of society. This problem can be avoided for a while as a so-called delicate question but social reality requires an answer more and more urgently'.[2]

It is accepted throughout Eastern Europe that a permanent apparatus is necessary for the efficient and effective administration of a complex industrial society. Lenin's vision of self-administration is not seen at present to be capable of realisation: the state is not about to wither away. Once this is admitted, the socialist is confronted with two problems: how to ensure that administration is conducted as efficiently and effectively as possible, and how to subordinate the administrative apparatus to the control of those in whose name it acts.[3]

These two objectives are likely to come into conflict insofar as effective administration requires that the apparatus have extensive rights, responsibilities and powers. But the contradiction cannot be resolved by laying stress on one objective rather than the other. If efficiency and effectiveness are neglected in the interests of democratic control, the administrative apparatus may lose its capacity to attain any social, economic or political purposes, whether democratically formulated or not. If efficiency and effectiveness are pursued at the expense of democratic control the apparatus will develop, and attempt to realise, aims and interests of its own, which may not correspond to those of other groups and classes in society.[4]

This contradiction is not of course unknown in capitalist societies, but it is more sharply focused in state socialism. There central administration is not obstructed by private ownership of the means of production, and the state has sought to exercise a control which is planned, conscious and detailed and thus farther-reaching than is possible in a liberal democracy.[5] In the exercise of this control, however, a powerful bureaucratic centralist state has been created, and democratic control has atrophied. The opportunities for democracy are nevertheless claimed to be greater than under capitalism because the chief contradiction of capitalism — that between capital and labour — is said to have been eradicated, and with it all structural conflicts of interest in the social system. The relationship between the practical opportunities for efficient and effective administration and the theoretical commitment to democratic control has been at the centre of reform theory and practice in Eastern Europe.

I shall look at the way in which efficient economic planning and administration and democratic control have been pursued by Eastern European reformers in the post-Stalin period. Political change in Eastern Europe cannot be explained in terms of these two factors alone, although they have undoubtedly been significant. Nor can it be said that the two objectives have been pursued with equal vigour: the search for more efficient economic planning and administration has commanded widespread support, but democratisation has not been seen by those with power as a goal that needed to be pursued. I shall not look at the question of regional devolution in spite of its obvious interest and importance, for two reasons. Firstly, although it is a problem of general relevance, the way in which it manifests itself tends to differ from one society to another. Secondly, regional devolution is contingent upon economic and political decentralisation; in a highly centralised planning system regional bodies can be little more than extensions of the central apparatus, and autonomy can be granted only through reform of the system as a whole.

The Stalinist Economic Model

The centralised system of economic planning and administration was an essential instrument for carrying through the Stalinist policy of industrialisation since it was the means whereby resources were concentrated in heavy industry — those sectors which provide the basis of economic growth and military power. The main features of the planning system were as follows.[6] Firstly, almost all economic decisions were concentrated at the central level, except for individual decisions in the fields of consumption and employment. The central authorities determined the rate and structure of investment, defined the proportions of individual and collective consumption, and decided the structure of current output. The criteria by which these decisions were made reflected the preference scale of the central political leadership, and they sought to realise their preferences not merely by creating general guidelines for economic development, but by giving detailed planning instructions to all economic units. From this flows the second main feature of the centralised model: the predominance of vertical relationships (between the central authorities and the enterprise) over horizontal relationships (between enterprises). Most enterprises found themselves under the direct control of the appropriate Ministry, which compiled detailed plans for its enterprises in accordance with the priorities laid down by the party and government leadership. It was these plans, rather than direct relations with suppliers or customers, that determined the enterprise's activity. The task of coordinating the plans was performed by the state planning commission.

The third main feature of the model was the imperative and administrative character of planning and management. The plan embodied the will of the party and government: the planning instructions were binding, and had to be implemented irrespective of the preferences of the enterprise. The economy was managed chiefly by administrative means, and material and moral incentives were used to buttress the plan instructions rather than to create a context for individual decision and initiative. Although not clear-cut, the distinction between 'administrative measures' and 'economic measures', which is often to be found in the reform debates, is an important one. An administrative measure is a direct instruction – for example, about the production of machine-tools; an economic measure affects the economic conditions which influence the decision-maker – for example, by changing the price structure or taxation system. Finally, in line with the administrative character of the system, economic calculation and planning were carried out in physical rather than value units. Prices were fixed centrally and changed infrequently; they did not reflect scarcities and were out of line with costs. They did not play an active role in decision-making, since they carried no information that could guide the planner or manager. The enterprises were not autonomous in the sense of being immune from interference from the central authorities.

Although in historical perspective this system can be seen as one designed to fulfil specific tasks of economic development, it was presented at the time as the epitome of socialist planning. Political economy and economic theory suffered greatly from Stalinist repression, and the system's advantages and disadvantages could receive no critical discussion. Greater centralisation was the dominant reflex to difficulties, and failures – which could not, after all, be given a structural explanation – were attributed to the work of 'wreckers' and 'saboteurs'. But the climate of freer discussion which followed Stalin's death made it possible to express doubts and criticisms which had hitherto been suppressed, and to assess the suitability of the existing system for the current tasks of economic development.

Criticism of the centralised planning system focused on two issues: complexity and efficiency. As the economy develops, the number of economic units (enterprises, state farms, retail outlets etc.) increases, and the number of inter-relations between them grows too — at a much faster rate. As a result, the central authorities are faced, in a centralised system, with more and more decisions. Besides, in the 1950s the priorities of economic development became more complex, as the draconian simplicities of Stalinist policy were abandoned. It began to be realised that the centralised planning system could not guide more complex economic relationships towards the attainment of more complex goals:

> 'economic reality does not by itself confront planners with the choice between "a small number of alternatives". Rather they are only capable of direct rational choice between a small number of basic alternatives and ... if they take responsibility for practically all acts of choice, the effects can be only detrimental.'[7]

Nevertheless, there is an inherent tendency in the centralised model to increase the scope of central control: it is preferable to make plans as detailed as possible lest operating with aggregates open the way to uncontrolled structural changes in the economy. There thus existed two contradictory processes: a growing complexity of economic relationships, and a tendency to attempt more detailed control from the centre.

The system of planning by instructions had certain harmful effects. None of the plan indices was unambiguous and they could thus be — legally — fulfilled in ways which might or might not correspond to the intentions of the planners. The incentive system failed to ensure that the interests of the enterprise manager were in line with those of the state. Besides, the bargaining process by which the plan was drawn up often resulted in plan targets which did not match the productive capacities of the enterprise — either because they were too ambitious as a result of pressure from the planners, or because they were too slack as a result of the manager's efforts to secure an easier life and a certain bonus for overfulfilling the plan.

The second focus of criticism was the efficiency of the system, in particular its ability to exploit the possibilities of intensive growth. The distinction between extensive and intensive growth has been prominent in the Eastern European reform debates: in the former, growth is based upon increases in land, capital and labour, whereas intensive growth is derived from increased productivity, greater efficiency and better utilisation of capital. It was clear in the 1950s that the latter factors were coming to play an increasingly important role in economic growth. But the centralised planning system was said to be unable to exploit these factors for two main reasons.

Firstly, the system could not secure the rational allocation of scarce resources because prices, which did not reflect scarcities, did not provide the planner or manager with the appropriate information on which to base his decisions. Secondly, the centralised model provided no incentive to technological innovation: the desire to fulfil plan targets often hampered innovation, and the predominance of vertical over horizontal relationships acted as a brake on the transfer of new scientific knowledge from the R & D establishments into industrial production.

The Role of the State

In the Soviet Union power has been exercised by permanent officials who, although they have ruled in the name of the working class and peasantry, and then of all the people, have in practice been controlled by, and responsible to, no one but themselves. In the 1920s the power of the permanent officials in the state administration and party apparatus grew stronger, and democratic institutions atrophied. Power passed into the hands of officials who identified themselves increasingly with the interests of the new state rather than with the cause of international revolution. The centralised planning system greatly expanded the sphere of state control. Moreover, the system was created after forced collectivisation had broken the *smychka* or alliance between working class and peasantry: the power of the state was thus increased at the very time when the social basis of its support was destroyed. The policy of industrialisation involved a conscious effort by the state to transform socioeconomic relationships and this, with the strict enforcement of priorities that went along with it, entailed the active exercise of coercive state power.

The Soviet state is remarkable for the degree of control it seeks to exercise over social and economic activities. In its hands lies control over the means of production and distribution, the means of mass communication and the instruments of violence. It strives to achieve detailed control and abhors spontaneity. Trotsky declared in 1932 that

> 'if there existed a universal mind — that projected itself into the scientific fantasy of Laplace; a mind that would register simultaneously all the processes of nature and of society, that could measure the dynamics of their motion, that could forecast the results of their interactions, such a mind, of course, could *a priori* draw up a faultless and exhaustive economic plan, beginning with the number of hectares of wheat and come down to the last button for a vest. In truth, the bureaucracy often

conceives that just such a mind is at its disposal; that is why it so easily frees itself from the control of the market and of Soviet democracy.'[8]

This bureaucracy comprises those in leading or managing positions in the party apparatus and state administration, or in voluntary but party-controlled bodies such as the trade unions. To speak of 'the bureaucracy' is not to deny that important cleavages and divisions of interest exist between its various parts. Nevertheless it may be argued that these divisions are less important than the cleavage between bureaucracy and the rest of society, since this latter cleavage marks off those with access — albeit differential access — to the instruments of power and control from those without.

The main structural cleavages in the bureaucracy may be defined as follows. Firstly there exists a tension between the party apparatus and the state administration which arises out of the party's attempt to play its 'leading and directing' role in society. This role involves: deciding the general lines of policy; providing personnel for leading positions; ensuring that policy is carried out; and mobilising support for policy. This role can come into conflict with the tendency of specialists and professionals to seek autonomy in their work, and is accentuated by differences in career patterns, training and education, and institutional loyalties. The strength of this cleavage varies from time to time, and has shown a secular tendency to diminish.

Secondly, a cleavage between generations emerges when new problems of administration arise requiring new techniques and approaches, or when there is, for whatever reason, a shift in the methods of government. A new generation of managers, planners, officers, *apparatchiki* comes forward with new skills, a new outlook and style of authority and a different historical experience. It may feel hampered and frustrated in its progress, while the older generation becomes anxious and hostile. The resulting tension can cut across the whole spectrum of the bureaucracy — as appears to have happened, for example, in the Soviet Union in the 1960s with the growing complexity of administration. There exist, thirdly, cleavages between different levels of the bureaucracy. A good example of this is to be found in relations between the central planners and the industrial managers.

Finally, there exist important tensions between different Ministries or departments. These conflicts centre primarily on resource allocation or the protection of departmental interests. They seem to occur at all levels, and it is therefore misleading to conceive of the central authorities as a unitary actor, moving purposefully towards the attainment of specific goals. What is known of political processes in the Eastern European bureaucracies suggests that they are extremely complex, with an important part taken by factions seeking to gain control of a department or policy. The conflicts are the more complex for the severe limitations that are placed on the activities of groups pursuing their own interests, even within the bureaucracies. Such activity is regarded as illegitimate; the opportunities for canvassing and organising support are restricted, and group activity consequently circumscribed.

Power relationships within the bureaucracy have changed since Stalin's death. The post-Stalin leaders decided almost at once to abandon terror — the arbitrary use of coercion — as an instrument of rule, and the police apparatus was brought under tighter party control. It ceased to be possible to resolve political arguments within the bureaucracy by the use of force. While power is still largely concentrated in the hands of a small number of leaders they cannot formulate their policies without appealing to the major constituencies within the bureaucracy — for example, the party apparatus, the central planners, the military leaders. To some extent at least, power has been diffused within the bureaucracy.

It follows from this that two sets of relationships must be taken into account in looking at the bureaucracy: those internal to it, and those between the bureaucracy and the activities it controls. The two sets of relationships are closely linked, and changes in one may affect changes in the other. Oskar Lange has written that

> 'the contradictions which may arise in the development of socialist society between the requirements of the economic base and antiquated superstructures, such as methods of management of the national economy, political superstructures and others, may also arouse opposition from vested interests of certain strata, which makes a change difficult. But these are not social classes — there are no class struggles. To overcome these obstacles there is not required a basic change in production relations, i.e. a social revolution, though it may lead to all kinds of friction in the superstructure during the period of transformation and of adaptation of the superstructure to the new requirements of the economic base.'[9]

The reforms and debates should thus be seen in the context of bureaucratic rule. The central issue has been to create a new mechanism which would enable the state to exercise more efficient and effective control over economic activity. But economic reform is a complex political process, in which different groups — partly officials, central planners, technical specialists, for example — do what they can to pursue and safeguard their own interests.

Economic Reform

By the mid-1950s the need for reform was accepted by planners, party leaders and economists alike in Eastern Europe, and two main approaches to reform emerged. These two approaches can best be understood if all economic decisions are divided schematically into three categories:[10]

> basic macroeconomic decisions which would determine the general direction of economic development: the rate of growth of the national income and the share of investment and consumption; the distribution of investment, and the principles of distribution of the consumption fund.
>
> current decisions about the size and structure of a sector's or enterprise's output, choice of supplier and customer, structure of labour force, and form and methods of payment.
>
> the decisions of the individual about consumption and employment.

What is at issue is the second category of decisions. It is agreed that a socialist economy could not, and should not, plan the last category; nor could it afford to lose control over the first category.

The first approach to reform (the devolved-centralised model) would give the enterprise greater autonomy in making decisions of the second category and lessen the degree of 'petty tutelage' exercised by the central authorities. This would be done by reducing the number of plan targets and indices, and assigning a special role to profitability as a synthetic indicator of enterprise performance. The enterprise would be given more freedom to regulate its relations with other enterprises, for example through free contracts. The incentive system would acquire a more important role in harmonising the interests of the enterprise with those of the state. There would be greater emphasis on economic instruments in directing economic activity towards the attainment of plan goals. Although this approach proposes decentralisation of economic decision-making, it does not call for a fundamental transformation of the system.

The second approach (the regulated market mechanism) is more radical in arguing for a greater role for the market. It is claimed that the market, with equilibrium prices which would adjust supply to demand, is the most efficient mechanism for taking decisions in the second category. The market would function within a framework laid down by the central authorities, and would help the planners to determine the most rational way of attaining their goals. Opponents of this approach have objected that it would in fact deprive the planners of the power to decide the main lines of economic development for, if the enterprise were given autonomy, it would have to have some freedom to redistribute profits between investment and wages, and this would take an important element of investment and consumption decisions out of the hands of the central authorities. To this the reformers reply that these decisions could be guided in the desired direction by central policies on prices, credit, tax and interest rates. A second objection is that central control over economic activity would be undermined because management through the market is *ex post,* and not planned *ex ante,* management. The reformers respond that the centralised planning system fails to secure precise control over economic activity, and that, moreover, they see the market as a complement to, not as a replacement for, planning; consequently, the socialist market would be quite different from capitalist free enterprise.

The economic reforms of the 1960s have followed both these approaches. Although the planning systems of Eastern Europe have been in a state of constant change since their creation, this was the most important period of reform. The process differed greatly from one country to another, but a major impetus was provided by declining growth rates (cf Table 1). The main lines of change are well illustrated by three reforms: the creation of the New Economic System (NES) in the German Democratic Republic in 1963, the Soviet reform of 1965, and the New Economic Mechanism (NEM) which was introduced in Hungary in 1968. The Soviet Union and the GDR have followed the first approach to reform, while the Hungarian NEM, like the abortive Czechoslovak reform of 1966-9, attempts to make use of the regulated market mechanism.

The Soviet reform of 1965 did not aim to transform the system of economic planning and administration, although many saw in it a first step towards fundamental change. It both recentralised and decentralised economic decision-making, for it replaced the territorial decentralisation that Khrushchev had introduced in 1957. This reform had been misconceived and tended to reproduce at the local level many of the defects inherent in the centralised system. Competition between the Ministries and Ministerial empire-building were transmuted into a 'localism' in which the regional economic councils *(sovnarkhozy)* put the interests of their own regions first, often against the wishes of the central authorities. There was much tinkering with the system between 1957 and 1965; but its functioning suggested that territorial decentralisation, within a system which relied upon administrative instruments, could provide no solution to the problem of economic planning and management, since the only mechanism for coordinating the activities of the different regions was the central plan.[11]

The 1965 reform abolished the regional economic councils and restored the economic Ministries. The number of compulsory indicators handed down to the enterprise by the central planners was, however, greatly reduced. Profits were to be calculated as a percentage of capital and a capital charge was introduced; interest-bearing credits were to play an increasing role in investment. The incentive system was recast so that profitability and sales should be better rewarded and thus feature more prominently in managerial behaviour.

In the course of implementation the reform has proved to be less radical than at first thought. The centralised system remains: prices are still fixed centrally, and do not reflect scarcities; material supply is still centrally controlled, and the power to allocate resources and take production decisions remains at the centre. The indicators handed down by the central authorities are frequently contradictory, and the incentive system, which is immensely complex, does not guarantee the realisation of the planners' wishes. Ministerial competition is still rife, and Ministries intervene much more than is allowed for in the plan; if anomalies and difficulties arise in the operation of the system, the central authorities step in to try to solve the problem by the means to which they are accustomed: administrative action. Debate about reform continues, but no fundamental change seems imminent. The present system undergoes constant adjustment, as for example with the creation in 1973 of industrial associations at an intermediate level between the central authorities and the enterprise.[12]

Like the Soviet reform, the New Economic System which was introduced in the GDR in 1963 represents an attempt to decentralise the planned system by changing the locus of bureaucratic control, not by moving wholeheartedly towards the regulated market mechanism. The extent of decentralisation is, however, greater than in the Soviet case. Central planning has concentrated on structure-determining and proportion-determining tasks, and much of the responsibility for drawing up the material balances and forming prices has devolved on the industrial associations. Central control over the supply system was relaxed, and the enterprise given greater freedom in production planning. Horizontal relations between enterprises grew more important, and legal regulations were changed in order to strengthen contractual relationships. The incentive system was revised and emphasis placed on profit rather than on gross output as the chief indicator of success, in order to encourage efficiency. A price reform was carried out between 1964 and 1967, and there has been continuous revision of prices since then. The principle of price formation has been the same as in the Soviet Union: average cost plus a percentage for planned profit.

The NES has not stood still. In 1967 it was renamed the Economic

System of Socialism. This did not, however, signify a major change in the system: it reflected the idea that socialism should be viewed not so much as a society in transition between capitalism and communism, but rather as a distinct — and prolonged — phase of social development. This concept was rejected by the new SED leadership at the Eighth Party Congress in 1971. Indeed since 1970 there has been a considerable recentralisation of economic decision-making: balancing and price formation have been withdrawn from the lower rungs, there has been an increased number of plan indicators, and incentives have been linked more closely to physical plan targets than to profits. This process may be temporary, a response to shortages caused by taut planning, or even reflect an inherent instability in the 'devolved-centralised model'. The recentralisation may, however, be reinforced by the greater emphasis on central party control apparent since the Eighth Party Congress.[13]

With the reversal of the Czechoslovak reform in 1969, Hungary is the only Comecon country to have the decentralised planning system with a regulated market mechanism. The NEM fits into the pattern of market socialism advocated by reformers throughout Eastern Europe: the market is to be used as a way of attaining central goals more efficiently. The centre is to retain control over the total of fixed investment in the economy and the share to be directed to a few specific growth areas and to major areas of social investment such as housing; the rest is to be distributed by market forces.

Central planning of supply has been abandoned, as have production plans for the enterprises. The enterprise now acts as both customer and supplier in the market, and competition has been encouraged, although the high concentration of industry in Hungary has made this largely oligopolistic. Plans are given to Ministries and their departments, but these are not binding. Prices are, in principle, allowed to fluctuate in response to supply and demand, but in fact it appears that price control has been exercised rather more tightly than originally envisaged. The state monopoly of foreign trade has been abandoned, and steps have been taken to tie the Hungarian economy into the world market.[14]

The NEM differs from the Soviet and GDR reforms in making a wholehearted attempt to harness the market to the attainment of centrally-determined goals. But while successful, the NEM has not so far functioned as well as the advocates of the regulated market mechanism had suggested. As Table 1 indicates, the Hungarian economy has not shown an increased potential for economic growth. Its performance in recent years is not markedly better than in the pre-reform period; it is not strikingly better than that of its main rival, the New Economic System in the GDR; nor is it as good as that of Czechoslovakia where the reform was largely abandoned and economic decision-making recentralised in 1969.

Of course, many factors other than the system of planning and administration contribute to — and hinder — economic growth; but one American economist, after a study of the NEM, has concluded that

> 'it is quite possible that other socialist countries will follow the example of the Hungarian reforms; but they will not be able to make this decision on the basis of the demonstrated success or failure of the new Hungarian system. Rather, I feel that other socialist counties will have no basis except that of ideology on which to decide whether to follow the Hungarian model.'[15]

This suggests that, from the economic point of view, the regulated market mechanism has not proved its superiority over the alternative approach to reform.

Although the NEM attempts to make use of the market, there are several political constraints which prevent market rationality from being fully realised. These constraints can be summarised as follows: the level of unemployment which will be tolerated will be much lower than in capitalist countries; little pressure may be put on workers or managers to change their place of work or to alter their skills; rapid increases in the prices of consumer goods are unacceptable; there must be no sudden turnover of management personnel. This last constraint has been observed in order to prevent the creation of a group of managers opposed to the reform. The other constraints may be seen as springing from the socialist commitment of the party and state, and also from the fear of popular, and in particular working-class, unrest in the face of unemployment or inflation. The Hungarian leadership has attempted to maintain security of employment by price control aimed at ensuring an excess of demand over supply for most products, and by a system of differential subsidies which allow marginal firms to continue to operate.[16] At the November 1972 plenum of the Party Central Committee steps were taken to control prices and to raise the wages of manual workers. Central control has thus been exercised to ensure that the operation of the market does not jeopardise certain strongly held social and political values.

Although the market functions within constraints which safeguard important socialist values, it also creates pressure for the removal of those constraints in order to allow market rationality freer rein. The reformers have argued that it is precisely this predominance of social and political values that distinguishes the socialist market. Thus Brus:

> 'a society which consciously constructs a mechanism for the functioning of its economy chooses between different combinations

of direct and market forms of allocation, and subordinates
commodity relations to autonomously defined goals and criteria
of rationality.'[17]

But it must be asked who makes this conscious choice, and who
defines the goals and the criteria of rationality. The constraints on the
operation of the market are presumably not immutable; and it may
perhaps be doubted whether the goodwill and ideological commitment
of the party and state bureaucracies are sufficient to maintain them.
A more effective safeguard might be provided if the workers themselves
had the power to prevent unemployment, job insecurity and higher
prices from being introduced in the name of economic efficiency. The
December 1970 strikes and unrest in the Polish Baltic ports, which
were sparked off by an increase in food prices, serve as a warning to
the political leaders of the other Eastern European states.[18] But the
very fact that they occurred indicates that the workers did not have
control over those who ruled in their name.

Economic Reform and Political Change

Economic reform is sometimes portrayed as an encounter between
economic rationality and totalitarianism. The bureaucracy, it is
claimed, opposes the introduction of the market, which would
allocate resources more rationally than the plan, because the market
would weaken its control over social and economic activity. This
argument, as the Hungarian reform suggests, is simplistic. But
it does point to two important issues: the definition of economic
rationality, and the political characteristics of the different economic
mechanisms.

Many Eastern European economists have accepted the argument
that without a market there can be no equilibrium prices and
consequently no rational basis for economic calculation, and
proposals have been made, and some steps taken, towards the
introduction of prices, rent, interest and profit as instruments of
economic administration. It does not follow from this that interest,
rent and profits should be paid to individuals as income; they should
accrue, the reformers argue, to the central state administration or to
the enterprise, there to be allocated in the general social interest. In
spite of its usefulness this concept of rationality is a narrow one since it
is linked to the idea of an economic equilibrium which is determined
by the forces operating in the market at any given time. It does not
concern itself with the equity of income distribution or with
economic growth; nor does it deal with the macroeconomic
problems of coping with unemployment and inflation.

The restricted nature of this concept of economic rationality has been recognised by many students of Soviet economic development.
It has been argued that rationality in economics has two meanings: optimal resource allocation within a given socioeconomic framework, without assuming any goals other than efficient functioning of the economy; and the economically most efficient way of achieving goals which are set from outside the economic system.[19] It is not necessary, for example, to assume that the Stalinist policy of industrialisation was carried through in the most efficient (or humane) manner to accept that market rationality was not central to a policy which involved profound discontinuous structural changes in the economy. Once the structural transformation has taken place, the question of efficient resource allocation within a stable socioeconomic framework reasserts itself: hence the concern with market rationality.

But even within a stable socioeconomic framework the socialist state will want to subordinate the market to particular social and political goals. Economic rationality cannot therefore be divorced from the social system as a whole or from the structure of political power. Godelier goes so far as to argue that

> 'the economic optimum is not the maximum possible use of the factors of production, but the use of these factors that is best adjusted to the functioning of the society's structure ... The intentional rationality of the economic behaviour of a society's members is thus always governed by the fundamental rationality of the hierarchical structure of social realtions that characterise this society. There is therefore no such thing as economic rationality "in itself", nor any "model" of economic rationality.'[20]

While this is no doubt true, it would be a mistake to suppose that the structure of a complex industrial society — and in particular of a society in transition between capitalism and socialism — is so firmly fixed and so cohesive that no tension will arise between the search for efficiency and the desire to maintain social and political values. The different systems of economic planning and administration cannot be seen solely as organisational and technical instruments for the attainment of policy goals; their political characteristics must also be taken into account.

Kornai has argued that the centralised planning system is a 'coherent, unified mechanism' which generates particular types of authoritarian social and political behaviour.[21] The 'excessive use of instructions', he claims creates a tendency for economic administrators to lose all enthusiasm for their work, and leads also to arbitrary and despotic behaviour towards subordinates. This behaviour has as its corollaries political apathy and a lack of initiative in the society at large. Kornai argues, moreover, that the centralised planning system tends to generate harmful uncontrolled processes — for example in managerial behaviour — which can be prevented and punished only by administrative methods. If the infringements are not punished, instructions will lose their power to regulate economic activity; consequently the central bureaucracy resorts to coercion to enforce its instructions. Some reformers have seen in economic reform a way of shifting the methods of government from an administrative to an economic basis and thus reducing the reliance on force as a means of attaining political goals.

Hungarian experience suggests that the introduction of the market mechanism has important political consequences. Economic activity is regulated by economic rather than administrative methods; consequently the use of coercion in economic administration is reduced. The decentralisation of decision-making creates pressure for institutional change. The greater autonomy of the enterprise, for example, alters the relationship between management and labour. The incentive system encourages the manager to seek higher profits because these affect his income directly; the workers, however, have no direct interest in higher profits, but do want higher wages. Now that the manager has greater autonomy the bargaining process has been brought into the enterprise, and this has created pressure for the trade unions to adopt a new role in industrial relations.[22]

The market also generates social behaviour contrary to socialist values. The NEM, for example, has given birth to *Nepmen* who have been able to engage in profitable trade. The government has attacked the private and cooperative enterprises, which grew up under the reform, for 'money-grubbing' and has curbed their activities on the grounds that they presented unfair competition to the state enterprises. Under the NEM income differentials have widened as a result of private and cooperative trading and of the new emphasis on material incentives. These differentials have created dissatisfaction among the workers which the party leadership has sought to counteract by modifying the incentive system and raising wages. The state thus acquires a new role in arbitrating between competing pressures.

Although the adoption of the devolved-centralised model brings some move from administrative to economic instruments of management, it does not have such far-reaching consequences, precisely because it does not mark a fundamental change in the system of planning and administration. But while the introduction of the market mechanism has social consequences which are politically important, it does not lead directly to political reform. Decentralisation

of economic decision-making does not constitute a political
programme, and it is now necessary to look at the way in which
the problem of ensuring democratic control over the system of
economic planning and administration has been treated in the
theory and practice of political reform.

Political Models of Socialism

It is a paradox of Eastern European development that Marxism-
Lenninism, committed in principle to the withering away of the state,
has inspired the development of immense state power. Khrushchev
encouraged greater voluntary participation in local government, and
this was presented as a step towards self-administration, but the
power of the central bureaucracy was little affected.[23] The three most
important political blueprints or models in state socialism at present
are the technocratic, the democratic socialist and the self-management
models. These are different from the models of economic planning and
administration already discussed since, as their names imply, they do
not all address themselves to the same issues; and for this reason they
are not necessarily incompatible. Moreover, although there is historical
experience which can help in assessing the models, they must be seen
as blueprints rather than as reforms already implemented.

The technocratic model: This seeks to realise, with the aid of cybernetics
and computer technology, the ideal of universal and all-embracing
control which Trotsky attributed to the Stalinist bureaucracy. It has
been influential in the Soviet Union, the German Democratic Republic
and Czechoslovakia.[24] In the Soviet Union it goes under the name
'scientific management of society', and its influence is attested by
the claim that

> 'the view of society as a complex cybernetic system with a
> multidimensional network of direct and feedback links and
> a mechanism of optimisation, functioning towards a set goal,
> is increasingly gaining prestige as the main theoretical idea of the
> "technology" of managing society.'[25]

The government of Soviet society has been portrayed in terms of
the interaction between two subsystems in the society — the controlling
or governing subsystem (the state and voluntary organisations led by
the Communist Party) and the controlled or governed subsystem
(the economy, science and other social activities). The essence of
government lies in such conscious, purposive activity by the controlling
subsystem as will ensure that social processes develop in an optimal

way. Scientific government requires that information about the state of the system be transmitted to the political institutions, that it be processed there into commands or decisions, that these be transmitted to the controlled subsystem, and that the loop be closed by feedback about the effect of the decisions or commands.

There are two crucial elements here: the policy-making process, and the control or administrative apparatus. The growing complexity of social and economic processes, along with the experience of Stalinist 'voluntarism' and Khrushchev's 'subjectivism', impels the search for improved decision-making. The cyberneticians argue that systems analysis, operations research and programming techniques will make it possible to come closer to the Marxist-Leninist ideal of scientific policy-making. They argue also that the principles of cybernetics — the science of control and communication — will help in the construction of hierarchical, multi-level administrative apparatuses which will enhance central direction of social and economic development. Complete centralisation of decision-making, which some cyberneticians initially saw as within their grasp, was soon realised to be impossible: the centre could not conceivably cope with the data which would need to be processed in drawing up disaggregated plans. The technocratic model seeks thus to restructure the information flows and decision-making points in the administrative machinery in order to ensure effective central control; it seeks also to improve the decision-making process to ensure that this control will be optimal.

Economic cybernetics is the most developed aspect of the technocratic model. Indeed the 'scientific management of society' school may be seen as a generalisation of the cybernetic approach to economic planning and administration — or rather, of the cybernetic approaches, for it is not possible to point to a single school of thought.[26] The optimal planning school, which is attempting to formulate proposals for an 'optimally functioning economic system', seeks to combine plan and market, to allow the market to operate at the microlevel in order to provide a basis for planners' evaluations and allocation decisions. But the favoured form of technocratic rationalisation at present is to integrate automated management information systems into the existing system, without a fundamental change in pricing or supply policy.

The extension of the cybernetic model into social management springs from a realisation that the economic system is part of the wider social system. Its successful functioning therefore depends on knowledge about, and control over, social relationships in order, for instance, to devise an effective incentive system. Social research has thus been advocated, and to some extent employed, as an adjunct

of government, for example in social policy and political education.
Moreover, some sociologists seem to suggest that, by analogy with the
market, social self-regulation should be allowed in some areas of
social life. In other words, there is advocacy of a shift from direct to
parametric control in economic and social life. This view, however,
has not been officially adopted.

The technocratic model is essentially an attempt to enable
the state to use the immense power it possesses in a controlled and
effective way. The model is congruent with the Marxist-Leninist
concept of policy-making that has developed in the Soviet Union.
In both there is an emphasis on control and management; both are
purposive and goal-oriented; both claim to be in some sense scientific;
both underline the need for a systemic or wholistic approach;
the one seeks correct policies, the other optimal solutions; the one
stresses democratic centralism, the other the hierarchical nature of
control systems. But insofar as the cyberneticians propose new
methods of government — a shift from administrative to economic
instruments, for example — they argue for a change in the mode of
bureaucratic rule. The cybernetic concept provides an ideological
justification for bureaucratic rule insofar as this is rule by the
competent and the technically qualified. At the same time, if
technocratic rationalisation is to take place, existing arrangements
have to be criticised and new proposals made. The technocratic model
legitimises the Soviet system as a whole, in the process of proposing
partial reforms, precisely by pointing to the possibilities that the
system offers for scientific and rational government. There has,
nevertheless, been opposition to some of the proposals put forward
under the technocratic model, both on the grounds that they would
not work, and lest, if implemented, they undermine the party's leading
role in society. In the GDR the emphasis on cybernetics and the
scientific-technical revolution has been greatly reduced since the
Eight Party Congress in 1971, and the role of the party and the
working class correspondingly stressed.[27]

The technocratic model is an attempt primarily to rationalise
the existing system of political relationships, not to change it. The
cyberneticians present themselves as heirs to the Leninist tradition,
and claim that they are using the achievements of the scientific-
technical revolution in the interests of efficient administration. They
have not made any public proposals about the way in which the
central political institutions work, although new decision-making
techniques might be expected to require some changes. Nor have
they raised the questions of accountability and democratic control.
Nevertheless, the technocratic model cannot be wholly isolated from
such questions as: who defines the criteria of optimality; what kinds

of different interests exist in society and how are these accounted for in policy-making; can an incentive system be so constructed that people will behave 'rationally' in accordance with state interests; what is the role of the specialist in policy-making? But discussion of these issues is severely restricted, for it might serve to weaken rather than to strengthen bureaucratic control. Unless these questions are answered in favour of democratic control, even a super-efficient administrative apparatus will be essentially bureaucratic, albeit with new forms of domination and new bases of legitimacy; it will develop, and attempt to realise, its own aims and interests in opposition to those of other groups and classes in society.

The democratic socialist model. The democratic ideas which underlay the Czechoslovak reform movement had their origin in the intellectual, cultural and political traditions of Czechoslovakia, and the political crisis of the mid-1960s enabled them to find expression. It was widely held in the reform movement that the democratic values of European civilisation, which Czechoslovakia, unlike Russia, had inherited, should be translated into reality. The tragedy of socialism was, in many eyes, that a socialist revolution had first taken place in a society as economically and culturally backward as Russia.

During the reform period various political blueprints and proposals were put forward which sought to show how a socialist society could safeguard democratic values, in particular the rights of the individual before the state, and the right of different interests to be heard.[28] The premise was generally accepted that a socialist society like Czechoslovakia is not *ipso facto* democratic, and that consequently democracy must be worked for and sustained by institutional arrangements in the political system. It was accepted further that although socialism had abolished the fundamental contradiction of capitalist society — that between capital and labour — a socialist society is not monolithic and the variety of interests in it should be recognised. It did not follow from this that the different interests should be permitted to express themselves through different political parties, but it was argued that institutional arrangements be created which would allow the different interests to be pursued.

The political model of democratic socialism was not fully worked out in the reform period, but its main lines, and the major practical problems facing it, became clear. In the documents prepared for, and presented to, the 14th Party Congress in August 1968 it was declared that

'the previous system by which monopolistic centres
of political power were formed through the fusion of Party and

State organs has been rocked to its foundations. This is in general accord with the needs of society, for under the old system there was a very inadequate impact on the decision-making process of the various interests, needs and opinions of different groups, even though the structure of society was already socialist; and scientific and professional analyses of problems earned equally short shrift. Indeed, the old system led to arbitrary decisions and to a progressive accumulation of unsolved disputes — economic, social and political — between groups. If we are to avoid a return to that state of affairs, a prospect which would provoke domestic political conflict in itself, we must evolve a qualitatively new political system.'[29]

The main object of the new system was to ensure that social minorities could express their wishes, while also ensuring that no political decision, and in particular no decision affecting the structure of power, could be taken against the wishes of the largest section of society — 'the industrial, agricultural and other groups of the "working masses"'.

The National Front, which comprises several small political parties besides the Communist Party and voluntary organisations such as the trade unions, would become the forum for policy-making by agreement between the different interests. These interests were to be expressed through parliamentary elections in which the voter would be presented with a list of candidates nominated by the member organisations of the National Front, and the Front would then form a government in accordance with with the results. The government would always be a coalition, for there was to be no competition for power, in the sense of parties presenting alternative platforms. The National Front would have a monopoly of political power and the right to expel parties or organisations which did not adhere to its common programme. The Parliament was to be multicameral, with the main chamber elected by universal suffrage, and three additional chambers: an Industrial Chamber, elected by factories and commercial enterprises, an Agricultural Chamber elected by collective and state farms, and a Social Services Chamber elected by institutions concerned with public health, education, culture and so on. This was to be the arrangement at both federal and national levels — for federation was one of the enduring achievements of the reform movement — but the details were not worked out. It was envisaged that the Parliamentary system should eventually be tied into the system of workers' self-management which was then in the process of being created.

The most difficult problem which the political reformers faced was how to reconcile the 'leading and directing role' of the Communist Party with the new democratic structures that they

wished to create. Some form of separation of powers was required
to prevent the concentration of power in a few hands. An independent
judiciary — and a downgrading of the state security organs — would
be necessary if the legal guarantees for such civil and democratic rights
as freedom of speech and association were to be enforced. Judicial
review would be required to ensure that legislation conform to the
new Constitution that it was intended to introduce. State and public
bodies should be able to maintain their independence from the
Communist Party if they were not to become its mere instruments.
If all these conditions were met, as it was intended they should be,
the Party's role would have to undergo a drastic change, for it
would have to operate 'in a political system in which administrative
management by command had ceased to be the main method of
deciding things'. The party would have to lead by example and persuasion
rather than by coercion and such administrative methods as control
over appointments.

The party's internal structure was not immune from the current
of political reform, and the draft party statutes prepared for the
14th Party Congress were an attempt to adapt the party to the new
conditions in which it would have to work.[30] Democratic centralism
was to remain, but minorities were to be given certain rights: a minority
could have their own views published along with the decision of the
majority; even after a decision had been taken the minority would have
the right to continue to advocate their views and demand renewed
discussion; the rights of minorities were to be respected as long as they
did not act in contravention of the party's statutes and programme, and
as long as they did not form themselves into factions, i.e. organised
groups. An attempt was to be made to improve control by party
members over the party apparatus and thus ensure greater inner-party
democracy. Moreover, no individual was to be allowed to hold several
political and economic positions at once, and in accordance with the
'rotation of cadres' no one — with certain exceptions — could stand
for election to the same office more than twice. The draft statutes can
be seen as trying to prevent excessive centralisation and concentration
of power within the party.

It was of course conceivable that the party would not be able
to exercise its leading role in the new political system. There were two
main lines of thought amongst the reformers on this question: one
group wished to use various institutional means to prevent the
Communist Party from finding itself in a minority, while others
envisaged a pluralist system in which the party would have to compete
with other socialist parties for political power. The authors of the
documents prepared for the 14th Congress wanted to institutionalise
the party's hegemony for a transitional period of five years, by

ensuring that the National Front continue to provide the framework for political organisation, and that the party retain its dominance over the Front. The new Constitution which was to be introduced in 1970 or 1971 would take account of the political experience of 1969 and 1970 in deciding on the structure of the political system. Two alternative schemes were envisaged. If the multiparty system within the National Front were to develop in such a way as to form a practical alternative to the Communist hegemony, the concept of the National Front as outlined above would be retained. If, on the other hand, the interest-group organisations and the idea of self-management were more influential, it would be possible to have the free formation of parties in accordance with criteria laid down in the new Constitution. Neither of these alternatives was at all clearly specified. The former seems to suggest a combination of one-party rule and multi-party pluralism, the latter a combination of one-party rule and self--government. The reform movement, however, never had the opportunity to try to resolve these ambivalences and dilemmas. And the invasion suggests that the Soviet leaders did not believe that the Czechoslovak reformers could achieve their reform goals without destroying the leading and directing role of the party.

The Hungarian reformers appear to have drawn the 'appropriate conclusions' from the invasion. Their reform has been carried through without any serious crisis in bureaucratic rule, and the party (the Hungarian Socialist Workers' Party HSWP) has made clear its determination to retain its leading and directing role in society. Nevertheless the introduction of the regulated market does create pressure for a change in the style of government. The decentralisation of decision-making leads to new social relationships — for example, between industrial managers and the state, and between managers and labour — which require a new approach to government. Thus:

> 'what kind of government do we consider a good government? Should it be conceived as a power factor acting as an initiator, a generator feeding new ideas into society with due regard to the changes that are taking place in the world and in society? Or should the government be considered rather as a balancing power helping to produce compromise permitting the confrontation of conflicting interests — achieving agreement eventually by arbitration? . . . The former type of government serves development in the first place, the second type ensures [social and economic] equilibrium. The present Hungarian government combines these types. It lays equal stress on initiative and equilibrium.'[31]

This has involved an attempt to combine the leading role of the party
with new methods of administration. The new style of government
has been summarised thus: the recognition that problems can be
solved in different ways and that the alternative solutions should be
clearly formulated; research into new ways of administering social
activities; increased attention to the interests of groups affected by
policy decisions; greater attention to public opinion — and more
active efforts to influence it; a more important role for legislation
and parliamentary committees.[32] The policy decisions taken at the
November 1972 plenary session of the Party Central Committee
reflect this style; so too do the new electoral and local government
laws, and the 1972 Constitution. These latter make small steps
towards firmer legal guarantees for civil rights, greater autonomy
in local government, and the freer expression of individual and group
interests (thus a choice of candidates is presented in local and
national elections, although the party doubtless exerts informal
pressure on the selection procedure).

Many of the Czechoslovak reformers saw a logical connection
between economic and political reform, and some went as far as to
argue that economic reform could not be successful without
political reform. The Hungarian experience suggests the contrary
(and the NEM is very close to the Czechoslovak reform): economic
reform can be carried through as long as bureaucratic control is not
destroyed and no threat thus presented to the other bureaucratic
regimes in Eastern Europe.

The self-management model. Workers' self-management, the most
distinctive feature of Yugoslav socialism, was long regarded in Eastern
Europe as taboo. The Hungarian and Polish uprisings of 1956 had
thrown up workers' councils spontaneously, but these had been
deprived of any effective power as the situation was 'normalised'.
With the move towards economic reform, however, the Yugoslav
experience came to be seen as something to be studied if not
emulated. Those who saw in the decentralisation of economic
decision-making an opportunity to democratise political power
pointed to the possibilities it offered for workers' participation in
industrial management. If the enterprise were given autonomy, it
was argued, management decisions would have a greater effect on the
workers' wages and welfare; workers should therefore be given a
voice in the management of their enterprises. Furthermore, it was
seen that workers' participation in industrial management would help
to strengthen the autonomy of the enterprise *vis-à-vis* the central
bureaucracy.

The Action Programme adopted by the Czechoslovak Communist

Party in April, 1968 declared the need for 'democratic organs' in the enterprise, now that the latter had been given autonomy under the economic reform.[33] In June, 1968 a provisional framework was published which set out principles for the establishment of workers' councils. They were to be elected by all the employees and to have between ten and thirty members, depending on the size of the enterprise. Most members would be elected from among the employees but enterprise specialists would be included, as would experts from outside, for example from banks or technical institutes. The council would elect the manager who would nominate his own deputies. In most matters the council could do little more than approve or make recommendations about the plans and measures that the manager was bound to submit to it; but the recommendations could eventually be turned down. The manager, it was stressed, would still run the enterprise, determine the production programme, control personnel policy, and could be dismissed by the council only in exceptional circumstances. Preparatory committees were required to work out their own programme and election rules. By June 1968 there were three hundred councils and three hundred preparatory committees in the seven hundred largest enterprises in Czechoslovakia. Not all the enterprises adhered to the principles in the framework, and some were more ambitious in moving towards self-management. In June 1969, however, economic decision-making was recentralised and the Husak leadership, under pressure from Moscow, began to press for the disbandment of the councils; this was completed by early 1970.

The workers' councils in Czechoslovakia did not spring up spontaneously, but were introduced on the initiative of the reform movement's leaders. Workers' participation was to be combined with the principle of professional, technically competent management. Many reformers had opposed self-management until early 1968 on the grounds that it would weaken managerial competence and sacrifice long-term growth to demands for immediate wage increases. But by early 1968 workers' councils seemed to be the most helpful and reliable bulwark against the reassertion of central bureaucratic control over the enterprise, and provided a way of enlisting working-class support for the reform movement. After August the councils became a focus of resistance to the occupation forces. Workers' councils have not been introduced in Hungary where managers are still appointed by the state, and central control over industrial management thus retained.

The Czechoslovak experiment was too short-lived to provide a basis for assessing workers' councils, but the Yugoslav experience suggests that, while it may help to foster democratic and participatory attitudes and provide a counterweight to the central bureaucracy, workers' self-management has not led to the radical redistribution of power expected of it and has not given the workers control over the development of the economy. Workers' councils were created in Yugoslavia in 1950, two years after the split with the Soviet Union and expulsion from the Cominform, in order to prevent the growth of a bureaucratic centralist state of the Stalinist type. Only subsequently was the market introduced, on the grounds that self-management without enterprise autonomy had little meaning. The tension between centripetal and centrifugal forces in the Yugoslav economy has been greatly exacerbated by the disparities of development between north and south, and by the sharp rivalries between the various national groups in the Federation. Central direction of economic policy was weakened by the 1965 reform, which marked a victory for the decentralisers. The economic and political crisis of recent years reflects the failure of the state and the League of Communists to act as an integrative force in Yugoslav society; whether the new and highly complex Constitution will succeed in alleviating social and political tensions remains to be seen.

The workers' councils, which may contain from fifteen to over one hundred members depending on the size of the enterprise, are elected by secret ballot of all the employees in an enterprise; all employees can stand for election, and a choice of candidates is normally available. Membership is for two years, with half the members elected each year, and no member is supposed to serve for more than two consecutive terms. The council elects a management board, which acts as an executive body, and appoints and dismisses the director. In principle the council establishes the main lines of policy, and the management board translates these into specific decisions which the director then carries out; but in practice the director and management board may be the source of initiative and work through the council. The council may concern itself with all aspects of management, and has broad decision-making powers: it approves production, wage and marketing policies and plans; it approves statutes about the organisation and work of the enterprise; it decides how earnings are to be distributed between wages and investment. Under the new Constitution it will have the right to determine the specific projects in which money is to be invested. The formal powers of the workers' councils have thus been steadily increased.

Nonetheless it has been clearly acknowledged in the discussions which preceded the drawing up of the new Constitution that within the enterprise the informal power of the managers and technical experts has grown markedly, thus belying the increase in the councils' formal powers. A recent Yugoslav study of strikes pointed out that in

the years 1960-70 there was a clear tendency for the relative
representation of workers in the formal centres of power to decline,
and that, moreover, the actual influence of workers on
decision-making in these centres is significantly lower than their level
of formal representation would suggest.[34] The vision of the self-
managed enterprise as a highly integrated and democratic organisation
has not become reality. It has been argued that

> the self-managing organs accepted full responsibility for all
> essential decisions without having an appropriate specialised
> knowledge or the social power needed for exerting this
> responsibility; and thus they increasingly changed into a
> facade for the leading group which — hidden behind the self-
> managing organs — were more or less irresponsibly managing
> the whole enterprise.[35]

It appears therefore that workers' self-management has not had the
revolutionary social consequences expected for it, and to a greater
or lesser degree serves to mask disparities in power rather than to
eradicate them.

Workers' councils are not to be dismissed out of hand as ineffectual
instruments of democratic power, but they cannot transcend the
environment in which they exist. In a market economy like that of
Yugoslavia the enterprise must try to operate profitably and take
the consequences if it fails. Workers' self-management can alleviate
the pains of redundancy, job insecurity and unemployment in a
market economy, but it cannot abolish them. In the decentralised
model with a regulated market mechanism the market functions
within a framework which is decided at the centre; and
consequently if workers are to control the economy and economic
policy, it is at the centre that they must exercise power. In such a case
self-management may be desirable but it is less important than
exercising influence on central decisions, and this is very clear, for
example, in the case of the Hungarian reform. It can be argued,
moreover, that the market breeds commodity fetishism: social and
economic relationships become competitive rather than cooperative,
and social and economic forces come to be seen as outside human or
social control. If the workers are directly involved in competitive
relations through self-management in the market, their solidarity will
be undermined and their power fragmented. There is therefore a case
for saying that trade unions are more effective instruments of
working class power than self-management bodies, because they create
at least some working class solidarity and make it possible to
influence decisions at the centre.

Conclusion

The period of economic reform is a most important stage in the development of state socialism. It involves, as Lange pointed out, a difficult process of adjustment by the political institutions to new economic conditions. It has been associated with the abandonment of some of the methods of Stalinist rule, and with the search for new forms of rule and new bases of legitimacy. Although economic reform can be seen as a shift in the methods of government, it has not led, as many expected, to fundamental political change. Where the political reformers have made any progress, it has been because of a crisis in bureaucratic rule which has opened the way for new ideas, interests and forces to come into play. Such crises may or may not spring from the process of economic reform, and it cannot of course be assumed that in such a crisis it is only democratic forces that will be effective, for nationalist or even racist ideas might triumph, or the army stage a *coup d'etat*.

Nevertheless the process of economic reform brings out some of the tensions and contradictions of bureaucratic rule. All the reforms have granted a greater role to technical expertise, and the technically expert, in economic management. But the experience in Hungary, Czechoslovakia and Poland suggests that workers have been far from enthusiastic about economic reform, seeing in it a relative worsening of their own position. In certain circumstances, bureaucratic resistance to reform may bring about a political alignment between workers and groups in the technical intelligentsia, as happened in Czechoslovakia. In Hungary too there have been attempts to fashion an alliance between workers and intellectuals to press for democratisation. But there is no reason to suppose that this kind of alliance is inevitable, and reformed bureaucratic rule, once established, may find strong social bases of support. Unless there is fundamental political change in the Soviet Union, Soviet hegemony in Eastern Europe is likely to prevent the emergence of anything akin to the democratic socialism envisaged by the Czechoslovak reformers. Consequently reform will tend to move in two directions: towards a form of bureaucratic rule responsive to pluralism, satisfying consumer demands, and oriented towards a social and political equilibrium; or towards a more technocratic, authoritarian rule in which the party may attempt to strengthen its support amongst the working class in order to provide some counterweight to technocratic groups.

The discussion and implementation of economic reform suggests that the most important political question is not whether greater use of the market mechanism under central control amounts to a restoration of capitalism, but whether or not the economic mechanism is under democratic control. The discussion and implementation of reform can be interpreted as a change in the methods of bureaucratic rule, rather than as a fundamental shift in power relationships. A change in the methods of rule is itself important; and the reform discussions point to some of the basic problems of state socialism. Centralisation of economic power makes easier the assertion of bureaucratic control over state-owned resources, while the decentralisation of economic power in a market economy generates pressure for the establishment of private claims over socially owned resources, and might deprive the state of the power to control economic activity.

No solution has been found to the problem of exercising democratic control over a powerful state apparatus, of ensuring that it does not degenerate into a bureaucracy with aims and interests of its own. Hegedüs has proposed that existing institutions such as party control, the trade unions and works' committees be reactivated, that officials be moved more frequently, and a democratic climate fostered;[36] and similar demands were put forward by the Polish shipyard workers in 1971.[37] But these measures would run up against the problems which the Czechoslovak reformers faced in redefining the role of the party and arranging for the representation of interests. The problem remains of creating a political infrastructure — a socialist civil society — in which different groups and organisations, including the party, could act to control a powerful administrative apparatus in the interests of the members of society, without being appropriated by the state and converted into instruments of bureaucratic rule.

Notes

1. By Eastern Europe I mean the Soviet Union, Poland, the German Democratic Republic, Hungary, Czechoslovakia, Rumania and Bulgaria. I have not attempted to describe or assess developments in all these countries, but have concentrated on the first five in order to provide a general picture of the theory and practice of reform. Nor have I discussed Yugoslav development, except with reference to self-management.
2. Hegedüs (1970), p.30.
3. This argument is well put forward by Samu (1966).
4. See Marx's comment that 'in bureaucracy the identity of state interests and particular private objectives if formulated in such a way that state interests become a particular private objective, in opposition to other private objectives'.
5. Over 90 per cent of the national income (produced) in all but one of the Eastern European countries is produced by the socialised sector. The exception is Poland, where the figure is about 75 per cent, because

agricultural land is still largely in private hands. See Wilczynski (1972), p.3.
6. See Brus (1972), pp.62-88; Kornai (1959); Nove (1965); Dobb (1970); Kosta *et al* (1973).
7. Brus (1972), p.87.
8. Quoted by Ellman (1971), p.60.
9. Lange (1970), p.88.
10. See Brus (1973), p.7.
11. See Nove (1965), chs. 2 and 7.
12. For a comprehensive discussion see Katz (1973).
13. See Sheren (1973); Broll (1973); Thomas (1972); Freier and Lieber (1973).
14. Granick (1973); Nove (1972).
15. Granick (1973), p.428.
16. Granick (1973), p.417.
17. Brus (1973), p.55
18. See Polish Workers (1972).
19. Nove (1965), pp.155, 309.
20. Godelier (1972), p.99.
21. Kornai (1959), pp. 199-214.
22. Robertson (1973); Bognar (1972).
23. See Churchward (1968), ch.12.
24. See for example, Afanas'ev (1967); Klaus (1965); and Richta (1966).
25. Berg (1967), p.303.
26. See Ellman (1971); Hardt (1967).
27. Thomas (1972), pp.24-6.
28. See Kusin (1971); Golan (1971 and 1973); Bystrina in Kusin ed. (1971); Remington (1969).
29. Pelikán (1971), pp.221-2.
30. Pelikán (1971), pp.128-86.
31. Bognár (1970), p.27.
32. Ibid.
33. See Pelikán (1973); Pravda (1973); Golan (1973).
34. Jovanov (1973), p.34.
35. Rus (1967), p.208.
36. Hegedüs (1970), pp.55-6.
37. Amongst the strikers' demands were: the return of food prices to the pre-December 1970 level; legal elections to trade-union posts and to the Workers' Councils, and democratic elections in the Party and youth organisations; full pay for workers for the period of the strike; honest information on the political and economic situation of the shipyards and the country as a whole; an end to the harassment and arrest of strikers by the security services. See Polish Workers (1972).

Select Bibliography

Afanas'ev, V.G.   *Nauchnoe upravlenie obshchestvom*, Moscow, 1967.
Berg, A.I. ed.   *Kibernetiku – na sluzhbu kommunizmu*, vol. 5, Moscow, 1967.

Bognár, Jozsef	'Initiative and Equilibrium. Major political and economic issues in Hungary'. *The New Hungarian Quarterly*, 1970, vol. XI, no.37.
	Economic Reform, Development and Stability in the Hungarian Economy, in *The New Hungarian Quarterly*, 1972, vol.13, no.46,
Bröll, Werner	*Die Wirtschaft der DDR*, Gunter Olzog Verlag, Munich and Vienna, 1973
Brus, Wlodzimierz	*The Market in a Socialist Economy*, Routledge and Kegan Paul, London, 1972.
	The Economics and Politics of Socialism, Routledge and Kegan Paul, London, 1973.
Churchward, L.G.	*Contemporary Soviet Government*, Routledge and Kegan Paul, London, 1968.
Dobb, Maurice	*Socialist Planning, Some Problems*, Lawrence and Wishart, 1970.
Ellman, Michael	*Soviet Planning Today. Proposals for an Optimally Functioning Economic System*, Cambridge UP, Cambridge, 1971.
Freier, Udo and Lieber Paul	*Politische Okonomie der DDR*, Makol Verlag, Frankfurt-am-Main, 1973.
Godelier, Maurice	*Rationality and Irrationality in Economics*, NLB, London, 1972.
Golan, Galia	*The Czechoslovak Reform Movement. Communism in Crisis, 1962-68*, Cambridge UP, London, 1971.
	Reform Rule in Czechoslovakia. The Dubcek Era, 1968-69, Cambridge UP, London, 1973.
Granick, David	'The Hungarian Economic Reform', *World Politics*, 1973, vol. XXV, no. 3, April.
Hardt, John P. *et al*	*Mathematics and Computers in Soviet Economic Planning*, Yale UP, New Haven and London, 1967.
Hegedüs, Andras	'Marxist Theories of Leadership and Bureaucracy', in R. Barry Farrell (ed.) *Political Leadership in Eastern Europe and the Soviet Union*, Butterworths, London, 1970
Jovanov, Neca	'Odnos strajka kao drustvenog sukoba i samoupravljanja kao drustvenog sistema', in *Revija za sociologiju*, 1973, 1-2.
Katz, Abraham	*The Politics of Economic Reform in the Soviet Union*, Praeger, New York and London, 1972.
Klaus, Georg	*Kybernetik und Gesellschaft*, Berlin, 1965.
Kornai, Janos	*Overcentralization in Economic Administration*, Oxford University Press, 1959.
Kosta, Jiri *et al*	*Warenproduktion in Sozialismus*, Fischer Taschenbuck Verlag, Frankfurt-am-Main, 1973.
Kusin, Vladimir V.	*The Intellectual Origins of the Prague Spring*, Cambridge UP, Cambridge, 1971.
(ed)	*The Czechoslovak Reform Movement 1968*, International Research Documents, London 1973.

Lange, Oskar	*Papers in Economics and Sociology,* Pergamon Press, Oxford, and Panstwowe Wydawnictwo Naukowe, Warsaw, 1970.
Ludz, Peter Christian	*Parteielite im Wandel,* Westdeutscher Verlag, Köln and Opladen, 1970.
Naor, Jacob	'How Dead is the GDR New Economic System?' in *Soviet Studies,* 1973, vol. 25, no.2, October.
Nove, Alec	*The Soviet Economy,* Allen and Unwin, London, 1965.
	'Economic Reforms in the USSR and Hungary, a Study in Contrasts', in Nove, Alec and Nuti, D.M. (eds.) *Socialist Economics,* Penguin, Harmondsworth, 1972.
Pelikán, Jiri	*The Secret Vysocany Congress. Proceedings and Documents of the Extraordinary Fourteenth Congress of the Communist Party of Czechoslovakia, 22 August 1968,* Allen Lane, The Penguin Press, London, 1971.
	'Workers' Councils in Czechoslovakia', *Critique,* Spring 1973, vo.1, no.1.
Pravda, Alex	'Some Aspects of the Czechoslovak Economic Reform and the Working Class in 1968', *Soviet Studies,* July 1973, vol.XXV, no.1.
Remington, Robin Alison	*Winter in Prague. Documents on Czechoslovak Communism in Crisis,* MIT Press, Cambridge, Mass. and London, 1969.
Richta, Radovan	*Civilizace na Roscesti,* Prague, 1966, the second 1968 edition has appeared in German, *Richta-Report. Politische Ökonomie des 20 Jahrhunderts* (1971), Makol Verlag, Frankfurt-am-Main.
Robertson, Alexander	'Hungarian Economic Reform, *Critique,* 1973, vol. 1, no. 1.
Rus, Veljko	'Institutionalisation of the Revolutionary Movement', in *Praxis* (International Edition) 1967, 2.
Samu, M.	Democratism of the Socialist State and Scientific Leadership in *Annales Universitatis Scientiarum Budapestinensis – Sectio Iuridica – tom. VII*
Sheren, Michael	'The New Economic System in the GDR: An Obituary', in *Soviet Studies,* 1973, vol.24, no. 4, April.
Thomas, Rudiger	*Modell DDR,* Carl Hanser Verlag, Munich, 1972
Wilczynski, J.	*Socialist Economic Development and Reforms,* Macmillan, London, 1972.

'Polish Workers and Party Leaders – A Confrontation'. Document in *New Left Review,* no. 72, 1972.

Table 1 Annual Rates of Growth of National Income Produced. Official Figures.

(Percentages)

	1961	1962	1963	1964	1965	1966
Czechoslovakia	6.8	1.4	−2.2	0.6	3.4	10.2
GDR	3.8	1.4	3.2	4.8	4.4	4.9
Hungary	6.1	4.7	5.7	4.7	1.1	8.4
USSR	6.8	5.7	4.1	9.4	7.0	7.5

	1967	1968	1969	1970	1971	1972
Czechoslovakia	5.2	7.2	7.3	5.5	5.2	5.6
GDR	5.4	5.1	5.2	5.6	4.5	5.8
Hungary	8.7	5.0	8.0	4.9	6.5	Ca 5
USSR	7.0	8.3	4.8	9.0	Ca 6	4

Source: *Economic Survey of Europe*. Various years. United Nations, New York.

6. THE EEC DIMENSION: INTENDED AND UNINTENDED CONSEQUENCES

Richard McAllister

Introduction

'The failure of the State' is not a new refrain in European politics. Without going back any further, it is clear that it played a prominent part in attempts at restructuring Western Europe after the Second World War. The most diverse currents fed this stream, but some basic notions were widely shared. These included the belief that the chaotic economic conditions of much of the inter-war period had been a direct cause of conflict; that economic rearrangement of an 'integrative' kind could bring about desirable and controllable, predictable changes in political attitudes; and that liberalisation of economic activity and economies of scale would in any case provide the surest path to Western European recovery. Certain widely recognised 'failures of the state' were, then, to be rectified by a particular strategy of integration. This chapter begins by looking at what that strategy consisted in, how it evolved, and what expectations were held of it. But it is far from clear that the process so far has had the expected results: even less clear that the projected programme of the Communities will bring about those results. The view has gained currency that no salvation from the present discontents is to be found in Community mechanisms; and even that the dynamic set in train by the Communities may be highly dysfunctional both for national systems and for the Community system itself. These issues are taken up in the latter part of the chapter.

Origins

The Community system as we know it today — in particular the EEC itself — emerged from a period in which many different lines of approach to co-operation in Europe were being put forward. To some extent the strategy pursued by the 'founding fathers' had a positive logic of its own; to some extent it was also a reactive one, a response to the perceived failures or shortcomings of any alternative approach.

The attempts of the 'integrationists' faced certain common problems. For example, there arose the question of whether the new institutions were designed primarily as an answer to demands for increased *efficiency;* or to demands for increased *participation.* Alternatively, they might assume that there was no conflict between such aims. Second, different kinds of institution tended to arouse different kinds of opposition, of blockage, to them. Third, any attempt at 'integration' required some notion both of the scope of the functions which it proposed to shift to a 'European' level, and of the manner by which these shifts should take place. These tend to be common themes, running through all the attempts to produce new machinery; but each attempt was also profoundly influenced by more temporary, contingent, but nonetheless critical factors, which have certainly modified the prospects for the 'European' dimension now.

The prehistory of the 'European movement' well illustrates the recurring problems. In the late 1940s the west Europeans were under maximum external pressure, from both the US and Soviet sides, to 'put their house in order'. It is not clear whether this experience can be held to confirm or disconfirm the alleged importance of 'external elites' in precipitating integration. The Brussels Treaty Organisation (BTO), set up in March 1948, showed the ambivalence of western European governments on the defence front; it was initially a response as much to fear of 'Germany' as of the Soviet Union – a response that was to reappear in the debates over the European Defence Community (EDC) proposal in 1953-4. At all events, the defence aspect began as it has usually continued – under a different organisational hat from the 'economic' aspects. For in the very next month, April 1948, a wider cluster of nations set up the Organisation for European Economic Cooperation (OEEC). Its main aims were to act as a clearing-house in the distribution of Marshall Aid, to help revive intraEuropean trade, and to coordinate investment in western Europe. Such organisations shared two characteristics which have been thought important: each was specific to certain functions – defence, trade and aid; and each operated essentially as a traditional intergovernmental body.

Not content with these two, the fertile spring of 1948 threw up a third, and more extravagant, strain: the Hague Congress of May, which eventually resulted in the Council of Europe in 1949. There was an air of idealism and unreality running through the Hague deliberations that was reminiscent of the ambitions of the German liberals in that other *annus mirabilis* exactly a century before. Opinions on the overall effectiveness of the Council of Europe have been nearly unanimous. An eminent international lawyer has described it as 'an organisation somewhat unhappily combining the characteristics of an unending diplomatic conference and a House of Lords'. Sir Robert (later Lord) Boothby wrote in 1958, 'After eight years of membership of the Consultative Assembly of the Council of Europe I have, for the time being, given it up. I can't take the frustration any more.'[1] Here, indeed, lay the rub. Far-reaching proposals for a European Parliament with muscle were eroded, largely due to British influence, to the anodyne Consultative Assembly. Hovering over this, like a damp cloud, was the

Committee of Ministers, opposing every proposal for an extension of the Assembly's powers. The use of the unanimity rule, procedure by recommendation only, and a general air of secrecy and confidentiality, guaranteed that this machinery would not cause any headaches to the bureaucrats of member states. A partial exception should be made for the 'parallel' body, the Court and Commission on Human Rights; that it was in danger of being somewhat effective may be adduced from the facts that the UK only permitted individuals to go to it in 1968, and that France consistently refused to sign the Convention. For this was an arrangement more similar to the style and political theory of the later community institutions.

By late 1949, there was considerable disillusion with OEEC also. The *Economist* opined, 'There can, unfortunately, be no doubt that the secrecy and the unilateral character of the British devaluation — [of that year] unavoidable though they may have been — have dealt European co-operation and OEEC in particular, a crippling psychological blow ...'[2] This was critical because one aim of OEEC 'has come to have an importance, at least in American eyes, equal to all the rest ... The official contribution expected of OEEC has come to be that of *a pooling of Europe's resources, some tangible proof of self-help ...*'[3]

Against this unpromising background, other plans were being forged. Jean Monnet, head of the French Planning Commission, and his coterie of close associates at the rue de Martignac were aware that any new attempt would have to break with past ones in several respects. Their approach was both eclectic and unconventional. They went some way with 'functional' thinking in espousing sector-by-sector integration. They sought a startingpoint of undoubted material importance where traditional diplomatic techniques were demonstrably failing;[4] their technique included a bureaucratic coup to launch the proposal, highly unorthodox negotiating postures to try to induce new perspectives in the initial stages and a new institutional balance and modes of operation to maintain momentum.[5] A cardinal article of their faith was that institutional form does affect performance, and that they possessed the 'open sesame'. We must next look at the motives behind their attempt to shift certain functions away from the national to a 'European' level; the kinds of function for which such shifts were thought appropriate; and the problems encountered in the attempt.

The Schuman Plan and the Treaties of Rome[6]

This is not the place to disentangle the Schuman declaration from the elaborate and tense diplomacy of the spring of 1950. But it is important to note here that it caught hold because it appeared to

answer many different needs; and that only some of those concerns
are of the kind we now have in mind in speaking of the failure,
or failures, of the state. When Robert Schuman, as French Foreign
Minister, made his proposal for a Coal and Steel Community at the
dramatic press conference on May 9, 1950, it appeared to most
continental observers to be a real break out of an impasse. The offer
was made to the newly-established Federal Republic of Germany
initially, and to any other European nation which wished, to join in
pooling coal and steel resources on identical terms. If the voice was
Schuman's, the plan owed most to Monnet.

It was not, however, some wave of a magic wand. Similar notions
had been put forward during the previous year or so in the Council of
Europe, where they predictably got bogged down. Chancellor Adenauer
early in 1950 had put forward a spate of proposals for virtual unification
of France and the nascent West Germany, which had among other
things the effect of embarrassing the French into having to react
somehow, to be 'seen to be doing something'. All of this represented
a frantic attempt to break a number of deadlocks simultaneously, and
until the Schuman proposal, all appeared to have failed. The matters
demanding attention and hopefully solution were extremely diverse.
They included, urgently, some settlement of the whole Franco-German
'border' problem – a context for defusing both the Saar and Ruhr
problems. French fears at any loosening of control here were
multiplied by clear hints from her allies that the Federal Republic
must again have armed forces. Fears seemed piled on fears in early
1950: despite great fears about Soviet intentions, the West Europeans
seemed too paralysed by fears of each others' motives to act in concert.
American irritation at this was mounting; a *demarche* was needed by
Europeans themselves to persuade the US that Marshall Aid should
be continued. As Gerbet has put it,

> 'The originality of the Schuman plan was that it represented an
> attempt at solution of all of these problems at once: control of
> German coal and steel, Franco-German reconciliation, pursuit
> of the European 'construction', working for the economic
> prosperity of Europe, and a peaceful initiative on the international
> front.'[7]

The motive for starting from some particular sector was clear; no-one
believed in unity overnight, yet everyone required some concrete
sign of achievement. Equally, the fate of the various 'European'
experiments thus far indicated that if anyone were to propose
'supranational'[8] authorities, such a proposal would have to be made
by one government and agreed to by others – it would not gain

acceptance emanating from a Council of Europe Consultative Assembly. The motives for the choice of coal and steel were less obvious. Materially, the French probably gained most, though they lost the apparent control and right of veto they had hoped for previously. From a technical point of view, these sectors were not an obvious choice. Most projections indicated that a crisis of overproduction in European steel was imminent: the new 'harmonisers' of the proposed High Authority would face painful choices of closures and cut-backs rather than easier choices about the increments of growth. (The Korean War boom promptly falsified these predictions, helping the fledgling Coal and Steel Community over what would otherwise have been a difficult period.) The advantages of 'Euroscale' and collaboration might seem more tempting in the new growth industries — aeronautics, electronics, atomic energy. Yet the choice had advantages, two especially for the French. The first was to draw the teeth of the German war machine. The second was that a project which began with the *'industries de base'* offered the prospect of enlargement, of a logical extension, which was not so apparent with an initial choice of *'industries de pointe'*.

These were also the kinds of sector on which the French Planning Commission had itself set to work; there was relevant expertise, concentrated in French hands. Whilst it is generally not the case that official pronouncements reveal much of the thinking behind them, Schuman's declaration is something of an exception; and this is not altogether surprising, considering the circumstances surrounding it. The original idea had been for 'an economic Lotharingia . . .', 'a regrouping of Germans, Frenchmen, Belgians and Dutch'.[9] Quickly it was realised that such an arrangement could not be restricted just to the specific regions concerned; 'Lotharingia was abandoned in favour of a market open of all the interested countries'.[10] On the 'ideological' front, compromise was the order of the day. Monnet and Reuter preferred a socialistic arrangement, but realised it would encounter German and US hostility: Pierre Uri wanted a free market: finally they settled on a single market to be jointly planned. With the passage of time, the 'planned proportion' diminished.

Both French and German negotiators gave primacy to political objectives in the ECSC. Schuman, in a speech to the French National Assembly in July 1950, said:

> 'The essential thing is the creation of a supranational authority which will be the expression of solidarity among the countries, and which will exercise a part of the powers of these countries. . . We must create communities of interest on concrete foundations without the preponderance of certain countries, for the

advantage of all.'[11]

Yet Hallstein made it clear that there were limits to what the West Germans would concede in strict economic terms. There would be no concessions to the French desire to cut Germany's competitive advantage by 'equalization' of wages and taxes. '... the High Authority in principle has no power to intervene in the labour and wage policies of the member countries ... No state may ... change the competitive conditions of its producers to their benefit.'[12] Odd though it seems from the perspective of the '70s, at this time it was the Benelux countries who were the most cautious about the 'degree of supranationality' and the position of the High Authority. The Dutch particularly insisted on injecting the Council of Ministers into the scheme, whereas Monnet's original hope had been to exclude such 'intergovernmentalism' altogether.

Thus, stated in the terms of the thinking of the founders themselves, the proposal sought to use economic means to break a political impasse. Whilst clearly directed to one country above others, it sought to 'close off' the project neither geographically nor sectorally. Indeed it expected expansion in both senses. It laid great store by independent expertise, again a borrowing from functionalist thinking, expecting that casting problems in a new mould would lead to new perceptions of them and in turn to more imaginative solutions.

But more aspects of the institutions proposed had Monnet's stamp all over them. His inter-war experience with the League of Nations inclined him entirely toward regional groupings, away from global arrangements; the High Authority and the consultative set-up were reminiscent of the environment of the French Planning Commission, not to mention the French stress on the role of Courts; but the initial Franco-German focus was in tune with the mind of Robert Schuman, the son of that frontier: Monnet's British and Atlantic preference, he knew, must await a more favourable array of forces in London. Again, the notion that setting resources in common would of itself eliminate antagonisms, was very much part of Monnet's credo. The episode was a gamble, and Monnet was a born gambler; consultation of interested Ministries or of other interested Governments had, to put it politely, been kept at a minimum. The fragile craft was launched. That the ECSC came into being, with a powerful High Authority endowed with levies as well as real independence in decision-making, owed much to Monnet, who became its first head. Other projects which tried to parallel this one fell by the wayside – 'pools' for transport, agriculture and health; and, most importantly, the Defence Community proposal with a 'Political Community' overseeing both it and ECSC. In the wake of these failures, a major rethink took place in 1955-6; its purpose was both to decide what the next steps should be, and what institutional shape they should take. In regard to both, those concerned borrowed heavily from the established structures of the ECSC, trying to adapt them to the wider functions of a general Common Market. The best single key to this stage of reflection is the report of the intergovernmental Committee, known as the Spaak Report.[13]

The 'Spaak Committee's' Report was issued on 21 April 1956, and accepted as a basis for the *relance europeenne* on 30 May. Since its work so closely matched the final Treaties — the EEC Treaty and the Euratom Treaty — it is worth having some insight into what the Committee felt needed to be achieved, why, and how; and to what extent it felt that other contingencies could be anticipated, or should be left to take care of themselves. The preface to the Report was a catalogue of the shortcomings of western Europe's economies (not its polities) — problems which the report anticipated could be ameliorated by institutional means. It spoke of achieving 'common bases for development' and of the 'progressive fusion of [Europe's] markets', and produced the justification that the Treaties it proposed to give effect to all of this were, while not the only possible solution, a 'linked and practicable one ... which can be got under way immediately'.[14]

It is a matter of contention just how far the Treaties of Paris and of Rome contained a built-in 'laisser-faire bias', and how far this may have exacerbated later problems, both for the Communities and the Member States. Briefly, it is clear that the earlier Treaty of Paris did set great store by the liberal free-market mechanisms, stressing advantages that might accrue from economies of scale, freer factor movements, better resource allocation; minimising attendant risks and tending therefore not to lace itself with exceptions and derogations. Nevertheless, the High Authority's powers and means were such as to enable it to take fairly vigorous action to mitigate the worst disruptions caused by industrial change; not, however, as effectively as British national policy in the same period. When we move to the EEC Treaty, the picture is more complex. The Spaak Report proposed, and the Treaty set up, a 'Common Market' without ever defining precisely what was meant by the term. It was a piece of elastic: everyone was sure that it comprised at least a customs union; and that, to please the French, agriculture must be included. Beyond that, between that minimal state which the Treaty sought to programme fairly closely, and some distant peak which came to be known later as 'full economic and monetary union', there was a good deal of mist and dead ground. Yet the Spaak Report contains some epigrams which give clues to its authors' thinking. For example, 'setting resources in common ensures equality of opportunity'; or again, 'the whole point of a large market is to reconcile mass production with the absence of monopoly'.[15] Prevailing economic doctrines and expectations change. Such propositions are not self-evident and would be disputed by many. That they appear in the Report indicates at least that, though its authors were prepared on occasion to justify state aids, regional assistance or derogations from the Treaty, they did not expect that, overall, the dynamic effects of the creation of such an economic Community would include possibly crucial disruptive ones. Of this issue, to which we must return, it may be truly said that it was 'not dead, but sleepeth'. For, as with the ECSC, in the short term at least, the prophets of doom were swamped under a cornucopia of consumer-durables, and the growth-escalator triumphed.

The Spaak Report had much else of interest to say. The advantages of a common market could only come about if requisite delays were allowed for adaptation. Hence the phasing of the transitional period would be matched, it was hoped, by changes in decision-making rules. It stressed, without elaborating, (students of 'optimal currency areas' would have much to say on this later) the need for 'geographical limitation', and restated the Monnet position that a common market was 'inconceivable without common rules, actions-in-common', and 'finally a system of institutions to watch over it'. Such an arrangement required states which 'feel sufficiently close to each other to bring about in their legislatures the appropriate adjustments, and to make the requisite solidarity prevail in their policies'.[16] If it was understandably vague on such questions as the problem of differentiating among various forms of state aids and subsidies, or on the compatibility of what was proposed (particularly in agriculture) with GATT, it produced an impressive list of the 'nature of the necessary action' which would have to be undertaken by the institutions.[17] The last of these was 'to obtain a convergence of (national) efforts for the maintenance of monetary stability, a high level of employment and activity'.

After listing the tasks, the Report, in the manner of a well-framed *these,* elaborated the principles required of the institutions to be established, and the institutional arrangement itself. These institutions drew upon the ECSC experience, but the 'balance of power' between the Council of Ministers, the only body officially representing Member States, and the Commission, representing the 'Community interest', was somewhat different from that of the Council and the High Authority of Coal and Steel. This was dictated largely by the 'open-endedness' of the EEC Treaty as compared to the specific sectors covered by the Treaty of Paris. The change reflected also reservations about giving powers in a wide field if such powers could be as ingeniously extended as they had been by Monnet and his collaborators of the High Authority. Indeed, by this stage, it was clear that Monnet had overshot. Attempting a first 'relance' after the EDC failure, he had proposed an expansion of the scope of the ECSC to cover *all* sources of energy. With this he had linked his own resignation as President of the High Authority, to take effect in February 1955.[18] Whilst most governments responded fairly positively to this, the French did not. Mendes-France and Faure made it so clear that they were not willing to be led down the 'supranational' road that Monnet had to resign without achieving the extension. Nevertheless, the authors sought to preserve much of the novelty, the gains as they saw them, of the Treaty of Paris. Thus Spaak, writing of the 'caractère supranational' of the Rome Treaties: 'It is essential in that it signifies giving up the absurd rule requiring unanimity for a decision. The unanimity rule is the bane of international organisations, the cause of their substantial ineffectiveness'[19]

Spaak readily admitted that, powerful though his own influence was, he did not write the report that bore his name. Its principal author was Pierre Uri. Uri's basically free-market views were noted above, and whilst it would be unfair to accuse him of deliberately setting out to further these via the Treaty, this helps to explain why the Treaty gave a secondary place to activities and policies designed to correct imbalances.

The EEC Treaty aimed at a precise timetable for the first stages of the programme; abolition of internal tariffs and the establishment of a common external tariff (CET). It also laid down principles and guidelines for the much more difficult attainment of a single market in agricultural goods. The question of parallelism between this and the industrial common market was passed over. More crucial was the strategy, which has been wordily called 'dynamic disequilibrium'. This held, essentially, that the 'logic' of things would require integration, once begun, to proceed, even though this could involve a series of crises. One could not logically stop at a customs union, the argument ran, because the absence of tariffs would mean that decisions about the location of new industry would now be influenced more by such differences as national fiscal, state-aid and social security policies, which must themselves, if they were not to distort competition, be 'harmonised'. In more crusading moods, the thesis held that such crises would be desirable, as they would lead to perceptions that the problems could only be solved at Community level, and thus to increased legitimacy for the Community's institutions.

Performance

Crises there have certainly been. They have not, however, in general had the desired effect in institutional terms. In barest summary, most of the record so far has consisted of 'negative integration' — the dismantling of certain barriers between Member States — relatively little has been in the field of 'positive integration', the establishment of major common policies with Community financing. An examination of the record does not suggest that it is going to be easy to transfer additional activities to Community level: nevertheless, the Paris Summit of November 1972 set forth an ambitious programme. At the very least, the tension between those aspirations and the many forces of resistance is going to be considerable.

To date, the Community can be said to have moved a long way toward two 'common policies' — commercial policy, and agriculture; and to have moved some way toward the establishment of the 'four freedoms' of which the EEC Treaty spoke — freedom of movement of goods, persons, services and capital. But that enumeration must at once be qualified. Despite the dismantling of tariffs and attainment of the common external tariff, non-tariff barriers to trade have given much more trouble and frequently led to ferocious rearguard actions in which national administrations have been ready backers of concerned local industrialists. The saga of the importation of Italian refrigerators into France is an early but informative example;[20] in this case French resistance was finally worn down.

In agriculture, the saga is well-known. The financing of the CAP was at least the pretext, if not the direct cause, of the worst crisis yet in the community — that of 1965-6, culminating in the so-called 'Luxembourg agreements'. As a result, it was accepted in practice that 'majority voting' in the Council of Ministers — the possibility of one state being forced to bow to the wishes of its partners — was a dead letter, at least insofar as 'very important matters' were concerned; and the definition of those is for the Member State itself.[21] The difficulties in the way of agreeing a common policy for agriculture were immense, arising both from the nature of the activities concerned and from the vast differences of practice which originally separated Member States. Getting agreement at all was a considerable achievement, and helps to explain the great reluctance to unpick the knitting of this *'acquis communautaire'* despite its well-known costs and shortcomings. Yet the crucial point is that just as the policy was being fully introduced in 1969, the CAP was washed over by the first waves of the international currency crisis. The setting of agricultural prices in terms of an external 'unit of account' had been designed precisely to prevent anyone gaining or losing from devaluations and revaluations; but it had also been hoped in Commission circles that it could help make such changes unlikely. In the event, the result was a series of 'temporary exemptions', an elaborate nexus of border compensation payments and a division of the 'single' market into four zones. In the area of the 'four freedoms' also, progress has been patchy. It has gone farthest for goods and labour; much less far to date for services and capital.

A key area is that of Articles 85 and 86, dealing with cartels and mergers. It provides a classic example of the need to balance contending *desiderata,* an unavoidable task in economic regulation but one which necessarily leaves enterprises at a high level of anxiety. Even one of the most crucial cases yet decided by the Court, that of Continental Can,[22] has done little to clarify the position. The Commission's own proposals in the merger field give it three months to decide whether it wishes to take proceedings, and a probably elastic further nine months to decide whether to ban a merger. They also indicate the view that definitions both of company size and market share are necessarily elastic.[23] Whilst the Treaty of Paris contained explicit provision for the control of mergers, the Treaty of Rome does not; its formula is the notion of 'fair' or 'workable' competition, rather than 'free' competition.[24]

In almost every other field, actual achievement of common policies, as opposed to the mouthing of sentiments of goodwill, can be said to be minimal to date (1974). In 1967 the Six agreed in principle to introduce the value-added tax (VAT); and Italy produced a classic stalling operation on it, for the next six years. No agreement has been reached on other fiscal measures. Progress in the area of transport policy has been almost non-existent, due to the diffuse 'catchment' of the term in general and Dutch resistance in key fields in particular. Both research and technology 'policy' and energy policy have suffered, too, from this lack of definition; but also from touching too closely on sensitive security and 'defence' related areas, from squabbles about the *juste retour,* and jurisdictional disputes. They were not, in any case, clearly spelled out as such in the founding Treaties, but have rather the status of 'felt needs'. 'Social policy' was to a large extent emasculated by the cost-crisis of the mid-sixties and the conveniently cheese-paring doctrine of 'social budgeting'. (There really should be some prizes for bureaucratic euphemisms.) That does not conclude the list; but before we examine the Paris Summit and its sequels, it is relevant to ask why the record should be so patchy.

Several factors help to explain this. A first approach concentrates on the question of institutional adequacy and responsiveness. Any deliberate shift of functions to some new level presupposes a degree of confidence in the new mechanisms available for handling those functions. Such confidence is far from universal in the case of the Nine. Since the crisis of 1965-6 the Commission has been much more wary of taking far-reaching initiatives, by and large much more reduced toward an 'administrative' and 'defensive' rather than an innovating role. The Assembly or 'Parliament' has not substantially expanded its powers, its budgetary grip probably extending only to

3-4 per cent of the total.²⁵ From an original situation of plurinational party groups, the Assembly has increasingly reflected national party particularities. It is caught in a vicious circle. Only a directly elected Parliament, runs one argument, will obtain meaningful powers *or* thus attract able personnel. The case can be argued in reverse; only an Assembly with powers is likely to seem to require anything like direct election; and so on. The infusion of British notions of parliamentary 'warfare' since enlargement has not improved its cohesion. Its best work is in its specialist committees; some effectiveness may be granted to the indefatigable question-masters, with Mr Vredeling of Holland heading this league table over the years.

The 1965-6 crisis did tilt the delicate institutional balance between the Council and Commission. Relations since have often been frigid or downright hostile. Recent examples include the January 1973 episode where, to avoid a drastic clamp-down on its information activities, the Commission agreed 'informally' to let Member States' delegations know in advance if it intended to reveal 'delicate' matters.²⁶ Questions of who should represent the Communities at the European Security Conference, or whether the Commission should be represented at all in the closing fanfare of the Paris Summit, are other examples. The 'Luxembourg crisis' marked an obvious turningpoint, but the direction then taken was probably reinforced by the Merger Treaty (of 1965, operative 1967), which recognised officially for the first time the all-important 'brokers' in the system, the Committee of Permanent Representatives, and again by the enlargement of 1973. There was a great deal of in-fighting over Commission positions at the time of enlargement, with national government jostling to 'colonise' particular posts or departments which they had earmarked as requiring their (presumably reliable?) nationals. Optimists could regard this as indicating vitality: if the Commission were really so unimportant, it would not be worth fighting over. But important for what? If as an engine for blocking or moulding proposals in particular ways, such a notion compromises the pristine 'independence' of the Commission.

It appears increasingly that, in contrast to earlier stages, the Commission, insofar as it is effective at all, is now perceived as a threat to be staved off:

> '... the Commission by its existence, sharpens the awareness of alternative courses of action (not only between Governments but also) among groups *within* the state; and when it enters into relationships directly with these groups, the Commission effectively highlights the extent to which the views of Governments and the views of some internal groups differ. Governments are on the defensive insofar as they *now* (my emphasis) have to make a

deliberate effort to preserve an appearance of state interest in the face of the Community. The integrity of national decision-making structures is challenged from without and erosion (sic) from within.'[27]

This, while fair as a description of what can happen, does not explain why. The force of the remark, 'now' in the quotation is that it leads to other major factors: the fact of enlargement, with its attendant diversification of interests; the economic dynamics of the situation, which clearly predated enlargement but have been accentuated by it; and the nature of the new tasks which the Communities face.

It is argued that it is too early to say what are the effects of enlargement upon the cohesiveness of 'Community Europe' and hence its importance as a counterweight to the nation-state. This seems too cautious. Previous disagreements could often be falsified by pretending that they represented the churlishness of 'one Member State'; that it was really a question of the Five plus the Commission versus France. This was almost never true, but now it is not even possible to pretend. It is quite clear that coalition-building, trade-offs, package deals, and log-rolling are the order of the day, and that the coalitions are different for different issues. The permutations are endless, but simply to consider the respective attitudes of the four largest members, France, BRD, UK and Italy over three issue areas — attitudes to institutional evolution, to reform of the CAP, and to economic and monetary union (EMU) should be sufficient. Almost any combination is to be found somewhere among the Nine; and certainly no two of the four 'majors' are in real agreement.

Next there is the question of the economic dynamics of the situation.[28] It is certainly possible to imagine an 'economic community' arrangement which would not be hostile to shifts of function, either upward from the nation-states to 'Community' institutions, downwards from central government to minor territorial or functional units, or all of these. But it is probable that the economic geography of such a community would have to look different from that of the present one. An area whose initially prosperous regions were its geographically peripheral ones, and whose relatively underprivileged areas were geographically central ones at the junction of State frontiers, would be most ideal. Here, the creation of a customs union could be expected *(cet. par.)* to produce a more equal distribution of economic activity. It should also provide a favourable environment for the surrender or sharing of functions by national governments to the Community, and for cooperation at lower levels, either inter-regional or even interfunctional, on a 'decentralised' basis.

Just to describe the prerequisites for this paradise is to indicate how far it is from the actual situation. A situation where the peripheral regions are also the initially disadvantaged ones is usually held to compound the problem. Many disparities increase as new industry (especially if it is either 'market tied' or truly 'foot loose')[29] locates near the market centre. The possibility also emerges of whole countries becoming 'underdeveloped regions' of the Community, and, as Herr von der Groeben of the Commission stated, 'There is no sense in having a coordinated economic policy if the structural and regional conditions in which it can be implemented are lacking.' Questions of inter-regional equity are critical for all attempts to shift governmental activities, either 'upwards' or 'downwards' from national central government. Either increasing economic disparities or sharp reversals of fortune can easily lead to a breakdown of political cohesion. There are the traditional arguments that this can happen as a result of new competition rendering categories of firms 'inefficient'; from increasing equalisation of factor earnings in participating countries; or as greater mobility of capital or services is added to the existing degree of mobility of goods and labour. There is also the growing problem, the tendency of national 'corrective' policies to conflict with each other, or to lead to wasteful 'outbidding' unless appropriate alternatives can be agreed.

To date, again, the Communities have been circumspect in their approach to these admittedly complex problems. Each bundle of available policy instruments has been handled with great care, many would say too much care. There are the financial instruments — so far, the actions of the Social Fund, European Investment Bank, ECSC, and the 'guidance' section of the Agricultural Guidance and Guarantee Fund; and, increasingly, the regional fund advanced in the Thomson Report.[30] Beginning with the 'Regional' Council meeting of 20 October 1971, some progress has been recorded at least on paper over the principles and magnitude of aids in the 'central' areas, and over the designation of agricultural 'priority regions'. It remains to be seen how robustly such notions as the 'opaqueness' or 'transparency' of aids will stand up to national interests in concealment. There has also been pressure on national governments about some of their more blatant contraventions in this area, such as the early battle with the Germans over the 'phantom railway rates' (the 'Als-Ob Tarife' Case);[31] or the later ones with the Belgians over the Loi Leburton[32] or with the Italians over the Venezia-Friuli region.

Prospects: The Budget and the Functions

No-one knows what the Communities will look like in five to seven years' time or if indeed they will exist at all. The Communiqué of the Paris Summit tried to establish agreed ground on the eve of enlargement. It was, significantly, taken more seriously — subject to much closer monitoring for what it did or did not say — than that of the Hague Summit three years earlier. Yet the fate of the Communities may well depend on the answer to three other questions. Firstly, regardless of how the West European 'construct' looks on paper, how will it be perceived by the relevant populations? And second, how far will their perceptions have any influence? Third, how far will outside factors blow it off course?

Those questions are even harder to answer than questions about the shape of the undertaking. Here at least we have some indicators, and while we may not be able to say much about their relative importance, we can make intelligent guesses. We are now (1974) in a situation of great uncertainty from the Community point of view. But it is clear that if 'Community Europe' is indeed to acquire new functions as its founders hoped, it will require financial means to carry them out. So it is with the prospects for the Community budget that we should start.

Over the medium term (five to seven years), will the Communities have at their disposal sizable or derisory budgetary means, which might be made available for compensatory policies? Secondly, over about the same time-span, will they have moved a long or short distance toward the elusive 'full economic and monetary union', the very definition of which appears so ambiguous?

Without taking any further factors into account, we have a two-by-two matrix; four quite distinct possibilities. It is generally agreed that an economic and monetary union in the absence of central compensatory activity is likely to lead to severe imbalances, especially where

a) the unit is large;
b) the peripheral areas are also the initially disadvantaged ones

Both conditions hold for the enlarged EEC. Conversely, very little progress toward 'full economic and monetary union', but with substantial budgetary means available for compensatory policies, would appear to present far fewer problems. The other two cases, (large progress/large compensation: small progress/small compensation) appear intermediate and more indeterminate. Of these latter two, the first is also unlikely, for reasons which follow.

Next, then, the question of probabilities. Is it likely that the Communities will, over the envisaged time-span, acquire considerable budgetary means; and is it likely that they would be used for what we have called compensatory policies? A recent study[33] suggested that in the late 1960s the share of 'European' revenue in national budgets was, for the Six, of the order of 0.8 per cent; and that this would probably rise to approximately 3.5 to 4 per cent by 1980. If this were so, it would be significant, though hardly dramatic. But an examination of the main components of the 'Community budget' makes that figure less likely. Over the relevant period (the remainder of the '70s) the Community's resources are to be made up of three components: the proceeds of the agricultural levies; the common external tariff (CET); and a proportion up to 1 per cent of VAT.

It may well be that, on reasonable assumptions, the first two components could shrink almost to vanishing point over the next few years. As world food prices rise, and the gap between them and Community agricultural prices narrows, so necessarily does the yield (per physical unit) of the variable levy. Second, a good deal of the CET yield may well have to be bargained away in the Nixon Round Tariff negotiations (timetabled to be concluded in 1975).[34] This is the more likely the more the US-European agenda over trade, monetary, and defence matters is seen as 'linked' — whether formally or not. So most of the weight will be thrown upon VAT, and upon arguments about the comparability of methods of levying it. Thus it may be doubted whether there will actually be much of a 'Community' budget; and to the extent that there is not, the Community as an *active* governmental system, able to take initiatives of its own, will be diminished. There will be no (quasi-) federation without taxation; that much is certain.

The Community would then retain a merely 'irritant' function, insofar as it indulged in any positive activity: (indeed it is already becoming infamous for this): frantically searching for something to be seen to be *doing,* it seeks to introduce ever more ludicrous 'harmonisations', of loaves under a certain weight, or of beer-making techniques. It would be pleasant to believe that a little more was left from the wreck of Monnet's 'grand design'.

It is doubtful, in any case, whether whatever budgetary resources are available will be spent on *new* compensatory policies. This is of importance for any consideration of which functions 'could' be shifted upwards or downwards. Policies with a strong compensatory element which were part of the rather explicit initial bargain, such as the CAP, are one thing. New policy areas, even though involving much smaller financial means, are, it seems, quite another — if the present state of the regional policy debate is anything to go by. Although orders of magnitude are notoriously hard to agree on in this area, a number of calculations suggest that the effort required for the fulfilment of even basically satisfactory regional policy aims during the seventies would be anything from four to six times as great as the present national efforts, assuming that things get no worse.[35]

These then are some of the central problems concerning the budget, without which it will not be possible for the Community directly to undertake, or to have shifted to it, additional functions requiring any considerable outlay. We may now turn to consider some problems involved in making projections about 'full economic and monetary union', another key element in portraying the shape of the Community in the medium term.

Economic and Monetary Union

As with so much else which the Communities now confront, 'Economic and Monetary Union' is not clearly set out as an aim of the Treaties. The EEC Treaty provided for a Monetary Committee and that was all. It is by no means clear that any of the implications at this level had been foreseen in the Spaak Report. This was not to be wondered at in a Europe just emerging from destitution. What has become much more evident over the last five years is the ability of certain economies within the West European area to take paths which are completely out of line with those of others. The Italian and British economies illustrate this dramatically.[36] Such a situation does not seem readily manageable by resort to the conventional wisdoms, and while academic economists have given a great deal of attention to such puzzles, it is not clear that there has been any drastic change in official thinking.

It is convenient to begin a discussion of EMU with the Werner Report[37] of October 1970, which threw its weight much more behind the 'monetarists' of the Barre plans than behind the 'economists' of the Schiller proposals. Where the 'economists' had emphasised the co-ordination of economic policies, the monetarists stressed the 'discipline' of fixed exchange rates, and also the importance of establishing a 'European (monetary) identity'. On this, Werner's own testimony was eloquent.[38] In his lecture at Lausanne University on 22 February 1971, he said,

> 'For myself, I have had the conviction since 1960 that the fullness of objectives of the Common Market could not be attained except through a far-reaching monetary co-operation, going beyond the prudent thoughts of the Treaty. The experience of my own country with economic unions was such as to make me particularly aware of this aspect of affairs. Everybody knows that the ambitions of the Treaty go beyond a free trade area, beyond a customs union. Certain of the objectives of articles 2 and 3 . . . are only attainable if one puts at the service "of the harmonious development of economic

activity in the community as a whole" a monetary standard
(étalon monétaire), which ensures at the same time equal
opportunities to the economic agents and competition without
distortion or discrimination.'

The centrality of these notions for Werner and the apparently
dominant school in Economic and Monetary Union questions is
reinforced by the Werner Report itself which asserts boldly (p.9):

'Economic and monetary union will make it possible to realise an
area within which goods and services, people and capital will
circulate freely and *without competitive distortions, without thereby
giving rise to structural or regional disequilibrium.* (my emphasis)
'The implementation of such a union will effect a lasting
improvement in welfare in the Community and will reinforce the
contribution of the Community to economic and monetary
equilibrium in the world.'

Such claims are of course disputable. How far does it appear that such
'integration' might go — with what results for national and subnational
systems? The first major problem that arises is the content of the notion
of 'economic and monetary union'. Werner voiced the problem, but
did not resolve it when he said,

'The report points to a centre of decision for Community economic
policy, and to a centre of decision for *monetary* policy. Whilst the
functions of the second are clearly envisageable, since this would
mean a "community system" of central banks, there remained a
wide margin of interpretation as far as the "decision-centre"
of economic policy was concerned. With regard to this, the
problem of democratic parliamentary control must be faced,
[an] indispensable [element] insofar as important decisions are
transferred to the Community level. In this area, conflicting
views will surface, depending upon first what concept people hold
of the Europe to be.'[39]

This is a masterly understatement. Monetary policy is, *selon* Werner,
not the coping-stone, but the very motor, of the integration process.
Will such an arrangement come about? This is hard to say in view of,
inter alia plurima: British reluctance, Italian policy, and the entirely
negotiable state of the international monetary regime. Does it make
much difference whether it comes about in this way or not?
This is also a distinctly complex issue to which the following pre-question

can be addressed:

> Will regional problems be aggravated by monetary integration?
> In answer to this there exist at least three main schools of thought:
>
> a) the notion that factor prices are competitively determined: if this is true, then monetary integration is largely irrelevant, because wages would (in principle) go down sufficiently to eliminate unemployment;
>
> b) the notion that what are critical as between regions are *exogenous* cost-trends or propensities to inflate: in which case flexible parities would still be crucial;
>
> c) the theory that monetary integration would lead to an equalisation of factor costs: in which case a set of factor prices would result which would not be appropriate to differing levels of productivity: hence unemployment *and* inflation would result (differentially) in certain regions.

A great deal depends upon which of these views is espoused; at present there is far from complete agreement among economists about it. But it would be generally agreed that almost any (combination) of the following three factors is enough to throw huge spanners in the works:

> a) differential rates of increase of money supply *and* (linked) government spending;
>
> b) differential rates of growth of productivity through time;
>
> c) differential propensities to inflate.

Yet again, the larger and more diverse the area, and the more diverse the policies which component units seek to pursue, the more likely are these factors to appear. Parity changes are recognised to be pretty rough justice in correcting 'global' (i.e. national) and regional imbalances, but they are usually regarded as helpful. Most versions of economic and monetary union would at least curtail the freedom of national government to change parities; and would thus tend to force them to use other 'rectificatory' weapons of dubious compatibility with the Treaties.

Such a 'discipline' has, however, the beguiling merit in some eyes of appearing to curb the trade unions, and may thus be espoused by governments tempted to do a 'Pontius Pilate' about their local situation. Nevertheless, it is hard in logic to disagree with the remark of the

the governor of the Danish central bank: 'I shall begin to believe in European economic and monetary union when someone explains how you control nine horses that are all running at different speeds within the same harness.'[40] The final paradox is that, despite this, a large number of national and Community bureaucrats are still determined to achieve such a union; it is not an accident that it figured at the head of the matters of substance referred to in the Paris Communique.

That it is on the agenda is beyond doubt, and agendas have a disconcerting way of dominating attention and consuming time. Thus for example, the Thomson Report's remit was drawn clearly under its shadow: '... a high priority should be given to the aim of correcting, in the Community, the structural and regional imbalances which might affect the realisation of Economic and Monetary Union.'[41] The linkage is made evident, but so is the subordination of the compensatory policy to the EMU shibboleth. Or there are the equally unsupported assertions of ex-Commissioner Ralf Dahrendorf: *'It is imperative* for the Community to pursue its own course towards Economic and Monetary Union along the lines which *have been suggested in the past,* (my emphasis) decided upon by the Council of Ministers, and confirmed by the Summit meeting in Paris. And it is important that the crucial step towards Economic and Monetary Union — a step towards a commitment in the monetary as well as the economic field — is taken at the time which has been set for it.
It should be clear that *the next two years* will be as decisive for the E.C. as for the world system in respect of monetary policy.'[42]

'Imperative' or not, this is an area which has suffered heavy hammer blows lately. Although these originated mainly outside the Community, they have had their effect. The rapid rise in world oil prices clearly played its part in the French decision (January 1974) to join Britain in 'floating', at the same time as growing realisation of the extent to which Britain's inflation was being fueled by her own float, which should therefore be reconsidered. The prospects for EMU in the midst of such fluctuating attitudes and such a howling gale look distant indeed.[43]

Supporting EMU there is an *apparent* coalition of interests, between for example the Commission (in the name of logic and 'completion'), the monetarists (in the name of discipline) and the City of London (in the name of the latter, with the bonus of a new arena in which to practice its time-honored skills of capital-export). It remains to be seen whether they can tempt into their camp a sizable proportion of British civil servants, disenchanted with the hard furrow of actually trying to influence the economy, and the Sisyphus-exertions of regional policy; and knowing that, if the tithe of the Stillman Report's forecasts for the shape of 'economic Europe 1985'[44] are true, their task will be more hopeless still.

It is hard to disagree with Hirsch when he states: 'The *direction* of this movement conflicts with the functional need of the major economies . . .'[45] and that 'To the question of when European monetary union can be expected to be economically and politically feasible, the answer should therefore be something like "when the economies of the present EEC countries are significantly more integrated with each other than are England and Scotland today".'

As to EMU and related proposals, either the Community is serious about the wildly flapping, almost flightless bird; or it is not. If they are serious, we are heading for stormy waters. If they are not serious, then 'Community aims' have reached an impasse which should be widely recognised. It will neither be possible to 'unpick the knitting' nor to advance. On the purely economic front – the motor of the original integrators – the Community will be living in limbo, and aware of it; aware that there is no salvation in future Community mechanisms; nor any escape from present ones. If any head of steam develops behind the proposals, there will be a period of menace for the weaker economies; hardly an atmosphere congenial to experiment. 'The next two years' may well be 'decisive' for the European Community – and more than just ' in respect of monetary policy.'

Conclusion

All major governments in western Europe have recently been undergoing considerable strain. Ominously, nautical metaphors have again come to the fore. This alone would be enough to prescribe severe limits to 'Community Europe', for some time to come; but it is not all.

We have seen that the European institutions were originally intended to help States to 'fade', gracefully and voluntarily. That was the strategic intention. But the Communities took the shape they did, in part for immediate tactical reasons which were to have important consequences for their development.

In the conditions of the 1960s, the experiment prospered as a customs union, and progressed in one or two associated areas, but outside these early projects, progress has been very slow. In particular, attempts to move 'beyond the economies of scale', into such areas as 'political union', defence and foreign affairs, have had negligible success.

Originally, the 'European experiment' was seen more as a 'growth engine' than as an engine of redistribution. At this stage it was plausible to argue that 'integration' had the force of almost universal benefit on its side. What is now at issue, however, is very different.

First it concerns the extent to which the dynamics of the 'growth engine' produce redistributions that favour its developed centre; while institutional paralysis limits agreement on measures to compensate for these more or less unanticipated effects. Second, we may in any case be moving off the 'growth escalator'; to the extent that this is true, the game approaches more and more a zero-sum situation. What was originally an 'engine of cooperation' becomes increasingly a new stake in the struggle of national interests.

Thus enlargement of the Community, in the conditions of the 1970s, has compounded the problems. To solve them would require a degree of political inventiveness as great as that of the founding fathers, and of that there is little sign. Instead, those who favour 'moving on' have up to now tended to back such techniques as economic and monetary union, which are increasingly unattractive. Where once the objectives of policy and its instruments appeared to be in reasonable harmony, now they are fundamentally at odds — assuming, that is, that the objectives still have something to do with 'the economic and social welfare of the inhabitants'.

The Treaties of Rome went into effect just months before de Gaulle, the first of the major politicians of 'movement', came to power. For him, the Treaties were acceptable insofar as they gave France a stronger base for her own political aims, which he would describe tantalizingly as a 'European Europe', but which he knew it would be impossible for the EEC partners to pursue at the same pace. As long as that remained a lone *defi* it could continue and not feed back into intolerable disruptions at the Community level. This too ceased to be the case, with the crisis of 1965-6 and with French wariness at West Germany's *Ostpolitik*.

The 'Community level' is less and less insulated from other levels of policy; less and less allowed to go on by itself, or to be regarded as subject to special rules. It is now a main battleground for national policies. These policies have a precarious strength — (just how precarious has been shown by the events since the 'Yom Kippur War') — but such strength as they have, has been built not least upon the relative successes of the Community in the 1960s.

On the political plane, there has been virtually no agreement as to how far evolving relationships require the deepening and extension of the Community. Because there is no agreed 'image of Europe', there is no agreed view of the place and nature of the Community in it. Both its institutional shape and the scope of its competences are in dispute. But equally, contending versions of the 'Community dimension' always figure somewhere in each national government's scheme of things. Meanwhile, the Community does have a life of its own, precarious and under question as it is. And that life of its own exercises an independent effect in the field of forces; a sometimes disturbing and disruptive one for national governments, which in turn contributes to their determination to retain strategic control in a number of fields. Thus the impact of the 'Community dimension' upon State structures is highly complex, full of paradox and irony. Above all, it does not correspond to the notions of the founding fathers, but rather to Burns'

> 'The best laid schemes o' mice an' men
> Gang aft a-gley.'

'Renegotiation', formal or not, is now on everyone's agenda.

Notes

1. Lindsay (1958), p.xiii
2. The *Economist*, Oct. 29 1949.
3. *idem*, my emphasis added.
4. Willis (1968), *passim*.
5. See *inter alia* Mayne (1967); Bromberger (1969).
6. Gerbet (1956): Haas (1958); Reuter (1951); Mayne (1966).
7. Gerbet (1956), p.538.
8. This term is used as convenient shorthand only.
9. Bromberger (1969), p.96.
10. Ibid, p.97.
11. Haas (1958), p.244.
12. Ibid, p.248.
13. Report of the intergovermental committee, 'Spaak Committee', Brussels, 21 Apr. 1956. French version.
14. Spaak Report, p.10.
15. Spaak Report, pp.13ff.
16. Ibid, p.14.
17. Ibid, p.23.
18. Haas (1958), pp.107-8.
19. Spaak (1969), vol.II, p.97.
20. See Meynaud and Sidjanski in Gerbet and Pepy (1969).
21. De la Serre (1972); Newhouse (1967); Lambert (1966).
22. *Financial Times*, 22 Feb 1973.
23. *Financial Times*, 10 Aug 1973.
24. Mally (1973), pp.98-9.
25. Vedel Report, Brussels, 1972, pp.53-4.
26. *Financial Times*, 24 Jan 1973.
27. Taylor (1968) as quoted in Mally (1973).
28. See McAllister (1971-2)
29. McLachlan and Swann (1967), *passim*.
30. Report on the Regional Problems in the Enlarged Community, COM(73) 550. Brussels, 3 May 1973.
31. *Common Market*, Nov. 1966.

32. Perin (1967-69), pp.71ff.
33. Seung Soo Han (1971), p.150.
34. See *30 Jours d'Europe,* June 1973, p.8.
35. Moore and Rhodes (1973); Rhodes (1973), mimeo.
36. *Financial Times,* 24 Jan. 1973.
37. Report to the Council & Commission on the realisation by stages of Economic and Monetary Union in the Community: Supplement to Bulletin 11-1970 of the European Communities, Luxembourg, 8 Oct. 1970.
38. Werner (1971), p.15.
39. Werner (1971), p.23.
40. *Financial Times,* 24 Jan. 1973.
41. Paris Summit Communiqué; and Thomson Report, p.1.
42. Dahrendorf (1973), p.52.
43. See e.g. letter from Dr. A.P. Thirlwall, the *Guardian,* 26 Feb.
44. Stillman Report: 'Europe 1985', Hudson Institute, 1973.
45. Hirsch (1973), p.426.

Select Bibliography

M. and S. Bromberger	*Jean Monnet & the United States of Europe;* New York, 1969; orig. publ. as *Les Coulisses de l'Europe;* 1968.
Ralf Dahrendorf	'The Foreign Policy of the EEC': *World To-day;* Feb. 1973, pp.47-57.
F. de la Serre	'Approaches theoriques de l'integration europeenne': *Revue Francaise de Science Politique;* 1972
P. Gerbet	'La Genese du Plan Schuman': *Revue Francaise de Science Politique;* 1956, pp.525-53.
P. Gerbet and Pepy	*La Decision dans les Communautes Europeennes;* Brussels, 1969.
E.B. Haas	*The Uniting of Europe;* Stanford, 1958.
F. Hirsch	'The political economics of European monetary integration': *World To-day;* Oct. 1972, pp.424-33.
J. Lambert	The Constitutional Crisis, 1965-6: *Journal of Common Market Studies;* May, 1966, pp.195-228.
K. Lindsay	*Toward a European Parliament;* Strasbourg, 1958.
G. Mally	*The European Community in Perspective;* Lexington, Mass., 1973.
R. Mayne	'The Contribution of Jean Monnet': in *Government and Opposition;* vol.2, No.3; Apr.-July 1967; pp.349-71.
R. McAllister	'Prospects for Decentralisation in a "united Europe":' in *The New Atlantis;* vol.2, No.3; Winter 1971/2, pp.136-44.

D. McLachlan and D. Swann	*Competition Policy in the European C Community;* London, 1967.
B. Moore and J. Rhodes:	'Evaluating the effects of British Regional Economic Policy': *Economic Journal;* March, 1973, pp.87-110.
J. Newhouse	*Collision in Brussels;* New York, 1967.
F. Perin	*Le Regionalisme dans l'integration europeenne;* Louvain, 1967-9.
P. Reuter	'La Conception du pouvoir politique dans le Plan Schuman', in: *Revue Francaise de Science Politique;* 1951, pp.256-76.
J. Rhodes	*Regional Policy in the EEC;* 1973 (Prepared for a study group of the Federal Trust.)
Seung Soo Han	*The Growth & Function of the European Budget;* Seoul, 1971.
P.H. Spaak	*Combats Inacheves;* vol.2: Paris, 1969
P. Taylor	'The Concept of Community and the European Integration Process': in *Journal of Common Market Studies,* vol VII, Dec. 1968, pp.83-101.
P. Werner	*Vers l'Union Monetaire Europeenne;* Lausanne, 1971.
F. R. Willis	*France, Germany & the New Europe;* (rev. ed.) Stanford, 1968.